Interdisziplinäre Studien zu Mediation
und Konfliktmanagement
is published by

Prof. Dr. Ulla Gläßer, Berlin
Prof. Dr. Lars Kirchhoff, Berlin
Kirsten Schroeter, Hamburg

Volume 7

Anne Holper | Lars Kirchhoff (eds.)

Peace Mediation in Germany's Foreign Policy

Uniting Method, Power and Politics

 **Nomos**

The Deutsche Nationalbibliothek lists this publication in the
Deutsche Nationalbibliografie; detailed bibliographic data
are available on the Internet at http://dnb.d-nb.de

ISBN   978-3-8487-8211-6 (Print)
          978-3-7489-2616-0 (ePDF)

British Library Cataloguing-in-Publication Data
A catalogue record for this book is available from the British Library.

ISBN   978-3-8487-8211-6 (Print)
          978-3-7489-2616-0 (ePDF)

Library of Congress Cataloging-in-Publication Data
Holper, Anne | Kirchhoff, Lars
Peace Mediation in Germany's Foreign Policy
Uniting Method, Power and Politics
Anne Holper | Lars Kirchhoff (eds.)
237 pp.
Includes bibliographic references.

ISBN   978-3-8487-8211-6 (Print)
          978-3-7489-2616-0 (ePDF)

Onlineversion
Nomos eLibrary

1st Edition 2021
© Nomos Verlagsgesellschaft, Baden-Baden, Germany 2021. Overall responsibility
for manufacturing (printing and production) lies with Nomos Verlagsgesellschaft mbH
& Co. KG.

Preface to the International Edition

In many countries and international organizations, peace mediation is undergoing an intense process of adjustment and sophistication. Alongside its gradually increasing political promotion and strategic relevance within the spectrum of instruments for crisis prevention, conflict resolution and stabilization, the examination, criticism and skepticism have gained substance and precision – an indispensable corrective to this major structural shift in the field. At the same time, while some critical steps in defining the mediation profile of Germany have already been taken, many decisions are still to be made. From a scientific as well as political perspective, this seems like a good moment to capture the recent and possible future developments in a book.

Evidently, peace mediation in Germany must be seen and can only be properly understood against the background of the international dimension. Nevertheless, we dedicated large parts of this volume almost exclusively to the German perspective, the domestic dimension of and discussions around peace mediation. Why? During our years of intense cooperation and exchange with several foreign ministries, organizations and multilateral networks, it became increasingly evident that the most impactful and reputable mediation approaches of any entities draw from and respond to two distinct sources of inspiration and information: the collective methodological wisdom that has been accumulated over the years in a global effort, and the highly specific conditions, dynamics and qualities of the very actor that tries to establish a (new) profile in the field.

Considering the wealth of literature already existing with regard to common denominators, questions and achievements in the international peace mediation community, we decided that an in-depth-analysis of the highly specific German history, constraints, potential and role in peace mediation was the missing piece of the puzzle in the effort to define the profile of Germany in the field. Therefore, the book takes a close look at the somewhat special situation of a medium power actor (as Germany is) with a unique and difficult history (which Germany has), actively searching to redefine (as Germany does) its responsibility and role in an international arena that is confronted with a whole set of new dynamics and challenges.

Naturally, we hope that the resulting struggle with regard to concepts, structures and narratives – summarized throughout this book as the struggle between politics, power and method – will not only help explain how

German peace mediation has developed and how it operates today; we hope that it will also serve as a useful reference frame for comparable processes in other countries and contexts. In the long run, only a deeply integrated and interconnected system of peaceful intervention in violent conflict will have a chance to make a difference in the contemporary field of international conflict.

Instead of dedicating this book to a person, we want to highlight the relevance of a central idea that runs through this volume: Frequently, as Hannah Arendt showed in tracing back the history of the term, power has been falsely equated with coercion, domination and control. Mediation, interestingly, implies an understanding of "power" as an effect of collective communication and cooperation. This book's deeper purpose is to pave the way for mediation methods and politics to complement their power to make peace with, not against, the will of the conflict actors and groups affected by conflict.

Berlin, June 2021
Anne Holper and Lars Kirchhoff

Preface to the German Edition, or: An Introduction to Peace Mediation from a German Perspective

Over the last ten years, the field of peace mediation has gone through profound changes around the world as well as in Germany, both practically and theoretically. The results extend from newly created structures at the Federal Foreign Office (FFO), the United Nations (UN), the Organization for Security and Co-operation in Europe (OSCE), the European Union (EU), the African Union (AU) and non-governmental organizations (NGOs) to the consolidation of mediation methodology and the professional design of peace processes.

These changes have been accompanied by a frank, controversial – and thus, in the best sense of the word, "genuine" – discourse on the challenges, dilemmas and potentials associated with the field. Naturally, these aspects always have played a decisive role in determining the course and results of peace mediation processes. But in the years of quick and pragmatic growth, more differentiated conceptual, methodological and strategic questions initially attracted little attention. Now the answers are being translated into generally applicable empirical values and practical actions, which in turn must undergo critical analysis. The subject of peace mediation thus finds itself in a dynamic, cyclical learning process to which this volume is intended to contribute.

Conflict, war and peace – themes that have always occupied humankind – are doubtless highly complex, not only analytically and practically but also politically as well as in legal and ethical terms. This complexity is contained in the key question from which peace mediation originally emerged: "How can peace be achieved without the use of violence?" Thus it is not surprising that the reemergence of this question has been and is being achieved not only in a network of state and civil-society actors but also through a close interplay of practice and science. For peace mediation processes, too many actors, perspectives and disciplines prove to be relevant for a silo-based approach to make sense.

It is precisely this kind of motivation – genuine discourse, cyclical learning and the cooperation of wholly disparate actors and their perspectives on political action – that is reflected in the composition of this volume on peace mediation. Alongside current contributions from scholars and practitioners from the German and Swiss mediation field, the "Fact Sheets on

Peace Mediation" form the core of the publication. These Fact Sheets were developed over several years in a cooperation between the Federal Foreign Office and the Initiative Mediation Support Deutschland (IMSD) and represent the status quo on peace mediation from a German perspective. They identify questions that set the course for the future and illuminate conflicting goals and trade-offs. The resulting snapshot deliberately shows achievements and potentials together with remaining ambiguities and gaps.

We would like to highlight two successful axes of cooperation that are reflected in this volume and that are tightly linked with the strengthening of the field of peace mediation in Germany. The first is the close cooperation network within German civil society that deals with the theme of peace mediation. A particularly visible expression of this is the Initiative Mediation Support Deutschland (IMSD), which is described on several occasions in the volume and without whose cooperation and productivity the results presented here could not have been accomplished. The second axis of cooperation is the one between the Federal Foreign Office, the IMSD and academia, in which a respectful exchange on an equal footing was established and instruments and approaches were refined and networked. This, too, is described in this volume.

Since the establishment of such an ambitious instrument as international mediation depends not least on the commitment of specific individuals, let us expressly mention here Ina Lepel, Rüdiger König, Thomas Zahneisen, Gregor Schotten, Clemens Hach, Jens Urban and Björn Gehrmann, who – in respective functions and phases of the project – have made significant contributions to the initiation, refinement and establishment of the topic of peace mediation at the German Federal Foreign Office.

The volume's subtitle stands for an explicit recognition of the different and sometimes conflicting realities in which mediation processes must assert themselves. Peace mediation always operates in an area of tension between methodology, power and politics, and thus is unavoidably characterized by both conflicting goals and trade-offs. If one recognizes this seeming dilemma in a first step as the presence of heterogeneous strengths in methodology, power and politics, new types of profiling and synergy potential arise in a second step. If Germany's role as a mediator is to realize this potential, a common determination must be made about whether, where and how German politics and mediation methodology can work together fruitfully in an integrated mediation approach or whether they can act more effectively independently of each other.

Power – understood as a variable strength ratio within a network of relationships that steers interaction dynamics and processes[1] – is thus the volatile capital with which politics and methodology work in very different ways. Mediative methodology is just another approach to generating and using power. When it comes to power, this creates a surprising connector for successful complementarity that can actually unite mediation methods and politics.

We wish to thank Anna Dick, Marike Blunck, Tanja Rollett and Hui Zhang for their dedication and diligence, which contributed greatly to the creation of this volume.

Berlin, June 2021
Anne Holper and Lars Kirchhoff

---

1 Peter Imbusch, "Machtfigurationen und Herrschaftsprozesse bei Norbert Elias", *Macht und Herrschaft: Sozialwissenschaftliche Theorien und Konzeptionen*, edited by Peter Imbusch (Wiesbaden: Springer Fachmedien Wiesbaden, 2013), 169–93.

Foreword from the German Federal Foreign Office

The Federal Foreign Office has deliberately invested quite some time to consider the question of what peace mediation means for German foreign policy, and what role Germany can, may and should play in it. We have taken many steps along the path toward finding answers, together with our partners. The latter includes partner states such as Switzerland, Norway and Finland that are active in the field of mediation; international organizations such as the UN, the OSCE and the EU; and civil-society groups, in particular the Initiative Mediation Support Deutschland.

While the publication of the German *Peace Mediation Framework* in 2019 was a widely visible conceptual milestone, it is the lived practice of German mediation that determines the relevance of the topic. At this very moment, Germany is active in various roles in more than 40 mediation and dialogue processes. We are working with local, national and international non-governmental organizations via the UN or the targeted promotion of formats and activities. Sometimes we engage in visible and leading roles, and sometimes we deliberately stay in the background. Thus, we have reached the phase of implementation and operationalization.

Germany brings three core strengths to the role of a peace mediator: the political weight of a middle power with a central position within the EU, a credibility that arises largely from the confrontation with our own history and the possibility of using a broad range of stabilization instruments in a networked and long-term manner. These are significant assets.

In addition to providing obvious opportunities, Germany's profile also raises many questions that demand timely, differentiated answers. These questions arise in no small part from today's significant shifts in the multilateral order: Where are the contemporary fields of action for engagement that fit to Germany's international role? How can our profile be translated into the concrete design of peace mediation processes? Which unique characteristics must be taken into consideration when a middle power with clearly defined interests and values becomes active as a mediator? Where are the tools for an improved interplay of the relevant instruments and actors?

Many of these questions can best be answered by the Federal Foreign Office on its own, using its in-house capacities. In other areas, a special form of cooperation has proven to be of added value in recent years: the active exchange of knowledge with universities. This was an integral part of my department's work from the start. Scientists bring solid insights drawn from hands-on research to our government activities and reflect the research needs of our own practical experiences back to their scientific community.

The structures that have thus arisen in the Foreign Office are a successful start, and a volume like this one is an expression of the productivity of this cooperative effort.

Berlin, June 2021

Rüdiger König

Ministerial Director, Directorate-General S for Humanitarian Assistance, Crisis Prevention, Stabilisation and Post-Conflict Reconstruction (2015–2020)

Foreword by the Initiative Mediation Support Deutschland (IMSD)

Only ten years ago, the term "peace mediation" barely came up in German mediation circles. Mediation activities occurring in the context of peace processes were too diverse and too seldom guided by professional principles to be established as an independent field of mediation. Today, the term is well established in Germany. This anthology represents the first comprehensive handbook to present this subject area with a focus on Germany.

What brought us to this point? In the past decade, the increased professionalization of non-state and state actors as well as international organizations has led to a specialization, to a major development in learning and thus to the emergence of the discipline of peace mediation. In the course of this development, general professional guidelines and principles of mediation also have increasingly been recognized for mediation processes in the context of peace building – an area that is particularly exposed to power politics and pragmatic constraints.

This professionalization was initiated by a few international actors, who defined basic principles and established structures. Chief among them was the UN, which in 2006 set up a Mediation Support Unit followed by a Standby Team and the Group of Friends of Mediation (a network of countries that are dedicated to the topic). The UN also produced numerous publications in this field. The central document is considered to be the *UN Guidance for Effective Mediation* (2012), upon which the German *Peace Mediation Framework* (2019) also draws. In addition, over the years both the OSCE and the EU have installed units and concepts in which the topic of peace mediation is firmly anchored.

In Germany, peace mediation – which in 2013 was a niche area for non-governmental players – became a subject of political debate, culminating in its institutionalization in the Federal Foreign Office in 2015. This occurred after some EU member countries promoted the founding of a European peace institute in 2013 (ultimately established as the European Institute of Peace – EIP). The German Bundestag and Federal Government had to develop a position on this proposal, and a group of non-governmental mediation support actors took this as an opportunity to advocate for the institutionalization and professionalization of the field in Germany. Five

German organizations that were dedicated to peace mediation either primarily or as part of their work joined to form the Initiative Mediation Support Deutschland (IMSD), in order to bring in their expertise and promote the development of peace mediation among state actors. These five groups were the Berghof Foundation, the Center for Peace Mediation (CPM) at European University Viadrina, CSSP – Berlin Center for Integrative Mediation, inmedio – institute for mediation. counselling. development as well as the Center for International Peace Operations (ZIF). In cooperation with the Subcommittee on Civilian Crisis Prevention, Conflict Management and Integrated Action, they put the topic on the political agenda and from then on supported it in the German Bundestag. The initial working meetings with the Federal Foreign Office in early 2014 led to a fruitful and trusting cooperation that can be described as a successful example of collaboration between civil society and state.

The results of this collaboration were several conferences (2014: Germany as Mediator; 2015: Expert Conference on Conflict Analysis and Mediation Entry Points; 2016: The OSCE as Mediator) as well as the Fact Sheets on various aspects of peace mediation – initially prepared as internal papers by the IMSD and the Federal Foreign Office – some of which are now published in this volume. Peace mediation is understood here as a generic term for various mediative interventions, including national dialogues, at various levels of society. This understanding, which is also reflected in this anthology, does not limit peace mediation to official peace or ceasefire negotiations but is based on the so-called "multi-track diplomacy" approach.

With the publication of the Federal Foreign Office's *Guidelines* and *Peace Mediation Framework* in 2019, peace mediation was systematically anchored in German foreign policy. From the standpoint of the IMSD, the years 2014 to 2019 thus could be seen as a start-up phase of peace mediation at the Federal Foreign Office. The focus is now turning towards many individual mediation processes and engagements – implemented or financially supported by the Federal Foreign Office itself – and to an increasing internal institutionalization in the Federal Foreign Office. In this new phase, too, the IMSD network of experts will continue to support the Foreign Office's capacity building.

Thus, this volume could not be more opportune. The current task is to further refine the discipline of peace mediation and support its application in the political realm, for it is clear that the practical translation of the *Peace Mediation Framework* is subject to the constraints of realpolitik and complex contextual factors. It is therefore all the more important to be clear about the technical guidelines and principles, in order to be able to demand that they be followed as much as possible. This volume is intended to contribute towards achieving that clarity and shaping of the concept of peace mediation.

Berlin, June 2021

Christoph Lüttmann and Dirk Splinter
(representing the approximately 20 individuals who have filled the IMSD with life and content since its founding)

Abbreviations

ANC	African National Congress
AU	African Union
BAKS	Bundesakademie für Sicherheitspolitik / Federal Academy for Security Policy
BMZ	Bundesministerium für wirtschaftliche Zusammenarbeit und Entwicklung / Federal Ministry for Economic Cooperation and Development
CPM	Center for Peace Mediation, European University Viadrina Frankfurt (Oder)
CSS	Center for Security Studies, ETH Zurich
CSSP	Berlin Center for Integrative Mediation
DSF	Deutsche Stiftung Friedensforschung / German Foundation for Peace Research
EEAS	European External Action Service
EIP	European Institute of Peace
EU	European Union
FDFA	Swiss Federal Department of Foreign Affairs
FES	Friedrich-Ebert-Stiftung / Friedrich Ebert Foundation
FFO	Federal Foreign Office
FriEnt	Arbeitsgemeinschaft Frieden und Entwicklung / Working Group on Peace and Development
GCSP	Geneva Centre for Security Policy
GIZ	Deutsche Gesellschaft für internationale Zusammenarbeit
GMF	German Marshall Fund of the United States
HD	Centre for Humanitarian Dialogue
ICRC	International Committee of the Red Cross
ifa	Institut für Auslandsbeziehungen
IGAD	Intergovernmental Authority on Development
IMSD	Initiative Mediation Support Deutschland
ISSG	International Syria Support Group
MSP	Mediation Support Project
MSU	Mediation Support Unit
NGO(s)	Non-governmental organization(s)
OSCE	Organization for Security and Co-operation in Europe
SADC	Southern African Development Community
SMM	Special Monitoring Mission
SWP	Stiftung Wissenschaft und Politik / German Institute for International and Security Affairs
UCDP	Uppsala Conflict Data Program
UN	United Nations
UNHCR	United Nations High Commissioner for Refugees

Abbreviations

UNITAR	United Nations Institute for Training and Research
UNSMIS	UN Supervision Mission in Syria
ZFD	Ziviler Friedensdienst / Civil Peace Service
ZIF	Zentrum für Internationale Friedenseinsätze / Center for International Peace Operations

Contents

Contents

The Volume's Structure and Line of Thought

Anne Holper & Lars Kirchhoff

This publication consists of three parts, each of which examines peace mediation in German foreign policy from a different angle. Part I focuses on concepts and structures, Part II analyses methodology and norms, and Part III integrates all these perspectives within a political-strategic evaluation of the status quo.

In **Part I: The Formation of a German Mediation Profile – Guidelines, Processes, Networks**, six authors from Germany and Switzerland present various approaches to the topic of peace mediation: 1) a compilation of key dimensions and guiding questions for shaping state mediation profiles; 2) an assessment of peace mediation in the current political landscape (including the resulting challenges and niches of action for Germany); 3) an inventory of the historical development and conceptual foundations behind Germany's role as a mediation actor; 4) an appeal to make (better) use of Germany's potential in the field of peace mediation; and 5) a current – by its very nature fractal – view of the role that mediation initiatives have played and could play in Syria.

Part II: The Fact Sheet Series "Peace Mediation and Peace Mediation Support" – Methodological Professionalization includes five items from a collection of policy briefs developed by the Federal Foreign Office and the Initiative Mediation Support Deutschland (IMSD). These were assembled in recent years on the basis of an intensive process of exchange and coordination between the relevant units of the Federal Foreign Office (in particular the Division S03, which is responsible for peace mediation) and the five organizations of the IMSD. Since their successive completion (in some cases they already have been revised and updated), these items have provided comprehensive orientation, served targeted capacity building (for example, for diplomatic training courses and embassies) and certainly contributed to the further development and refinement of the German approach to peace mediation.

Against the background of the first part and the Fact Sheets, the goal of **Part III: Peace Mediation as a Balancing Act Between Methodology, Power and Politics** is to situate the current state of development of peace mediation – in general and in Germany – conceptually, politically, methodologically, and scientifically. To that end, the relevant fields of tension are laid out and a tentative prognosis is offered, which open questions could shape the future axes of development. In addition, remaining core questions concerning the differentiation of Germany's roles in peace mediation are addressed.

The **Annex** to this volume contains the **"Peace Mediation Framework" of the Federal Foreign Office**. As the framework represents a milestone in the development of peace mediation in Germany and practically all other texts in this publication relate to this concept, its inclusion is essential.

As the Fact Sheets serve to clarify central terms and concepts in peace mediation and to illustrate their complexity based on concrete examples, the first part of this volume does not need to offer a traditional explanation of terms. Instead, it can be completely dedicated to the framing and contextualization of contents that will be concretized later on. In the synopsis of the two parts, the potentials of theory and practice (isolated and considered together) for the future development of the topic also crystallize, as will be illustrated in the concluding Part III.

With this intentionally heterogeneous compilation of contributions on the conceptual framework, the structural fabric, the political-strategic debate, the methodological and normative professionalization as well as the scientific exploration of the field, an overview of the current landscape of peace mediation appears feasible and worthwhile.

Part I:
The Formation of a German Mediation Profile –
Guidelines, Processes, Networks

Overview Part I

Anne Holper & Lars Kirchhoff

The contributions in this section analyze and contextualize the process and results of establishing and differentiating German peace mediation activities to date. Alongside historical and political aspects, the topic calls for an international perspective as well.

In his contribution, **"Developing a State's Mediation Profile: Core Dimensions and Key Questions", Simon Mason** offers a frame of reference for the later remarks on German engagement by starting with the initial and ultimately central questions of motivation and suitability: Why do we do mediation, and how does it suit our country? Ultimately, the resulting dimensions – roles, resources and strategies – can only be defined in a goal-oriented fashion if these pivotal questions of peace mediation have been clarified in an honest, comprehensive and sustainable manner.

David Lanz takes up this theme in his contribution, **"Peace Mediation in the International Political Context: Challenges and Niches for Germany"**, but emphasizes the systemic dependencies between the development of a German mediation profile and the current dynamics in the international arena. Changes in the anatomy of conflicts are covered just as much as the development of a multipolar world order and related tendencies towards a democratization of peace processes. Lanz's impulses directly encourage Germany to better locate ongoing and future activities in the field of peace mediation in comparison with the activities of other countries and to actively explore niches that suit the country.

Against the background of these two conceptual outlines (to put it bluntly: "How do states develop their own mediation profiles? And what is needed in the world – where are gaps to fill?"), **Julia von Dobeneck's** survey of **"Germany as a Mediation Actor: Development and Conceptual Foundations"** provides concrete insight into which contours and structures have emerged in Germany, and why those and not others. Germany's current profile has been significantly shaped by developments such as the "review process" and the strategic restructuring of the Federal Foreign Office. Thus, the first three contributions make the area of tension between the dynamics of the international system and those of national politics tangible.

The next contribution, **Almut Wieland-Karimi's "Exploiting Potential: Peace Mediation in German Foreign Policy"**, takes the current situation and looks for ways to develop the potential and coherent emphases of Germany as a mediator, without ifs or buts. The demands of this approach are as concrete as they are ambitious, and any conflicting political dynamics are clearly identified. It pinpoints the right time for a genuine shift in emphasis towards peace mediation as "now".

This section concludes with an article by **Marike Blunck** and **Carsten Wieland** on **"Complexity and Asymmetry: Challenges of UN Mediation in Syria and the Role of Germany"**. Using the example of the conflict in Syria, which given its complexity and geopolitical dynamics is highly relevant to the topic, the text illustrates that – and how – mediation initiatives have up to now "lag behind" the realities of the conflict. In addition, the article addresses what kind of adaptation of process design is required in scenarios of fragmentation – and what role Germany could play specifically in such situations.

Developing a State's Mediation Profile: Core Dimensions and Key Questions

Simon J. A. Mason

This contribution[1] aims to support the reflections of policy makers and members of the wider public who seek to understand and shape their state's mediation profile. It does this by outlining some of the relevant dimensions and questions with which the contours of a country's mediation profile can be mapped out, providing illustrative answers from the perspectives of Switzerland, Norway, Germany, South Africa, Russia and the USA. The idea is not to fully cover these different countries' mediation profiles or to compare them in detail[2] but rather to illustrate the variety of possible answers, in order to clarify the meaning and relevancy of the questions. The working hypothesis is that by reflecting on and responding to these questions from a country's specific perspective, this country's mediation profile will gain in clarity and effectiveness. The questions are clustered into four sections, which address 1) the motivation of a country to engage in mediation, 2) the role the country seeks in the field of mediation, 3) the resources for mediation it has at its disposal and 4) the ensuing mediation strategy.

1 Work on this article took place in the context of the Mediation Support Project, a joint project of the Center for Security Studies ETH Zürich and swisspeace, funded by the Swiss Federal Department of Foreign Affairs (FDFA). Thanks go to the following experts whose helpful discussions have shaped this paper: Georg Stein (FDFA), Julian Th. Hottinger (FDFA), Christopher Moore (CDA), Laurie Nathan (Kroc Institute, University of Notre Dame), Andreas Wenger (CSS ETH Zürich), Anne Holper and Marike Blunk (European University Viadrina).
2 An empirical overview of different types of mediators, including different states, can be found in Isak Svensson and Monika Onken, "Global Trends of Peace Negotiations and Conflict Mediation", *Global Trends 2015: Prospects for World Society*, edited by Michèle Roth et al. (Bonn/Duisburg: Development and Peace Foundation, Institute for Development and Peace, Käte Hamburger Kolleg/Centre for Global Cooperation Research, 2015): 65–79. An attempt to compare different mediators can be found in: Simon J. A. Mason and Damiano Angelo Sguaitamatti, *Mapping Mediators: A Comparison of Third Parties and Implications for Switzerland* (CSS Mediation Resources, Center for Security Studies [CSS], ETH Zürich, 2011).

Simon J. A. Mason

1. *Motivation: Why do we as a state engage in mediation, and how does it suit our country?*

- Which mix of norms and direct and indirect national interests motivate and guide our actions in the field of mediation? How explicit, how defined and how stable is this mix?
- How does mediation fit in with other actively used foreign-policy tools, with the government's policies and with the legal and constitutional basis of our country?
- If the mediation work is in tension or conflict with other foreign-policy goals or interests, how are priorities set?
- What aspect of our country's historical trajectory shapes our mediation profile?
- What degree of support is there from domestic constituencies and taxpayers?

Since the motivation of a state to engage in mediation shapes the answers to all the other questions, it is the most important and foundational question. Generally, a country is motivated to choose mediation as a foreign-policy instrument and a measure in specific conflicts for a variety of reasons. In essence, these are values and norms (e.g., peace, security and justice), direct national interests (e.g., in the outcome of the conflict) and indirect national interests (e.g., international reputation and access to key actors). In the cases of Switzerland and Norway, for example, this motivation results from humanistic values as well as indirect national interests. Switzerland's obligation to promote peace is also anchored in its constitution.[3] The key interests behind these two countries' peace work is securing a good international reputation and access to important actors (e.g., the governments of the USA and Russia); direct interests in the outcome (e.g., economic entry points after the peace agreement) are rarely the main motivation for an engagement. For both countries, engaging in peace promotion is one way to contribute to global burden sharing.

---

3 Art. 54, para. 2 of the Swiss Federal Constitution of April 18, 1999 states: "The Confederation shall ensure that the independence of Switzerland and its welfare is safeguarded; it shall in particular assist in the alleviation of need and poverty in the world and promote respect for human rights and democracy, the peaceful coexistence of peoples as well as the conservation of natural resources".

A country like South Africa, which focuses its mediation efforts on the African continent, has a different motivation, which also changes from one engagement to the next. As far as values and norms are concerned, South Africa's motivation is rooted in the vision of an "African renaissance" and in the commitment of the African National Congress (ANC) to help those fellow Africans in conflict today who once helped South Africa to overcome apartheid. In conflicts close to its borders, such as in Zimbabwe, where South Africa could be adversely affected by migration movements, security problems at its borders and economic impacts, the country also has a direct national interest in helping to shape the outcome of conflict mediation.

In its *Peace Mediation Framework*, Germany also explicitly acknowledges that the decision to use mediation is shaped, on a case-by-case basis, by "our own interests [...] and our obligations resulting from political alliances and multilateral treaties".[4] Countries like the USA and Russia use mediation as part of their overall regional and global diplomatic and military strategy, with often very specific national interests in the outcome of the conflict. Many would argue that this calls into question the very notion of mediation as being built on the consent of the conflicting parties – but these countries are nevertheless involved as third parties in diplomatic activities that they call "mediation". Hence, when the word "mediation" is used, it is vital to understand who is defining it and with what purpose.

2. *Role: What does mediation mean for us, and what is our role in the mediation field?*

- What is our understanding of mediation?
- What is our state's position in the world, and how is it perceived by our citizens? How is it perceived by other countries? What does this position allow or prevent us from doing?
- How directive or facilitative is our mediation approach?
- Do we go beyond mediation and use power diplomacy? If so, how do we combine or differentiate between mediation and power diplomacy (demarcated/merging, independent/coordinated)?

---

4 Federal Foreign Office, *Peace Mediation Framework* (Berlin: Federal Foreign Office, 2019).

- Which mediation roles are we willing to take on (e.g., lead mediator, support to others, case-specific work, focus on generic professionalization, bilateral or multilateral work)?
- What connections to other countries can we mobilize for our mediation work?

There is broad academic and policy consensus that the parties to a conflict must give their "consent" to the mediator and the mediation process for a mediation activity to be described as such.[5] However, since all actors are normally under a certain degree of pressure, it is unclear if a signaled "consent" means a 10-percent or a 90-percent consent and how this might vary in the course of a process. Often only minimal consent is given at the start, which then expands as the process gains momentum and the parties realize what they can get out of it. If a mediation actor has a direct interest in a specific outcome of a mediation process (as in the case of the USA, Russia or South Africa), this can increase the actor's willingness to accept low or asymmetrical levels of consent from the conflict parties as a basis for proceeding. The USA's bias towards Israel in the Israel-Palestine peace processes is one example. Countries like Switzerland and Norway, with little leverage other than their impartiality, financial resources and expertise, need to base their work on higher levels of consent and greater efforts to be impartial if they are to work effectively and remain acceptable as mediators. Since these countries' small size prevents them from working alone, they must generate as much approval as possible for their mediation activities within the international community, or at least ensure that other actors do not see their interests threatened.

The question of consent is also closely related to the question of the mediation style that a state employs. Norway and Switzerland usually use a facilitative approach. The USA and Russia, on the other hand, mainly employ a directive approach, often using so much leverage that their efforts go beyond the limits of mediation[6] and can be understood as a power-based intervention, or high-powered diplomacy. Countries with a moderate degree of influence, such as Germany on a global level and South Africa in Africa, have the option of choosing between facilitative and direc-

---

5 United Nations, *United Nations Guidance for Effective Mediation* (New York: United Nations, 2012): 4.
6 The formulations "with their consent", "assist" and "mutually agreeable" of the *United Nations Guidance for Effective Mediation* implicitly mark the boundaries between mediation and power-based intervention.

tive mediation styles and of varying them as each case requires. At the same time, their dominant position in their region can impede them from taking on certain mediation tasks. Germany and Russia, for example, would scarcely be seen as impartial mediators when it comes to mediating the conflict within Ukraine.

Due to their high dependency on multilateralism, small countries are likely to engage in mediation that is rooted in and supports multilateralism. In so doing, they follow the mediation guidelines outlined in the UN Guidance for Effective Mediation or participate in a so-called "group of friends". Great powers like the USA and Russia, especially in the current geopolitically polarized context, tend to use mediation also outside of multilateral formats as part of their own foreign-policy agenda. For Germany, a key question is to what extent it engages directly in mediation activities as an independent agent or indirectly within the framework of the EU system. Due to its economic interdependency with and unique role in the EU, it is to be expected that Germany will often choose to work primarily through the EU; in any case, it will certainly not engage in mediation activities that would harm its relations with that organization. Since the EU is one of the largest funders of mediation processes worldwide, its funding mechanisms make it a key shaper of those processes.

Small states engage in both mediation processes and numbers of other mediation-related activities. Norway, for example, also has chosen to take on more low-profile mediation support tasks, after having experienced some of the failures of more prominent mediation lead roles, such as in Sri Lanka.[7] Switzerland, for its part, has recently outlined to what extent dialogue support, facilitation, negotiation support, mediation support and mediation are distinct but related activities that can complement one another.[8] The core argument is that not everything that is called mediation is mediation, and a more precise use of terminology helps increase the effectiveness and legitimacy of the use of different tools. In contrast, it is unlikely that countries like the USA, Russia and South Africa, which tend towards a much more politicized form of mediation, would advocate for definitional clarity about what mediation is and is not. Where does Germany

---

7 Lena Merkle, "The Nordic Model of Peace Diplomacy: Pride and Hegemonic Prejudice", *Beyond Peacebuilding: Challenging a Critical Mainstream. ASPR Report*, no. 3 (2019): 15–20.

8 Working group "Switzerland's 2028 Foreign Policy Vision" (AVIS28), *Switzerland in the World 2028. Report by the Working Group "Switzerland's 2028 Foreign Policy Vision"* (Bern: AVIS28, 2019).

stand on this question? Its *Peace Mediation Framework*[9] outlines its definition of mediation and guiding mediation principles. This policy document indicates that Germany decides on a case-by-case basis whether it can take on a mediating role in a principled, impartial manner, while also recognizing that there are cases where this approach is not possible and other approaches should be used.

3. Resources: Who drives mediation, and which resources can we as a state use for mediation?

> - Who drives mediation at which level of the government: president, minister, undersecretary of state (related to who is in charge of foreign policy)?
> - What mediation support structures are being set up and used (in the Federal Foreign Office or outside it – NGOs, the academic world, etc.)?
> - What resources do we have? What are our sources of influence and leverage (expertise, money, political clout, alliances, military peacekeeping)?

A country's motivation for mediation and understanding of mediation shapes the resources that a country invests in it. The knowledge-based understanding of mediation in Switzerland and Norway allows them to use internal (e.g., within their foreign offices) and external (e.g., academic or NGO[10]) support structures and to invest in the professionalization of mediation using training formats and research. South Africa's presidential and personal approach to mediation under Nelson Mandela, Thabo Mbeki and Jacob Zuma meant high-level political involvement, combined with quick and powerful political control of mediation processes, but less investment in internal and external technical support structures.

The long-term build-up of resources and reputation in the area of mediation requires broad and sustained domestic support. Hence a key question for all countries is how strong the domestic political consensus

---

9 Federal Foreign Office, *Peace Mediation Framework*.

10 E.g., the Swiss FDFA–funded "Mediation Support Project" of the Center for Security Studies ETH Zürich (CSS) and swisspeace, which, together with the FDFA, organize the annual Peace Mediation Course, www.peacemediation.ch (accessed June 29, 2020).

for peace promotion work is in all political parties across the political spectrum and in their respective administrations, and if such work relates to the personal preferences of different leaders. Switzerland and Norway illustrate how such a broad and consistent consensus can be achieved, even if the argumentation and the mix of values and national interests as a source of motivation for mediation may vary over time. In Switzerland, such cross-party consensus is achieved through a federal system of government where there is a governing coalition. Due to the political system's design, no party can hope to obtain a very large majority. In Norway, the consensus is built on cross-party negotiations, so that even though there might be changes of government and rotations within the executive branch, mediation continues. Thus political changes may lead to different priorities of Norwegian mediation policy, rather than a discontinuation. Because of the nature of their domestic support structures, Switzerland and Norway choose to engage in mediation and to intervene in its processes only when there are high degrees of approval and participation by all relevant parties. Depending on the case, this requirement for a strong level of inclusivity can be either a stumbling block or an advantage.

4. *Strategy: How do we as a state approach conflict mediation?*

- What are our criteria for engagement and case selection in relation to the types of conflict we are interested in and the levels at which we are involved (e.g., Tracks 1–3, language region, geography)?
- How process-oriented are we, to what extent guided by substantive principles and norms?
- How risk-friendly or risk-averse are we? What are the possibilities for gains or risks to our political reputation?
- Is there coherence among our country's different mediation-related activities and between our country's mediation and other peace promoting activities?
- What do we have to offer (e.g., money, expertise, political authority), and how is this added value perceived by the conflict parties?
- Who do we work with and how do we work with them (e.g., individually, cooperatively, competitively, using division of labor, sharing information)?
- How long do we engage? Which phase or phases of a process (pre-pre-negotiations, pre-negotiations, negotiations, implementation) do we focus on?

- How biased or impartial are we as mediators?
- How do we work on entry points?
- What is our approach to "do no harm", and what are our exit, distribution and handover strategies?

The phases of a peace process to which a country's mediation efforts contribute as well as that country's degree of risk-preparedness shape its strategic approach to mediation and mediation-related activities. Norway engages in all phases of a peace process: preparation, negotiation and implementation. Thus far, Switzerland has focused more heavily on the preparation and negotiation phases than on the implementation phase. Norway has invested more resources than Switzerland and has for a long time been more risk-friendly, even if Switzerland argues in its latest policy report that peace promotion "requires a certain willingness to take risks".[11] Switzerland likes to work with others and not necessarily carry the burden alone, while Norway works both alone or with other countries and seems more willing to take on a leading and more visible role (e.g., Israel-Palestine, Sri Lanka, Colombia). Depending on the case and context, countries like South Africa, the USA and Russia tend to act alone or through regional or global organizations: South Africa, for example, in the case of Zimbabwe, has acted through the Southern African Development Community (SADC), while Russia and the USA, in the case of Syria, have at times acted via the UN, while at other times outside the UN.

Small and medium-sized states involved in mediation tend to focus on professionalization efforts, either through the UN Mediation Support Unit and the UN Mediation Standby Team or through supporting programs such as the Master of Advanced Studies ETH Mediation in Peace Processes, in which Switzerland, Germany, Finland, Sweden and the UN have a strategic partnership with the ETH Zurich to train the next generation of peace mediators.[12] Great powers like the USA and Russia also use mediation expertise, but because these countries rely more on diplomatic leverage and a strong foreign-policy agenda, mediation tools tend to become part of their diplomatic, economic, military and counter-terrorism strate-

---

11 Working group "Switzerland's 2028 Foreign Policy Vision" (AVIS28), *Switzerland in the World 2028*.
12 ETH Zürich, Department of Humanities, Social and Political Sciences, "MAS Mediation in Peace Processes. Preparing the Next Generation of Mediators", https://mas-mediation.ethz.ch/ (accessed January 6, 2020).

gies, rather than being focused primarily on achieving a locally owned peace.

Conclusion

The above list of questions and illustrative responses is far from comprehensive, but should be seen instead as a source of inspiration for a more systematic reflection on relevant dimensions in the development of a state's mediation profile. It is also important to emphasize that there is an interdependent relationship between these different dimensions and their related questions, from which a certain order for their clarification results: If the motivation for engaging in mediation changes, this will have an effect on the role, the use of resources and the strategic decisions. In other words, there first needs to be clarity about a country's motivation and overarching objective in this field before its strategic orientation can be determined. The clearer the mediation profile, the easier it should become to foster cooperation among different state mediation actors and ensure good fit between mediators and conflict.

References

ETH Zurich, Department of Humanities, Social and Political Sciences. "MAS Mediation in Peace Processes. Preparing the Next Generation of Mediators". https://mas-mediation.ethz.ch/ (accessed January 6, 2020).

Federal Foreign Office. *Peace Mediation Framework*. Berlin: Federal Foreign Office, 2019.

Mason, Simon J. A., and Damiano Angelo Sguaitamatti. *Mapping Mediators: A Comparison of Third Parties and Implications for Switzerland*. CSS Mediation Resources, Center for Security Studies (CSS), ETH Zürich, 2011.

Merkle, Lena. "The Nordic Model of Peace Diplomacy: Pride and Hegemonic Prejudice", *Beyond Peacebuilding: Challenging a Critical Mainstream. ASPR Report*, no. 3 (2019): 15–20.

Svensson, Isak, and Monika Onken. "Global Trends of Peace Negotiations and Conflict Mediation", *Global Trends 2015: Prospects for World Society*, edited by Michèle Roth, Cornelia Ulbert, Tobias Debiel and Stiftung Entwicklung und Frieden, 65–79. Bonn/Duisburg: Development and Peace Foundation, Institute for Development and Peace, Käte Hamburger Kolleg/Centre for Global Cooperation Research, 2015.

United Nations. *United Nations Guidance for Effective Mediation*. New York: United Nations, 2012.

Working group "Switzerland's 2028 Foreign Policy Vision" (AVIS28). *Switzerland in the World 2028. Report by the Working Group "Switzerland's 2028 Foreign Policy Vision".* Bern: AVIS28, 2019.

Peace Mediation in the International Political Context: Challenges and Niches for Germany

David Lanz

Introduction

The field of peace mediation has grown in recent years. International organizations – in particular the United Nations (UN) but also the European Union (EU) and the Organization for Security and Co-operation in Europe (OSCE) – have expanded their capacities. Moreover, many states, including Germany, have incorporated mediation in their foreign policy. They see it as a pragmatic and broadly legitimate approach to preventing, containing and resolving international conflicts. These states act either directly through official state representatives who conduct or support mediation processes, or they fund non-state actors to mediate between conflict parties. Indeed, the increasing availability of funding has resulted in a multiplication of non-governmental organizations (NGOs) working on mediation over the past 15 years. Today, NGOs specializing in "private diplomacy" employ hundreds of experts around the globe. Taking these developments together, one can conclude that mediation has become a social and professional "field", characterized by a complex, mostly non-hierarchical architecture of actors whose mandate, resources and interests may differ, but who agree on certain norms and methods, have a common discourse and thereby set themselves apart from other fields of international cooperation.

At the same time, because of the growth the field, peace mediation has tended towards a certain degree of self-referentiality, occasionally losing sight of its original goals. Self-interest as a motivation to engage in mediation processes is not in itself problematic. It can even be positive, since it ensures long-term commitment (see the article by Simon J. A. Mason in this volume). Yet mediation must not become an end in itself and serve primarily its own purpose: to procure funding for NGOs, legitimize states' foreign policy or secure politicians' legacies. The purpose of peace mediation is to resolve international conflicts and to promote peace and security in international relations. Accordingly, a state should engage in peace processes only if it can play a meaningful role in a given political context. For this reason – and the present contribution makes this case – peace mediation should be conceived of and practiced more explicitly in relation to its political context. Against this background, this contribution addresses the following questions: How has the context of peace mediation developed in recent years? Which challenges and which niches have emerged? What does that mean for Germany's role in peace mediation?

The difficult international political environment of peace mediation

Five recent and interlinked developments characterize the international political context of peace mediation: changes in international conflicts; geopolitical tensions; the growing role of mediation in the foreign policy of different states; the growth of private diplomacy; and the emphasis on inclusive processes.

The *first* development pertains to changes in international conflicts, which have become more violent since the Arab Spring in 2011. One consequence is the significant increase of forced displacement worldwide. There were more than 70 million refugees and internally displaced persons in late 2018 – the most since the establishment of the UNHCR (United Nations High Commissioner for Refugees) in 1950.[1] The number of war casualties has risen as well. According to Uppsala University, known for providing conservative estimates, over 30,867 people were killed in wars in 2010. That number increased fourfold in 2014, and in 2018, it was still more than 2.5 times the 2010 figure.[2] The total number of conflicts increased as well. According to a study by the International Committee of the Red Cross (ICRC), the number of non-international wars, i.e., civil wars, more than doubled between 2001 and 2016. Moreover, conflicts have become more complex. For example, the same ICRC study stated that the number of conflict parties in general as well as per conflict has significantly increased since 2010.[3] Today, there are also more "international-

---

1 UNHCR, "Figures at a Glance", June 18, 2020, www.unhcr.org/figures-at-a-glance. html (accessed June 26, 2020).
2 These figures are taken from the Uppsala Conflict Data Program website: Uppsala Conflict Data Program (UCDP), "Recorded Fatalities in UCDP Organized Violence 1989–2018", https://ucdp.uu.se/exploratory (accessed June 26, 2019).
3 International Committee of the Red Cross (ICRC), *The Roots of Restraint in War* (Geneva: ICRC, 2018).

ized" conflicts – civil wars in which foreign powers intervene militarily, either directly or using proxy groups.[4]

What do these changes mean for peace mediators? They are the primary reason why classic mediation approaches face significant challenges. In many countries – including Afghanistan, Yemen, Syria, Libya and South Sudan – conflicts have become highly complex systems. They are characterized by multilayered causes, self-perpetuating spirals of violence, a large number of armed and often extremist groups, overlap and interplay of geopolitics and local interests, as well as economies that have adapted to the war, creating situations in which individuals and organizations materially benefit from it. Efforts to solve these conflicts through conventional peace negotiations faces serious limitations, leading the Centre for Humanitarian Dialogue – a prominent mediation organization based in Geneva – to posit the "end of the big peace". The conventional approach according to which the government and a small number of rebel groups that can legitimately claim to represent certain constituencies in society negotiate a comprehensive peace agreement to end a war is no longer a realistic proposition in many places.[5] That does not mean that peace mediators should retreat. Their work remains highly relevant, because they can defuse conflicts, stabilize specific regions, secure humanitarian access and help ensure that violence does not escalate at the societal level. However, mediators may need to adapt their objectives. In the most difficult contexts, it is no longer a question of comprehensive conflict resolution but rather of partial measures within larger and longer-term processes, which are intended to contain and prevent violence and to stabilize the situation. Such an adaptation of objectives necessitates questioning established approaches to peace mediation. And it requires the ability to tackle difficult political and ethical dilemmas. For example, the question arises as to how mediators can engage with extremist groups while avoiding legitimizing their violent tactics.

The *second* development results from the shifts in global political tectonics that have led to "a world out of joint", as Frank-Walter Steinmeier put it.[6] The dominance of Western powers has waned, and the international

---

4 Kendra Dupuy and Siri Aas Rustad, "Trends in Armed Conflict, 1946–2017", *Conflict Trends* 5 (Oslo: Peace Research Institute Oslo [PRIO], 2018).
5 Christina Buchhold et al., *The End of the Big Peace? Opportunities for Mediation*, Meeting Report Oslo Forum 2018 (Geneva: Centre for Humanitarian Dialogue, Norwegian Ministry of Foreign Affairs, 2018).
6 Frank-Walter Steinmeier, "Vorwort von Bundesaußenminister Dr. Frank-Walter Steinmeier", *Zeitschrift für Außen- und Sicherheitspolitik* 8, no. 1 (2015): 1–3.

power structure is shifting towards a multipolar world order with the formation of new blocs. Relations between the West and Russia were severely damaged by the Ukraine crisis in 2014, and they remain broken. The tensions between the US and China have also intensified, culminating in a trade war in recent years. In addition, regional powers – such as Saudi Arabia and Iran in the Middle East – are fighting over supremacy.

These geopolitical tensions hinder efforts towards peace in two ways. Firstly, local conflicts become proxy wars when international powers intervene. This promotes the escalation of conflicts and makes their resolution more difficult, because a solution has to take into account not only the interests of local actors but also those of the international powers. This often amounts to squaring the circle. As the sad example of Syria shows, mediators are also hampered by international powers' seeking to leave their mark on a peace deal. The second way geopolitical polarization hinders efforts towards peace is by blocking multilateral organizations. For instance, in a number of crises and conflicts, for example in Venezuela, the UN Security Council has only a limited ability to act because of divisions between its permanent members. This prevents the UN from either mediating itself, furnishing other actors with a robust mandate or promoting a peace deal through other measures. In the absence of functioning multilateral formats, governments are increasingly drawing on ad-hoc formats bringing together the most important international powers to negotiate a settlement. One example is the Normandy Format dealing with the war in eastern Ukraine and involving representatives of Germany, France, Russia and Ukraine (see also the article by Marike Blunck and Carsten Wieland on the Syrian conflict in this volume).

The *third* development concerns the prominence of peace mediation in the foreign policy of an increasing number of states. Twenty years ago, peace mediation was a foreign policy niche occupied by just a few countries such as Switzerland and Norway; today, however, a large number of countries is committed to it. Headed by Finland and Turkey, the Group of Friends of Mediation has grown to 50 members.[7] These countries not only work on peace mediation in different ways but have highly diverging motives (see the article by Simon J. A. Mason in the present volume). Yet all these states have reacted to the fact that peace mediation now has positive connotations, enjoying broad international support and legitimacy. This is

---

7 See the website of the *Group of Friends of Mediation*: United Nations Peacemaker, "Group of Friends of Mediation", https://peacemaker.un.org/friendsofmediation (accessed June 26, 2019).

evidenced by the unanimous adoption of different UN General Assembly resolutions on mediation since 2011. Mediation is attractive because it permits states to actively address violent conflicts while focusing on civilian measures and respecting the consent of the parties to the conflict. In this way, state sovereignty is maintained, and controversial debates, such as those about the concept of the Responsibility to Protect (R2P), are avoided. Peace mediation thus fits well into the new multipolar world order, in which sovereignty is gaining importance. In addition, a dynamic of "positive contagion" has emerged in recent years: Since the mediation work of pioneering states is perceived positively, it has encouraged other states to commit to it as well. Peace mediation has thus become part of the foreign policy mainstream; today it is a standard (re)action of the community of states to crises and conflicts.

The *fourth* development concerns the growth of private diplomacy, primarily conducted by NGOs specializing in peace mediation. Today hundreds of experts work for these organizations. The Centre for Humanitarian Dialogue, for example, has a global staff of more than 250, while the Crisis Management Initiative, founded by Martti Ahtisaari, employs approximately 100. Two factors have supported the growth of private diplomacy. First, the increasing prominence of peace mediation within foreign policy, as described above, has made financial resources available. Many states now have substantial budgets to promote mediation activities. A significant portion of this money goes to NGOs, which use it to implement projects. The German Federal Foreign Office supports numerous NGOs through its Directorate-General for Humanitarian Assistance, Crisis Prevention, Stabilisation and Post-Conflict Reconstruction.

The second factor supporting the growth of private diplomacy is connected to the development of armed conflicts described above. Peace processes are now less centralized and necessitate diverse engagements with civil society actors as well as with individual armed groups, including those that advocate extremist ideologies. NGOs are more agile than states in this environment. They can react more quickly and take greater risks. This includes speaking with proscribed actors, which is often too politically sensitive for states to do. This modus operandi creates an advantage for NGOs on the peace-mediation "market" and explains their rise in recent years.

The "privatization" of peace mediation has had mixed results. On the positive side, mediation is increasingly employed in the early phases of conflicts, and a broader range of experts is available. This enables opportunities for fruitful cooperation between state and non-state actors. On the other hand, an increase of uncoordinated mediation initiatives risks confusing conflict parties and lessening their commitment to existing negotiation formats, because they may hope to obtain a better deal from other third parties.[8]

The final and *fifth* development concerns the "democratization" of peace processes, which has left its mark on the political discourse of recent years. The notion that peace negotiations should take place behind closed doors and that only a few representatives of the most important armed groups, usually men, should participate, has fallen into disrepute. The inclusion of broad strata of the population is demanded above all by representatives of civil society in countries involved in conflicts. They insist on having a say in peace processes that determine the future of their countries. Their demands have been strengthened by an international push for inclusion that resulted in UN Security Council Resolution 1325 and subsequent resolutions to promote the participation of women in peace processes. This is how "inclusivity" became a fundamental norm in the field of peace mediation – reflected, for example, in the *UN Guidance for Effective Mediation.*[9]

The practice of peace mediation, however, is less progressive than its normative discourse. It is true that mediators increasingly consult a large number of actors and promote dialogue processes with civil society, in which women are now more strongly represented. However, official peace negotiations are still the domain primarily of male representatives of armed groups. Moreover, a large number of societal actor who are affected by conflict and whose support is necessary for sustainable conflict resolution are often not included in peace negotiations. The discrepancy between discourse and practice has not been resolved to date. One reason for this is that the dilemmas associated with inclusion – such as the danger that broad participation promotes the splintering of existing groups and that negotiations will be impossible for mediators to manage because of the large number of negotiating parties – have not been taken seriously enough.

---

8   On the causes and effects of competition in peace mediation, see: David Lanz and Rachel Gasser, *A Crowded Field. Competition and Coordination in International Peace Mediation* (Pretoria: Centre for Mediation in Africa, 2013).

9   United Nations, *United Nations Guidance for Effective Mediation* (New York: United Nations, 2012): 11–13.

Niches for Germany

A comprehensive discussion of the impact of global political developments on the field of peace mediation goes beyond the scope of this contribution. Yet it is possible to ponder what the above-described developments mean for Germany and for its aspiration to be actively involved in mediation processes. Four niches can be discerned here: cooperation with other mediation actors, differentiation of mediation roles, mediation at the geopolitical level and exchange with the scientific community.

The *first* niche involves promoting cooperation between actors in mediation. The growth of the field occasionally results in different mediators' seeking to play a role or claiming a mandate to mediate in the same conflict. Uncoordinated action should however be avoided in these contexts. Instead, what is needed is a joint and coordinated approach as various mediation actors support each other in the interest of peace. Creative opportunities for cooperation between state and non-state actors are particularly relevant. Germany has already established far-reaching partnerships with NGOs and often works closely with them in peace processes – for example in Yemen, where the German Federal Government cooperates with the Berghof Foundation. Therefore, Germany can become a role model for how private and official diplomacy cooperates fruitfully in peace mediation.

The *second* niche concerns the differentiation of roles in mediation processes. Not everyone who seeks to get involved will play a lead mediation role. According to the *UN Guidance for Effective Mediation,*[10] peace talks ideally should be led by one organization and one responsible person. Third parties not involved directly at the negotiation table can, however, make essential contributions. The *UN Guidance* points out the importance of strategic partnerships allowing a broad range of third parties to support peacemaking efforts. In addition, Switzerland has developed a model that defines different supporting roles. They range from deploying technical experts in mediation teams to supporting individual negotiating parties to taking charge of the logistics of peace negotiations.[11] In its *Peace Mediation Framework*, Germany, too, has committed to different roles: leadership in mediation processes, support provided to other mediators, in particular

---

10 United Nations, *United Nations Guidance for Effective Mediation*: 18–19.
11 FDFA, "Mediation as Part of Switzerland's Good Offices", January 1, 2021, www.eda.admin.ch/dam/eda/en/documents/aussenpolitik/menschenrechte-mensc hliche-sicherheit/mediation-als-teil-der-guten-dienste_EN.pdf (accessed February 24, 2021).

multilateral organizations, and conceptual development.[12] In each case, the challenge is to find a role that constitutes a good fit for Germany *and* is relevant to the process. The *Peace Mediation Framework* mentioned above makes interesting proposals here, such as focusing on conflicts that have gained less attention and cooperating systematically with multilateral organizations. This kind of approach could become the hallmark of German peace mediation. One limitation, however, should be pointed out. A certain amount of coherence regarding a country's different policies in a given conflict context is necessary for that country's credibility. This concerns military interventions in particular. They do not contradict peace mediation per se. On the contrary, peacekeeping missions, for example, can help to create a conducive environment. However, military interventions to force regime change are not compatible with a mediation approach.

The *third* niche concerns geopolitics. As described above, civil wars are increasingly exposed to antagonistic geopolitical interests. In this context, it is important that there are countries among the major powers that work to accommodate divergent geopolitical interests, proposing negotiation formats and bringing about compromise within these formats. This is a unique niche for Germany because it has access to circles that remain inaccessible to smaller states such as Norway, Switzerland or Finland, which have been involved in peace mediation longer but are less influential in terms of power politics. Germany has already successfully taken on the role of the "geopolitical mediator" in recent years – for example, within the Normandy Format or the E3/EU+3 Format for the Iran nuclear negotiations – and could do so more often in the future.

The *fourth* niche concerns exchanges with scientific actors. Global politics is changing constantly and dynamically – and with it, international conflicts and efforts to prevent and resolve them. In addition, despite its emphasis on the consent of conflict parties, peace mediation is an intervention with far-reaching impact that one must be aware of in order to do no harm. Indeed, successful peace mediators make a constant effort to understand the dynamic developments in conflict contexts and adapt their work accordingly. This requires regular well-founded analysis as well as further conceptual and methodological development, which is best achieved through the cooperation between science, practice and politics. For example, the Swiss Federal Department of Foreign Affairs supports research and

---

12 Federal Foreign Office, *Peace Mediation Framework* (Berlin: Federal Foreign Office, 2019): 4–5.

analysis in the framework of the *Mediation Support Project*.[13] Germany also maintains close exchanges with scientific actors in the area of peace mediation. This cooperation could be expanded in order to jointly recognize trends, explore planned mediation initiatives, and further develop established approaches.

If Germany succeeds in working systematically in these four niches, it could serve as a role model for other countries and make an even more important contribution to a peaceful world through mediation.

References

Buchhold, Christina, Jonathan Harlander, Sabrina Quamber, and Øyvind Ege. *The End of the Big Peace? Opportunities for Mediation*. Meeting Report Oslo Forum 2018. Geneva: Centre for Humanitarian Dialogue, Norwegian Ministry of Foreign Affairs, 2018.

Dupuy, Kendra, and Siri Aas Rustad. "Trends in Armed Conflict, 1946–2017", *Conflict Trends* 5. Oslo: Peace Research Institute Oslo (PRIO), 2018.

FDFA. "Mediation as Part of Switzerland's Good Offices". N.D. www.eda.admin.c h/dam/eda/en/documents/aussenpolitik/menschenrechte-menschliche-sicherheit /mediation-als-teil-der-guten-dienste_EN.pdf (accessed February 24, 2021).

Federal Foreign Office. *Peace Mediation Framework*. Berlin: Federal Foreign Office, 2019.

International Committee of the Red Cross (ICRC). *The Roots of Restraint in War*. Geneva: ICRC, 2018.

Lanz, David, and Rachel Gasser. *A Crowded Field. Competition and Coordination in International Peace Mediation*. Pretoria: Centre for Mediation in Africa, 2013.

Steinmeier, Frank-Walter. "Vorwort von Bundesaußenminister Dr. Frank-Walter Steinmeier", *Zeitschrift für Außen- und Sicherheitspolitik* 8, no. 1 (2015): 1–3.

UNHCR. "Figures at a Glance", June 18, 2020. www.unhcr.org/figures-at-a-glance. html (accessed June 26, 2020).

United Nations. *United Nations Guidance for Effective Mediation*. New York: United Nations, 2012.

Uppsala Conflict Data Program (UCDP). "Recorded Fatalities in UCDP Organized Violence 1989–2018". N.D. https://ucdp.uu.se/exploratory (accessed June 26, 2019).

---

13 The *Mediation Support Project* (MSP) is a joint venture of the Swiss Peace Foundation swisspeace and the *Center for Security Studies* at ETH Zurich with support from the Swiss Federal Department of Foreign Affairs. The main activities of the MSP are process support, training and applied research. The author serves as the co-coordinator of MSP.

Germany as a Mediation Actor[1]: Development and Conceptual Foundations

Julia von Dobeneck

Introduction

The Federal Foreign Office is involved in a variety of peace processes around the world and is continuing to expand its capacities in the field of mediation. Three main documents provide a mandate and conceptual framework for this development. On June 14, 2019, the Federal Foreign Office launched the last of those documents, the *Peace Mediation Framework*,[2] in which its approach – based on values, interests and methods – was made accessible to the public. The *Peace Mediation Framework* represents a further development of the demand to make greater use of peace mediation in foreign policy, which was formulated first in the *Action Plan for Civilian Crisis Prevention, Conflict Resolution and Peacebuilding* (2004)[3] and later in the *Guidelines on Crisis Prevention, Conflict Resolution and Peacebuilding* (2017).[4]

Mediation has always been a central element of German diplomacy. After the collapse of the Eastern bloc and following the war in former Yugoslavia in the 1990s, German diplomats and politicians have taken on

---

1 This article describes developments in peace mediation at the Federal Foreign Office. It does not include the entire Federal Government or other departments, unless explicitly stated. Since the Federal Foreign Office often uses the term "Germany as an actor" in this context, it is also used as an equivalent for the activities of the Federal Foreign Office in some places.

2 Federal Foreign Office, *Peace Mediation Framework* (Berlin: Federal Foreign Office, 2019).

3 Federal Government of Germany, *Action Plan "Civilian Crisis Prevention, Conflict Resolution and Post-Conflict Peace-Building"* (Berlin: Federal Government of Germany, 2004), hereafter: *Action Plan*.

4 Federal Government of Germany, *Guidelines on Preventing Crises, Resolving Conflicts, Building Peace.* (Berlin: Federal Government of Germany, 2017); hereafter: *Guidelines.*

more visible roles in resolving crises and conflicts.[5] Also, the Federal Foreign Office's promotion of mediation by independent organizations did not just begin with the founding of Directorate-General S in 2015,[6] which is, among other matters, responsible for mediation. Non-governmental organizations (NGOs) already had been involved in facilitating dialogue and mediation processes, for example in the Balkans,[7] in Yemen and in Afghanistan,[8] as well as through the program of the Institut für Auslandsbeziehungen (ifa), zivik.[9] However, responsibility lay with various Federal Foreign Office departments,[10] which had fewer funds available in those days.[11]

So, what is new? In 2014 the Federal Foreign Office set the goal of acting more promptly, decisively, and substantially in foreign policy. It was in this context that mediation activities, too, were to be pooled and expanded.[12] Since that time, close cooperation with civic organizations has been established. The methodological expertise and experiences of such organi-

---

5 These include Hans Koschnick as EU Administrator in Mostar/Bosnia-Herzegovina (1994–1996); Ambassador Michael Steiner as Head of the UN Interim Administration Mission in Kosovo, UNMIK (2002–2003) and as Special Representative for Afghanistan (2010–2012), following Ambassador Bernd Mützelburg (2009–2010); or Christian Schwarz-Schilling as High Representative in Bosnia-Herzegovina (2006–2007), to name but a few. A more detailed account of the various engagements would be worthwhile in any case but cannot be provided in the framework of this contribution.

6 Directorate-General for Humanitarian Assistance, Crisis Prevention, Stabilisation and Post-Conflict Reconstruction; hereafter: *Directorate-General S.*

7 For example, through funds from the Stability Pact for South-Eastern Europe. See: "Stabilitätspakt für Südosteuropa", June 10, 1999, *Sicherheit und Frieden (S+F) / Security and Peace* 17, no. 3, Der Krieg im Kosovo (1999): 214–16.

8 Federal Government of Germany, *Action Plan*: chapter IV.

9 https://www.ifa.de/en/fundings/zivik/.

10 This article focuses on the peace mediation commitment of the Federal Foreign Office. The Federal Ministry for Economic Cooperation and Development (BMZ) and the Deutsche Gesellschaft für internationale Zusammenarbeit (GIZ) have been promoting dialogue measures for conflict transformation for some 20 years, including through the Civil Peace Service (ZFD).

11 It is not possible to determine the exact amount of funding since mediation and dialogue projects have always been financed from various budget headings. According to Rüdiger König, Ministerial Director of Directorate-General S, expenditures were more than 30 million euros when the *Peace Mediation Framework* was published in June 2019.

12 Maria Böhmer, "Grußwort", *Germany as Mediator: Peace Mediation and Mediation Support in German Foreign Policy*, Conference Report 2014 (Berlin: Federal Foreign Office and IMSD, 2015); Deutscher Bundestag, "Antwort der Bundesregierung auf die Kleine Anfrage der Fraktion DIE LINKE", *Bundestag docu-*

zations are considered in the Federal Foreign Office's approach. The current *Peace Mediation Framework* also emphasizes that mediation skills are not the same as diplomatic skills; rather, mediative competence must be learned.[13] What was the path that led towards this approach?

The development presented chronologically below focuses on peace mediation that arose from civilian crisis prevention,[14] a more differentiated definition was only coined when the Framework was published. Also shaping the approach were political developments that pressed Germany to play a stronger role as a multilateral mediator, as well as the international professionalization of peace mediation.[15] In this context, one must not forget the catalyzing effect of foreign-policy ad hoc requirements when dealing with crises and, at least as important, the wealth of ideas and dedication of individuals behind the scenes at the parliament and ministry.[16]

Stations on the Path to the Peace Mediation Framework

1.) The Action Plan "Civilian Crisis Prevention, Conflict Resolution and Peacebuilding": An Initial Milestone

Building on the *Comprehensive Concept of the Federal Government on Civilian Crisis Prevention, Conflict Resolution and Post-Conflict Peace-Building*

---

ment 18/2993; Frank-Walter Steinmeier, "Vierter Bericht der Bundesregierung über die Umsetzung des Aktionsplans", *Minutes of plenary proceedings* 18/86.

13 Federal Foreign Office, *Peace Mediation Framework*: 6.

14 The term "civilian crisis prevention" (Zivile Krisenprävention) is based on the title of the Federal Foreign Office's Directorate-General S for Humanitarian Aid, Crisis Prevention, Stabilisation and Post-Conflict Reconstruction and the Subcommittee on Civilian Crisis Prevention, Conflict Transformation and Integrated Action (formerly Subcommittee on Civilian Crisis Prevention and Networked Security). It is generally used as an umbrella term that also includes approaches to conflict resolution.

15 David Lanz, "Ten Recent Developments in Peace Mediation", *perspective mediation* 17, no. 3 (2017); as well as David Lanz's contribution to this volume. On the history of its origins, see also David Lanz et al., *Understanding Mediation Support Structures* (Bern: swisspeace, 2017).

16 The author followed the development between 2013 and 2017 from a civil-society perspective and has been a participating observer of internal developments at the Federal Foreign Office since 2018 as part of an embedded research and transfer project ("Mediation Hub") of European University Viadrina. Some of the information compiled here is based on these observations or on internal discussions and thus not documented in published sources.

(2000),[17] the aim of the *Action Plan* was to concretize and implement the methodological approaches to crisis prevention[18] and the existing commitment of the German Federal Government.[19] Instruments and institutions were to be expanded or newly created. Particularly noteworthy is the approach already pursued in the comprehensive concept: to not only anchor crisis prevention more firmly in foreign policy, security policy and development policy but also – in the interest of coherence – to integrate economic, financial and environmental policy.[20]

The desire to expand the instruments of diplomacy and development policy, which is documented in two coalition agreements,[21] in the *Comprehensive Concept* as well as in the *Action Plan* can be traced in particular to the experiences in wars in former Yugoslavia. Since the 1990s, this expansion has been prepared and further supported by cross-party commitment,[22] by the targeted creation of individual instruments and institutions

---

17 Federal Government of Germany, "Comprehensive Concept of the Federal Government on Civilian Crisis Prevention, Conflict Resolution and Post-Conflict Peace-Building", idem (2004): *Action Plan*, Annex XIX-XXI (Berlin: Federal Government of Germany, 2004), hereafter: *Comprehensive Concept.*

18 Under the umbrella terms of crisis prevention, conflict resolution and peace consolidation, the *Action Plan* and its underlying *Comprehensive Concept* include the use of effective strategies and instruments for preventing and containing violent conflicts, peaceful conflict resolution and, in addition to peace consolidation, reconstruction. The *Action Plan* is based on "an extended security concept that embraces political, economic, ecological and social stability" (Federal Government of Germany, *Action Plan*: chapter II.3).

19 Federal Government of Germany, *Action Plan*: chapter I.

20 Federal Government of Germany, *Action Plan*: chapter I. In the Federal Government`s *Comprehensive Concept* from 2000, the approach is even more extensive: "Civilian crisis and conflict management requires a comprehensive political strategy which is coordinated at national and international level and tailor-made for each individual situation. This strategy has to dovetail instruments from foreign, security, development, financial, economic, cultural and legal policy fields." Federal Government of Germany, "Comprehensive Concept", idem, *Action Plan* (Berlin: Federal Government of Germany, 2004): Annex, XIX.

21 SPD/Bündnis 90/Die Grünen, *Aufbruch und Erneuerung – Deutschlands Weg ins 21. Jahrhundert.* Coalition agreement (Bonn, 1998); SPD/Bündnis 90/Die Grünen, *ERNEUERUNG – GERECHTIGKEIT – NACHHALTIGKEIT. Für ein wirtschaftlich starkes, soziales und ökologisches Deutschland. Für eine lebendige Demokratie.* Coalition agreement (Berlin, 2002).

22 CDU/CSU/FDP parliamentary groups, "Verstärkung deutscher Beiträge zu Krisenprävention und Friedenspolitik", *Bundestag document* 13/6389, December 4, 1997; SPD parliamentary group, "Priorität für eine Politik der zivilen Krisenprävention und Konfliktregelung", *Bundestag document* 13/6999, February 19, 1997; Bündnis 90/Die Grünen parliamentary group, "Maßnahmen der Entwick-

and the emergence of civic associations.[23] The inclusion of civil-society expertise was settled upon in the coalition agreement of 2002[24] and has been part of further developments in civilian crisis prevention[25] and peace mediation.

In terms of content, the *Action Plan* – with its 161 tasks – conveys a comprehensive claim that ultimately could not be fulfilled in practice: It was missing clear prioritization, content coherence and a robust implementation plan.[26] Often the *Action Plan* was described as a collection of activities that were already taking place. Its anchoring as a cross-sectional task only succeeded to a limited degree, and the Interministerial Steering Group[27] that was designed to, among other things, carry out and monitor the implementation of the *Action Plan*, lacked both decision-making powers and resources.[28]

Still, the *Action Plan* clearly represented an important "catalyst" for the new government coalition in the years that followed, enhancing its ability

---

lungszusammenarbeit als Beitrag zu einer Politik der Krisenprävention und zivilen Konfliktbearbeitung", *Bundestag document* 13/6713, January 14, 1997. On the origins of the *Action Plan*, see the excellent text by Winfried Nachtwei: "Lehren aus 10 Jahren Aktionsplan Zivile Krisenprävention – Wie weiter?", *Sicherheit und Frieden* 32, no. 3 (2014); idem: *Stellungnahme zur Öffentlichen Sitzung des Unterausschusses Zivile Krisenprävention, Konfliktbearbeitung und vernetztes Handeln*, May 5, 2014; idem: *Zivile Krisenprävention – grüner Markenkern in der Friedenspolitik?*, March 16, 2019.

23 Forum Ziviler Friedensdienst (1996); German Platform for Peaceful Conflict Management (1998); Civil Peace Service (CPS), founded in 1999; German Foundation for Peace Research (DSF), founded in 2000; Working Group on Peace and Development (FriEnt), founded in 2001; zivik support program of the Institut für Auslandsbeziehungen (ifa), founded in 2001; and Centre for International Peace Operations (ZIF), founded in 2002.

24 SPD/Bündnis 90/Die Grünen, *Coalition agreement* 2002: 85.

25 Federal Government of Germany, *Action Plan*: chapter V; Federal Government of Germany, *Guidelines*: chapter III; Federal Foreign Office, *Peace Mediation Framework*.

26 German Platform for Peaceful Conflict Management, *Stillschweigender Abschied vom Aktionsplan Zivile Krisenprävention?*, Stellungnahme zum 3. Umsetzungsbericht "Zivile Krisenprävention, Konfliktbewältigung und Friedenskonsolidierung" der Bundesregierung vom 23. Juni 2010 zum Aktionsplan "Zivile Krisenprävention, Konfliktbewältigung und Friedenskonsolidierung" (Berlin/Cologne: German Platform for Peaceful Conflict Management, 2010); Bündnis 90/Die Grünen parliamentary group, "Kleine Anfrage zur Umsetzung des Aktionsplans Zivile Krisenprävention", *Bundestag document* 16/9171, May 9, 2008.

27 The group was composed of representatives of the departments for civilian crisis prevention in all relevant ministries (*Action Plan*, Action 136).

28 Nachtwei, *Lehren aus 10 Jahren Aktionsplan*.

to act in the field of civilian crisis prevention.[29] Even 13 years after its adoption, the plan was described as a "milestone in foreign policy" by actors not directly involved in its creation.[30]

The *Action Plan* contains three strategic approaches: 1) creating state structures; 2) promoting peace potential in civil society, media, culture and education; and 3) safeguard people's opportunities in life by taking appropriate measures in the realms of economy, society and environment. Conflicts are seen as "part and parcel of all processes of transition" that become "productive if resolved by means of peaceful, inclusive debate conducted in a spirit of solidarity with the aim of finding the best solution."[31] Conflict management or mediation by third parties, and the prerequisites for their use, are not described systematically but rather emerge at various points and in connection with specific measures (such as dialogue programs). The *Action Plan* focuses primarily on creating state and democratic structures in crisis countries – which in turn provide mechanisms for peaceful conflict resolution – and on promoting appropriate non-governmental and informal instruments and reform-minded individuals in conflict regions. The detailed definitions of conflict management, conflict resolution and mediation, as found in the Glossary to the *Action Plan*,[32] should be highlighted as they represent an understanding of conflict mediation that incorporates essential principles of mediation. Thus, the *Action Plan* already includes important conceptual elements for the further development of peace mediation as a foreign-policy instrument.

2.) The "Review Process" and the Establishment of Directorate-General S: Strategic Change Processes in the Federal Foreign Office

At the Munich Security Conference in January 2014, Federal President Joachim Gauck, Foreign Minister Frank-Walter Steinmeier and Defense Minister Ursula von der Leyen called for a stronger and earlier foreign-pol-

---

29 Deutscher Bundestag, "Antwort der Bundesregierung auf die Kleine Anfrage der Fraktion Bündnis 90/Die Grünen", *Bundestag document* 16/9363.
30 Kathrin Vogler (member of parliamentary group DIE LINKE) at the Federal Government of Germany's briefing on the *Guidelines, Bundestag minutes of plenary proceedings* 18/244.
31 Federal Government of Germany, *Action Plan*: chapter I, 1.
32 Federal Government of Germany, *Action Plan*: Annexes.

icy engagement by the Federal Government of Germany.[33] This announce-
ment was preceded by a conceptual foreign-policy exchange initiated by
the German Marshall Fund of the United States (GMF) and the Stiftung
Wissenschaft und Politik (SWP), with support from the planning staff of
the Federal Foreign Office.[34] In February 2014, Foreign Minister Frank-
Walter Steinmeier inspired the next decisive stage on the road to peace mediation with the reform process *Review 2014 – Außenpolitik Weiter
Denken*.[35] This process was meant to reflect critically on German foreign
policy and propose changes based on the questions "What, if anything, is
wrong with German foreign policy? What needs to be changed?" Participants were national and international experts, the general public and
members of the diplomatic service itself, who exchanged views on reshap-
ing Germany's role as well as on a more strategic foreign and security policy. One conclusion was that Germany should take a more active role in
foreign policy, including crisis prevention and peace promotion.[36] This review process and Germany's reflections on its Afghanistan engagement, as
well as an intensive and comparative examination of international stabilization policy, particularly regarding approaches by the United Kingdom,[37] led to the establishment of Directorate-General S in March 2015.
Within this section, the work of peace mediation was also to be en-
hanced,[38] not least inspired by the Foreign Minister's mediation experience in the Ukraine crisis.

---

33 FAZ, *Gauck fordert neue deutsche Außenpolitik*, January 31, 2014; Jochen Bittner
    and Matthias Naß, "Kurs auf die Welt", *DIE ZEIT*, February 6, 2014.

34 Institute for International and Security Affairs and German Marshall Fund of the
    United States, *New Power, New Responsibility: Elements of a German Foreign and Se-
    curity Policy for a Changing World* (Berlin/Washington, 2013).

35 Federal Foreign Office, "Review 2014 – Außenpolitik weiter denken", www.ausw
    aertiges-amt.de/blob/269656/d26e1e50cd5acb847b4b9eb4a757e438/review2014-ab
    schlussbericht-data.pdf (accessed September 1, 2019).

36 For the results of the review process and critical reflections on Germany's role, see
    also Annegret Bendiek, *The "2014 Review": Understanding the Pillars of German For-
    eign Policy and the Expectations of the rest of the World* (Berlin: Institute for Interna-
    tional and Security Affairs, 2015).

37 Philipp Rotmann and Léa Steinacker, "Stabilization, Doctrine, Organization and
    Practice. Lessons from Canada, the Netherlands, the United Kingdom and the
    United States", *Global Public Policy Institute* (December 2013).

38 Frank-Walter Steinmeier, "Rede bei der Abschlussveranstaltung zu Review 2014 –
    Außenpolitik weiter denken", February 25, 2015, www.auswaertiges-amt.de/de/ne
    wsroom/150225-bm-review-abschlussveranstaltung/269638 (accessed September 1,
    2019).

The task of Directorate-General S with its division S03, which became responsible for grants to support crisis prevention, stabilization,[39] and post-conflict peacebuilding projects, was to establish a more targeted use of and further develop existing funding instruments scattered across various departments, so as to provide "foreign policy with resources".[40] But a new edition of the *Action Plan* and a conceptual implementation mandate were not yet available. In the Directorate-General S's development phase, however, civil-society mediation actors were able to contribute to the conceptual design of peace mediation as an instrument within the section.

3.) *Initiative Mediation Support Deutschland (IMSD): A Call for a More Refined Definition of Peace Mediation*

Inspired by the establishment of the European Institute for Peace,[41] German civic mediation organizations joined in late 2012 to form a thematically focused initiative. Their goal was to process methodological knowledge and experience from mediation and dialogue processes in order to sharpen the definition of peace mediation as an instrument of crisis prevention and to demonstrate its possible applications. "AG Friedensmediation", known today as the Initiative Mediation Support Deutschland

---

39 The Federal Government of Germany defines stabilization as measures to support "political processes of conflict resolution, while providing an incentive for parties to cease engagement in armed conflict. (…) Stabilisation measures may also serve to consolidate legitimate political authorities by supporting them in their efforts to offer the population a more persuasive and inclusive vision which is more attractive than competing models of exercising political power" (Federal Government of Germany, *Guidelines*: 69).

40 Ekkehard Brose, "Krisen verhindern, Konflikte bewältigen, Frieden fördern", *Das Weißbuch 2016 und die Herausforderungen von Strategiebildung*, edited by Daniel Jacobi and Gunther Hellmann (Wiesbaden: Springer VC, 2019), 239.

41 European Institute for Peace (EIP), www.eip.org; MediatEUr, "A European Institute of Peace? Value-added, Risks and Options", September 5, 2012, http://themed iateur.eu/a-european-institute-of-peace-value-added-risks-and-options/ (accessed July 21, 2019). The EIP should, among other things, act as a "hub for mediators" and complement the commitment of the European External Action Service (EEAS) in the field of mediation by rapidly dispatching mediation experts and by debriefings after assignments. The EIP was launched by the Swedish Foreign Minister Carl Bildt, the Green MEP Franziska Brantner and the French MEP Alain Lamassoure.

(IMSD),[42] included individuals who also had been intensively involved in the *Action Plan* and were continuing their commitment to crisis prevention with the new initiative.[43] The involvement of practice-oriented academics and organizations experienced in methodological training[44] added a methodological component to the crisis prevention approach, inspired by many years of experience in dialogue facilitation. The members also wished to integrate into foreign policy both the international professionalization of peace mediation and the extensive experience with various mediation procedures within Germany.[45]

During the 2014 Bundestag election campaign, Green and Social Democratic legislators called for improved coordination of existing competencies, capacities, and potential to sharpen peace mediation as a crisis prevention tool. Soon after the election, in November 2014, the IMSD and the Federal Foreign Office held a joint conference on "Germany as a Mediator: Peace Mediation and Mediation Support in German Foreign Policy". Its goal was to more clearly define Germany's foreign-policy profile as a conflict mediator. One result was that a cross-track peace mediation approach was consolidated. This was meant to be embedded in the international environment of bilateral and multilateral approaches.[46] While follow-up con-

---

42 At the beginning, the association consisted of CSSP – Berlin Center for Integrative Mediation, the Berghof Foundation, the Center for Peace Mediation (CPM) at European University Viadrina and the Center for International Peace Operations (ZIF). About a year later, they were joined by inmedio – institut für mediation. beratung. entwicklung. The association was named Initiative Mediation Support Deutschland (IMSD) in 2014.

43 The Berghof Foundation and the ZIF, as long-standing actors in civilian crisis prevention, deserve mention here.

44 CPM and inmedio.

45 A first occasion to formulate proposals for shaping this field was provided by a workshop on April 22, 2013 in the German Bundestag, marking the establishment of the European Institute for Peace: *Die EU als Friedensmacht: Mediationskapazitäten stärken*, under the auspices of the Subcommittee on Civilian Crisis Prevention and Integrated Action. Subsequently, an expert hearing on peace mediation structures in international comparison took place in May 2013, also under the auspices of the Subcommittee on Civilian Crisis Prevention and Integrated Action. For background on the hearing, see Initiative Mediation Support Deutschland (IMSD), *Friedensmediation: Kurzinformation und Vorschläge für die Politik*, April 30, 2013.

46 Federal Foreign Office and IMSD, *Germany as Mediator: Peace Mediation and Mediation Support in German Foreign Policy*, Conference Report 2014 (Berlin: Federal Foreign Office and IMSD, 2015).

ferences focused more on other topics,[47] the November 14 conference – seen in retrospect as a "kickoff" for visible German mediation engagement – was a platform for participants to formulate demands that still remain current: Germany should not duplicate existing mediation work, it should use its political and economic weight in a targeted manner, and it should strive for better networking and coordination of governmental and non-governmental mediation actors. In order to dispatch experts quickly on a mediation mission, a pool of experts and service contracts outside the diplomatic career path was recommended – along the lines of the Human Security Adviser approach of the Swiss Federal Department of Foreign Affairs (FDFA).[48]

Over the years that followed, the IMSD developed Fact Sheets, some of which are published in this volume, in order to broaden the knowledge of diplomats working in the area of peace mediation within the Federal Foreign Office. In addition, various training and consulting formats were established for the Foreign Service. Looking back, one may conclude that the IMSD has clearly contributed towards sharpening the definition of peace mediation as an instrument, even though the number of articles published and events held has decreased over the years and impulses increasingly have come from the Federal Foreign Office itself.

4.) *The Federal Government's Guidelines: Preventing Crises, Managing Conflicts, Promoting Peace – A Clear Mandate for Directorate-General S*

The United Nations' 2030 Agenda for Sustainable Development (2015) and the *European Union Global Strategy* (2016) are international targets that framed the 2017 *Guidelines*.[49] Like the review process, the *Guidelines* were de-

---

47 The expert meeting *Identifying Entry Points*, held on October 5, 2015, focused on themes of conflict analysis and entry points, while the conference *The OSCE as Mediator: Instruments – Challenges – Potentials*, held on July 6, 2016 during the German OSCE chairmanship, was dedicated to mediation processes and potentials in the OSCE area. The conference reports are available at: www.peace-mediation-germany.de.

48 Federal Foreign Office and IMSD, *Germany as Mediator: Peace Mediation and Mediation Support in German Foreign Policy*: 23, 29.

49 Rüdiger König, "Ein Wiki der Krisenprävention", *Deutschlands neue Verantwortung. Die Zukunft der deutschen und europäischen Außen-, Entwicklungs- und Sicherheitspolitik*, edited by Wolfgang Ischinger and Dirk Messner (Berlin: Econ, 2017): 280.

veloped in a participatory manner through the *PeaceLab2016*[50] platform and coordinated cross-departmentally by Directorate-General S.[51] This was preceded by the interdepartmental guidelines *For a Coherent Policy towards Fragile States*,[52] as well as by basic documents of the Federal Ministry of Defense[53] and the Federal Ministry for Economic Cooperation and Development.[54]

The goal of the *Guidelines* is to increase the coordination and coherence of individual measures and to strengthen foreign-policy instruments in crises. The *Guidelines* emphasize the peace mandate in Germany's Basic Law and prioritize the political over the military.[55] Then-Federal Foreign Minister Sigmar Gabriel described them as a "compass for modern peace diplomacy" during the plenary debate in the German Bundestag.[56] With these *Guidelines*, he said, the government was also building on the peace infrastructure that had been developed over decades and for which Germany had earned worldwide recognition.[57] Crisis prevention is seen as the preferred foreign-policy approach in conflict regions, not least for cost considerations.[58]

According to the protagonists involved, the path to adoption of these *Guidelines* was sometimes arduous. It took a considerable effort to reach consent on interdepartmental goals and definitions, because of different departmental cultures and preferences. But when it comes to the desired coherence of government action, the value of this process should not be

---

50 Under the motto *PeaceLab2016: Krisenprävention weiter denken!*, 27 events were held with 1,800 participants. Experts, members of parliament and ministers published articles on the topic in the accompanying blog: https://peacelab.blog/debatt e/peacelab-2016.

51 For a detailed history of the development of the *Guidelines*, see also Brose, *Krisen verhindern, Konflikte bewältigen, Frieden fördern*: 287–96.

52 Federal Government of Germany, *Für eine kohärente Politik der Bundesregierung gegenüber fragilen Staaten – Ressortübergreifende Leitlinien* (Berlin: Federal Government of Germany, 2012).

53 Federal Government of Germany, *Weißbuch zur Sicherheitspolitik und zur Zukunft der Bundeswehr* (Bonn/Berlin: Federal Government of Germany, 2016).

54 BMZ, "Entwicklung für Frieden und Sicherheit. Entwicklungspolitisches Engagement im Kontext von Konflikt, Fragilität und Gewalt", *BMZ-Strategiepapier* 4/2013 (Bonn/Berlin).

55 Federal Government of Germany, *Guidelines*: chapter II.

56 Sigmar Gabriel during the consultation following the briefing of the Federal Government of Germany on the *Guidelines*, *minutes of plenary proceedings* 18/244.

57 Sigmar Gabriel, introduction to the *Guidelines*: 5.

58 König, *Ein Wiki der Krisenprävention*: 280.

underestimated, nor should the usefulness of the resulting document, to whose common definitions one can refer.

Both the Bundestag and civil society praised the *Guidelines* for their clearly formulated peace-policy model, for the close involvement of the Bundestag and civil society[59] and for the continuous increase in funding over the years. However, critiques were made about the fact that the German Federal Government was rarely self-critical and only summarized what it was already implementing.[60] Another complaint related to the lack of an implementation plan for interministerial coordination or of approaches for efficient handling of increased demands, tasks and growth in funding.[61]

Similarly to the *Action Plan*, the *Guidelines* see conflicts as a natural component of societal change processes. As part of its engagement for peace, the Federal Government supports the notion that such processes can be accomplished constructively and without violence, through cooperation between foreign, security and development policy, and through the contributions of internationally effective educational, cultural, trade, environmental and economic policy.[62] The *Guidelines* are divided into a description of

---

59 See, for example, Frei (CDU/CSU) in his statement during the consultation following the Federal Government of Germany's briefing on the *Guidelines, minutes of plenary proceedings* 18/244; Winfried Nachtwei, *Meine Stellungnahme zu den Leitlinien Friedensförderung der Bundesregierung: Deutlicher Fortschritt, aber mit Handicaps*, June 29, 2017.

60 Kathrin Vogler (member of parliamentary group DIE LINKE) during the consultation following the Federal Government of Germany's briefing on the *Guidelines, minutes of plenary proceedings* 18/244.

61 Oliver Knabe, "Gut im Grundsatz, enttäuschend im Handeln", *press release of the German Platform for Peaceful Conflict Management*, June 24, 2017; Franziska Brantner (member of parliamentary group Bündnis 90/Die Grünen) during the consultation following the Federal Government of Germany's briefing on the *Guidelines, minutes of plenary proceedings* 18/244; Marina Zapf, "Leitlinien Friedensförderung. Ungenau, unkritisch, ziellos", *WELT-SICHTEN*, June 20, 2017, www.welt-sichten.org/artikel/32964/leitlinien-friedensfoerderung-ungenau-unkritisch-ziellos (accessed September 14, 2019); Hans Jörg Friedrich, "Kabinett verabschiedet friedenspolitische Leitlinien der Bundesregierung", *Weltfriedensdienst e.V.*, June 15, 2017, https://wfd.de/kabinett-verabschiedet-friedenspolitische-leitlinien-der-bundesregierung (accessed September 14, 2019); Tobias Schulze, "Deutsche Regierung als Streitschlichter. Frieden schaffen ohne Waffen?", *taz.de*, June 15, 2017, https://taz.de/Deutsche-Regierung-als-Streitschlichter/!5418355/ (accessed September 14, 2019). On the reactions to the *Guidelines*, see also https://peacelab.blog/2017/06/reaktionen-auf-die-leitlinien (accessed September 14, 2019).

62 Federal Government of Germany, *Guidelines*: 59.

the world order in transition and the German Federal Government's model response to it. A description of goals and instruments follows, as well as of those structures and partnerships in which the Federal Government is involved. It concludes with 50 voluntary commitments.

Unlike the *Action Plan*, the *Guidelines* include a clear definition of peace mediation: Thanks to its international reputation and its political and economic influence, Germany could take up the role of a constructive mediator that coordinates closely with its partners – a definition of its own role that also comes up later in the *Peace Mediation Framework*. Mediation could contribute to "bridging the often-deep political and social rifts between conflict parties and creating a basis of trust".[63] A list of the essential elements of peace mediation then follows: the qualification of mediators, the local institutionalization of mediation processes and support for negotiations (Good Offices or Mediation Support). Furthermore, it is announced to advance Germany's own peace mediation skills and to engage more in mediation processes using an inclusive approach.

However, in comparison with previous conferences and statements[64] as well as clear proposals by the IMSD for further development,[65] the wording on peace mediation in the *Guidelines* is very brief. The goal of further expanding peace mediation, which Directorate-General S has pursued ever since, should be highlighted here. Thus, as of 2018, for example, a conceptual underpinning and sharpening of the definition of peace mediation has been developed, along with quality standards for the implementation of mediation and dialogue projects. A peace mediation team within the Federal Foreign Office is gradually being established. The aforementioned international professionalization of peace mediation as well as numerous exchange formats between states engaged in the field also play an important role here (see David Lanz's article in this volume).

---

63 Federal Government of Germany, *Guidelines*, Box on *Peace Mediation and Negotiation Support*: 77.

64 Steinmeier, *Rede bei der Abschlussveranstaltung zu Review 2014*.

65 Initiative Mediation Support Deutschland (IMSD), "Das deutsche Bekenntnis zur Friedensmediation ausbuchstabieren – eine Positionierung der Initiative Mediation Support Deutschland", 2016, www.friedensmediation-deutschland.de/filead min/uploads/friedensmeditation/dokumente/Friedensmediation_ausbuchstabiere n__IMSD-Positionspapier_Leitlinienprozess.pdf (accessed September 14, 2019); Lars Kirchhoff, Anne Isabel Kraus (now Holper) and Julia von Dobeneck, "Von Elefanten und Papiertigern in der Friedensmediation", December 22, 2016, https://peacelab.blog/2016/12/von-elefanten-und-papiertigern-in-der-friedensmediation (accessed September 14, 2019).

Julia von Dobeneck

Peace Mediation in the Foreign Policy Activities of the Federal Foreign Office

In 2019, the Federal Foreign Office used peace mediation in a variety of ways. Aside from the suitability of peace mediation for addressing a particular conflict, the question of whether an engagement is started depends on three essential components, in the view of this author: 1) existing accesses to and trust on the part of the conflict parties, 2) the possibility of taking a multi-partial role (which may be limited or excluded by alliance principles such as majority decisions at the EU level) and 3) foreign policy interests regarding the resolution of the conflict. The roles that are exercised range from direct mediation, mediation support to other third parties (UN, other states, NGOs), the establishment of so-called back channels to various types of mediation preparation. At the moment, the role of the "supporter of supporters" is particularly important: Directorate-General S alone is currently supporting some 30 mediation and dialogue processes worldwide, with about 30 million euros.[66] The distribution of tasks and roles between the Federal Foreign Office and NGOs operating as third parties is varied, ranging from an exclusive focus on financial support to political and methodological coordination in process design issues to joint action.

In Yemen, for example, the Berghof Foundation has received funding since 2012 from the Federal Foreign Office for its mediation activities,[67] supporting a Track 2 process[68] that involves high-ranking politicians from all parties and is considered the only inclusive and still-functioning exchange platform in that conflict. Furthermore, the Federal Foreign Office is contributing to a political solution to the Yemen conflict, flanking the process with stabilization measures[69] and supporting UN Special Envoy

---

66   There are no figures or data available on how many dialogue processes (at the civil-society or municipal level) are supported by other departments or even by the BMZ. Taken together, however, there are likely to be more than the 30 cited in the text.

67   Berghof Foundation, "Yemen Political Dialogue Support Programme (PDSP)", https://berghof-foundation.org/work/projects/yemen-political-dialogue-support-programme-pdsp/ (accessed January 31, 2021).

68   For a description of the tracks, see the Fact Sheet on *Basics of Mediation: Concepts and Definitions* in this volume.

69   Handelsblatt, *Deutschland sichert 4,5 Millionen Euro für Jemen-Hilfen zu*, January 16, 2019, www.handelsblatt.com/politik/international/friedensbemuehungen-deutschland-sichert-4-5-millionen-euro-fuer-jemen-hilfen-zu/23873932.html?ticket=ST-670425-czIyjibt33n3xCuXKbCr-ap4 (accessed July 24, 2019).

Martin Griffiths and his exchange with representatives of the Track 2 process.[70]

At the end of 2018, with the signing of a pre-negotiation agreement in Berlin between the insurgents in the Darfur region and the Sudanese administration, the Federal Foreign Office offered the parties to that conflict a neutral venue for their official preparations for peace negotiations.[71] The agreement followed a two-year mediation process in which the Berghof Foundation played a key role in mediation support.[72]

With regard to the crisis in and around Ukraine, Germany[73] is represented in the Normandy Format talks (alongside Russia, Ukraine and France) and in the Economic Working Group of the Trilateral Contact Group (TCG). The latter is facilitated by the Special Representative appointed by the OSCE chairman (additionally supported at the working level by Germany). Within the OSCE, Germany contributes personnel at various levels (working-level mediation support team in the Conflict Prevention Centre of the OSCE Secretariat in Vienna, Deputy Head of Mission, and working-level Special Monitoring Mission – SMM). It also finances various NGOs' dialogue support at different societal levels on diverse conflict themes. Of these NGO-led processes, some are closely linked to the implementation of the Minsk Process and, consequently, to the highest political level (Track 1), while others are more oriented towards civil society.[74]

In 2018, the Federal Foreign Office supported preparations for a national conference in Libya of the UN-led process over the commitment of the

---

70 Silke Mertins, "Jemen-Krieg: Eine elende Generation wächst nach", *NZZ*, January 5, 2019, https://nzzas.nzz.ch/international/jemen-krieg-elende-generation-waechst-nach-ld.1449223#swglogin (accessed July 24, 2019).

71 Federal Foreign Office, "Foreign Minister Maas on the agreement to hold new peace talks on Darfur", *press release*, December 6, 2018, https://www.auswaertiges-amt.de/en/newsroom/news/maas-dafur-peace-talks/2167902 (accessed January 31, 2021).

72 Africa-live, "Sudan/Darfur, Einigung auf neue Friedensverhandlungen", December 6, 2018, www.africa-live.de/sudan-darfur-einigung-auf-neue-friedensverhandlungen/ (accessed July 24, 2019).

73 The Chancellery oversees this process, working closely with the Federal Foreign Office.

74 For example, the dialogue on conflict transformation between women from government-controlled and uncontrolled areas in Ukraine and from the Russian Federation, facilitated by OWEN – Mobile Akademie für Geschlechterdemokratie und Friedensförderung: *Women's Initiatives for Peace in Donbas(s)*, www.owen-berlin.de/projekte/wipd.php (accessed July 24, 2019).

Centre for Humanitarian Dialogue (HD),[75] while in 2019, the Federal Government initiated the Berlin Process.[76] For the resumption of the UN-led, results-oriented negotiation process in the Cyprus conflict, Germany is acting as host country and offering the UN Secretary General the opportunity to meet with the leaders of the two Cypriot ethnic groups.[77] In the current conflict between civil society and government in Nicaragua, Minister of State Niels Annen is involved at the political level.[78] The Federal Foreign Office is also active in such countries as Afghanistan, Somalia, Colombia and Nigeria, to name a few.

In addition, experts are sent to accompany processes or institutions involved in mediation and dialogue, such as the mediation support team of the EEAS, the aforementioned OSCE Mediation Support Team in Vienna, the OSCE Special Monitoring Mission in Ukraine[79] and the team of the United Nations Special Envoy for Syria, or to head the OSCE Mission to Moldova, which handles – among other issues – questions about the frozen Transnistria conflict.

Current and past ambassadors, members of parliament and other experts play important mediation roles. Some examples are Ulrich Brandenburg, who followed the economics expert Per Fischer (May 2015–January 2019) as coordinator of the above-mentioned Economic Working Group of the Trilateral Contact Group (TCG) for resolving the crisis in Ukraine; Johannes Haindl in the Macedonia crisis (2016); and Tom Königs, a member of the German Bundestag, who served as Special Representative of the Federal Government for the peace process in Colombia (2015–May 2019).

There are also individuals who regularly play important roles in mediation or support but remain more in the background, providing their politi-

---

75   Centre for Humanitarian Dialogue (HD), "Lybia", www.hdcentre.org/activities/li bya/ (accessed July 24, 2019).

76   Federal Foreign Office, "Government press conference", November 22, 2019, www.auswaertiges-amt.de/de/newsroom/regierungspressekonferenz/2281144 (accessed November 29, 2019).

77   Ibid.

78   Niels Annen, tweet from July 1, 2019, https://twitter.com/nielsannen (accessed September 1, 2019); Birke, "Kein Grund zum Feiern in Nicaragua", *Deutschlandfunk*, July 18, 2019, www.deutschlandfunk.de/40-jahre-sandinistische-revolution-k ein-grund-zum-feiern-in.724.de.html?dram:article_id=454216 (accessed November 19, 2019); Federal Foreign Office, "Peace mediation: Working for peace", June 18, 2019, https://www.auswaertiges-amt.de/en/aussenpolitik/themen/krisenpraeventio n/peace-mediation/2227412 (accessed January 31, 2021).

79   ZIF carried out all three of the above-mentioned secondments.

cal experience, access to the region or expertise either directly to the Federal Foreign Office or via NGOs.

The substantial financing earmarked by the Bundestag is advantageous, since it provides opportunities to support peace processes sustainably, not only through mediation but also through flanking stabilizing measures in the security sector, rule-of-law reforms or reconciliation work. In this context, the anchoring of peace mediation within Division S03, which focuses on stabilization instruments, is helpful.

From the perspective of the Federal Foreign Office, this use of taxpayer money and German political weight brings with it the responsibility to clearly define its own role and to provide a conceptual framework for mediation work.[80] The *Peace Mediation Framework* is intended to fulfill this responsibility. Aside from containing values and norms, as well as explanations on how UN mediation principles translate to Germany's political role, the Framework includes a structuring description of previous practices. The approaches sketched out in the Framework are therefore based in no small part on the experiences of many NGOs and their work, from which the Federal Foreign Office has learned through joint collaborations over recent years. In this way, though civil society may not have been directly active in formulating the preceding documents (*Action Plan, Guidelines*), it nevertheless participated indirectly in the content of the Framework.

Outlook

Following the publication of the *Peace Mediation Framework*, the Federal Foreign Office is called upon to consistently implement its own standards not only in the allocation of funds but also, increasingly, in direct contributions or in mediation support. It is important to show *that* – and *how* – political weight, economic influence and any existing bilateral or alliance commitments can be reconciled with an approach guided by values, interests and methodology (with a view to multipartiality). It is also necessary to demonstrate precisely how this combination can contribute to the resolution of conflicts in a different way than, for example, the approaches of Switzerland and Norway, which have been heavily involved in peace mediation to date.

---

80 According to Rüdiger König, Ministerial Director of Directorate-General S, at the publication of the *Peace Mediation Framework* on June 14, 2019.

At the latest since the conference on "Germany as Mediator" (2014), national and international actors in peace mediation have raised their expectations for a defined German portfolio. The *Peace Mediation Framework* and the statement of acting Minister of State Niels Annen upon its publication make it clear: There is not likely to be any stipulation on a specific type of conflict or regional focus in the foreseeable future. This is understandable because Germany is a visible actor with diverse political interests, political alliances and multilateral commitments that must be considered when it comes to addressing specific crises. Context matters and does not always allow for Germany to take on all possible roles. The preconditions for a German mediation role, as stated in the publication of the Framework (specifically, the limitation of German engagement to those constellations in which one is welcome and is not duplicating the work of other actors), are to be seen against this background. At the same time, they express German foreign policy's long-standing hesitation both to play a visible role as an actor with primarily responsibilities and to bear all risks in conflict mediation.

The further development of peace mediation in the Federal Foreign Office is also dependent upon internal constellations, a functioning infrastructure and – importantly – budgetary solutions that allow for rapid and flexibly designed mediation assignments or support for such interventions by others. Rotation-related challenges, a relatively thin staffing structure (which affects far more than the field of peace mediation) and complex legal limitations on the design of related contracts and grants have thus far restricted the Federal Foreign Office's ability both to provide expertise, experienced mediators or mediation support teams[81] on an uncomplicated and short-term basis and to institutionalize and coordinate corresponding structures.

In addition, there is an ongoing learning process within the Federal Foreign Office as to how the instruments assembled in Directorate-General S and the methodological expertise of the peace mediation team can be integrated most efficiently into political processes. Here it is about learning from processes that will certainly be brought to Germany in the future, and also about consistently orienting ongoing mediation to one's own methodological and conceptual demands – not least in order to define the criteria for assigning actions to peace mediation or to classic diplomacy, respectively. One also could evaluate more deeply and systematically the pros

---

81 To see how this fits with the steps taken in other states, see David Lanz et al., *Understanding Mediation Support Structures* (Bern: swisspeace, 2017).

and cons of other countries' structures and strategies, as well as those of multilateral organizations like the OSCE, the EU or the UN and their support structures, in order to design a fitting infrastructure for the German Federal Foreign Office.

It is possible that also in the future, the core of the Federal Foreign Office's mediation approach will be to act as a supporter of supporters, working closely with independent third parties in assigned roles or exclusively as a funder – and therefore working more or less behind the scenes. In any case, the financial scope of a German peace mediation engagement offers the opportunity to secure greater influence and political maneuverability as a strong donor within the group of supporters – not least in order to claim a potential mediation role. Ultimately, German engagement could also involve even more multilateral support for mediation processes led by others, such as the UN (see the article by David Lanz in this volume). Germany's role in providing methodologically sound and values-led mediation support that contributes to the coordination of processes large and small seems to make sense for the foreseeable future, given today's unsettled multilateral system, fragmented conflict parties and the increasing number of geostrategic conflicts.

While it is not impossible to imagine Germany taking on a leading or more visible mediation role in the future, this is likely to remain the exception. Nevertheless, there is one central task ahead: to promote the development within one's own system so that mediation potential is recognized, clear roles are defined and distributed between the government and other third parties, and German peace mediation engagement is further professionalized altogether. Ultimately, it is important to proceed coherently in the spirit of the 15-year-old *Action Plan* and the *Guidelines* and to involve the other relevant ministries where this creates added value, without sacrificing foreign-policy leadership. With mediations led by the German Chancellery, for example, the Federal Foreign Office and Directorate-General S should be encouraged to provide support not only in the financial sense but also in terms of methodology, and to use available networks of specialists and non-governmental mediation actors in tailor-made set ups.

References

Africa-live. "Sudan/Darfur, Einigung auf neue Friedensverhandlungen", December 6, 2018. www.africa-live.de/sudan-darfur-einigung-auf-neue-friedensverhandlung en/ (accessed July 24, 2019).

Annen, Niels. Tweet, July 1, 2019. https://twitter.com/nielsannen (accessed September 1, 2019).

Bendiek, Annegret. *The "2014 Review": Understanding the Pillars of German Foreign Policy and the Expectations of the Rest of the World*. Berlin: Institute for International and Security Affairs, 2015.

Berghof Foundation. "Yemen Political Dialogue Support Programme (PDSP)". https://berghof-foundation.org/work/projects/yemen-political-dialogue-support-programme-pdsp/ (accessed January 31, 2021)

Birke, Burkhard. "Kein Grund zum Feiern in Nicaragua", *Deutschlandfunk*, July 18, 2019. https://www.deutschlandfunk.de/40-jahre-sandinistische-revolution-kein-g rund-zum-feiern-in.724.de.html?dram:article_id=454216 (accessed November 19, 2019).

Bittner, Jochen, and Matthias Naß. "Kurs auf die Welt", *DIE ZEIT*, February 6, 2014. www.zeit.de/2014/07/deutsche-aussenpolitik-sicherheitskonferenz (accessed July 20, 2019).

BMZ (Bundesministerium für wirtschaftliche Zusammenarbeit und Entwicklung / Federal Ministry for Economic Cooperation and Development). "Entwicklung für Frieden und Sicherheit. Entwicklungspolitisches Engagement im Kontext von Konflikt, Fragilität und Gewalt", *BMZ-Strategiepapier 4/2013*. Bonn/Berlin.

Böhmer, Maria. "Grußwort". *Germany as Mediator: Peace Mediation and Mediation Support in German Foreign Policy*, Conference Report 2014. Berlin: Federal Foreign Office and IMSD, 2014.

Brose, Ekkehard. "Krisen verhindern, Konflikte bewältigen, Frieden fördern", *Das Weißbuch 2016 und die Herausforderungen von Strategiebildung*, edited by Daniel Jacobi and Gunther Hellmann, 287–96. Wiesbaden: Springer VC, 2019.

Bündnis 90/Die Grünen parliamentary group. "Maßnahmen der Entwicklungszusammenarbeit als Beitrag zu einer Politik der Krisenprävention und zivilen Konfliktbearbeitung", *Bundestag document* 13/6713, January 14, 1997.

Bündnis 90/Die Grünen parliamentary group. "Kleine Anfrage zur Umsetzung des Aktionsplans Zivile Krisenprävention", *Bundestag document* 16/9171, May 9, 2008.

CDU/CSU/FDP parliamentary group. "Verstärkung deutscher Beiträge zu Krisenprävention und Friedenspolitik", *Bundestag document* 13/6389, December 4,1997.

Centre for Humanitarian Dialogue (HD). "Lybia". www.hdcentre.org/activities/lib ya/ (accessed July 24, 2019).

Deutscher Bundestag. "Antwort der Bundesregierung auf die Kleine Anfrage der Fraktion Bündnis 90/Die Grünen", *Bundestag document* 16/9363, May 28, 2008. http://dipbt.bundestag.de/doc/btd/16/093/1609363.pdf (accessed June 22, 2020).

Deutscher Bundestag. "Antwort der Bundesregierung auf die Kleine Anfrage der Fraktion DIE LINKE", *Bundestag document* 18/2993, October 28, 2014. http://dip 21.bundestag.de/dip21/btd/18/029/1802993.pdf (accessed June 22, 2020).

Deutscher Bundestag. "Minutes of plenary proceedings of the 86th session", February 6, 2015. *Minutes of plenary proceedings* 18/86.

Deutscher Bundestag. "Minutes of plenary proceedings of the 244th session", June 30, 2017. *Minutes of plenary proceedings* 18/244.

FAZ. "Gauck fordert neue deutsche Außenpolitik", January 31, 2014. www.faz.net/aktuell/politik/inland/muenchner-sicherheitskonferenz-gauck-fordert-neue-deutsche-aussenpolitik-12778741.html (accessed July 20, 2019).

Federal Foreign Office. "Foreign Minister Maas on the agreement to hold new peace talks on Darfur", *press release*, December 6, 2018. https://www.auswaertiges-amt.de/en/newsroom/news/maas-dafur-peace-talks/2167902 (accessed January 31, 2021).

Federal Foreign Office. "Peace mediation: Working for peace", June 18, 2019. https://www.auswaertiges-amt.de/en/aussenpolitik/themen/krisenpraevention/peace-mediation/2227412 (accessed January 31, 2021).

Federal Foreign Office. *Peace Mediation Framework*. Berlin: Federal Foreign Office, 2019.

Federal Foreign Office. "Government press conference", November 22, 2019. www.auswaertiges-amt.de/de/newsroom/regierungspressekonferenz/2281144 (accessed November 29, 2019).

Federal Foreign Office. "Review 2014 – Außenpolitik weiter denken". www.auswaertiges-amt.de/blob/269656/d26e1e50cd5acb847b4b9eb4a757e438/review2014-abschlussbericht-data.pdf (accessed September 1, 2019).

Federal Foreign Office and IMSD. *Germany as Mediator: Peace Mediation and Mediation Support in German Foreign Policy*, Conference Report 2014. Berlin: Federal Foreign Office and IMSD, 2014.

Federal Government of Germany. *Action Plan "Civilian Crisis Prevention, Conflict Resolution and Post-Conflict Peace-Building"*. Berlin: Federal Government of Germany, 2004. http://www.konfliktbearbeitung.net/downloads/file711.pdf (accessed November 12, 2020).

Federal Government of Germany. "Comprehensive Concept of the Federal Government on Civilian Crisis Prevention, Conflict Resolution and Peace Consolidation", idem: *Action Plan*, Annex XIX-XXI (Berlin: Federal Government of Germany, 2004). http://www.konfliktbearbeitung.net/downloads/file711.pdf (accessed November 11, 2020).

Federal Government of Germany. *Für eine kohärente Politik der Bundesregierung gegenüber fragilen Staaten – Ressortübergreifende Leitlinien*. Berlin: Federal Government of Germany, 2012. www.bmz.de/de/zentrales_downloadarchiv/Presse/leitlinien_fragile_staaten.pdf (accessed June 22, 2020).

Federal Government of Germany. *Guidelines on Preventing Crises, Resolving Conflicts, Building Peace*. Berlin: Federal Government of Germany, 2017. https://www.auswaertiges-amt.de/blob/290648/057f794cd3593763ea556897972574fd/170614-leitlinien-krisenpraevention-konfliktbewaeltigung-friedensfoerderung-dl-data.pdf (accessed November 12, 2020).

Federal Government of Germany. *Weißbuch zur Sicherheitspolitik und zur Zukunft der Bundeswehr*. Berlin: Federal Government of Germany, 2016. www.bundesreg ierung.de/resource/blob/975292/736102/64781348c12e4a80948ab1bdf25cf057/w eissbuch-zur-sicherheitspolitik-2016-download-bmvg-data.pdf?download=1 (accessed June 22, 2020).

Friedrich, Hans Jörg. "Kabinett verabschiedet friedenspolitische Leitlinien der Bundesregierung", *Weltfriedensdienst e.V.*, June 15, 2017. https://wfd.de/kabinett-vera bschiedet-friedenspolitische-leitlinien-der-bundesregierung (accessed September 14, 2019).

Handelsblatt. "Deutschland sichert 4,5 Millionen Euro für Jemen-Hilfen zu", January 16, 2019. www.handelsblatt.com/politik/international/friedensbemuehung en-deutschland-sichert-4-5-millionen-euro-fuer-jemen-hilfen-zu/23873932.html?t icket=ST-670425-czIyjibt33n3xCuXKbCr-ap4 (accessed July 24, 2019).

Initiative Mediation Support Deutschland (IMSD). "Das deutsche Bekenntnis zur Friedensmediation ausbuchstabieren – eine Positionierung der Initiative Mediation Support Deutschland". 2016. www.friedensmediation-deutschland.de/filead min/uploads/friedensmeditation/dokumente/Friedensmediation_ausbuchstabier en__IMSD-Positionspapier_Leitlinienprozess.pdf (accessed September 14, 2019).

Initiative Mediation Support Deutschland (IMSD). "Friedensmediation: Kurzinformation und Vorschläge für die Politik", April 30, 2013. www.zif-berlin.org/filea dmin/uploads/analyse/dokumente/veroeffentlichungen/Kurzinfo_Mediation_30 042013.pdf (accessed November 19, 2019).

Institute for International and Security Affairs and German Marshall Fund of the United States. *Neue Macht – Neue Verantwortung. Elemente einer deutschen Außen- und Sicherheitspolitik für eine Welt im Umbruch*. Berlin/Washington, 2013. www.swp-berlin.org/fileadmin/contents/products/projekt_papiere/DeutAussenS icherhpol_SWP_GMF_2013.pdf (accessed July 20, 2019).

Kirchhoff, Lars, and Anne Isabel Kraus (now Holper), and Julia von Dobeneck. "Von Elefanten und Papiertigern in der Friedensmediation", December 22, 2016. https://peacelab.blog/2016/12/von-elefanten-und-papiertigern-in-der-friede nsmediation (accessed September 14, 2019).

Knabe, Oliver. "Gut im Grundsatz, enttäuschend im Handeln", *press release of the German Platform for Peaceful Conflict Management*, June 24, 2017. http://konfliktb earbeitung.net/initiativen/gut-grundsatz-enttaeuschend-handeln (accessed September 14, 2019).

König, Rüdiger. "Ein Wiki der Krisenprävention", *Deutschlands neue Verantwortung. Die Zukunft der deutschen und europäischen Außen-, Entwicklungs- und Sicherheit- spolitik*, edited by Wolfgang Ischinger and Dirk Messner, 280–84. Berlin: Econ, 2017.

Lanz, David. "Ten Recent Developments in Peace Mediation", *perspektive mediation – Beiträge zur Konfliktkultur* 17, no. 3 (2017): 146–52.

Lanz, David, Jamie Pring, Corinne von Burg, and Mathias Zeller. *Understanding Mediation Support Structures*. Bern: swisspeace, 2017.

MediatEUr. "A European Institute of Peace? Value-added, Risks and Options", September 5, 2012. http://themediateur.eu/a-european-institute-of-peace-value-a dded-risks-and-options/ (accessed July 21, 2019).

Mertins, Silke. "Jemen-Krieg: Eine elende Generation wächst nach", *NZZ*, January 5, 2019. https://nzzas.nzz.ch/international/jemen-krieg-elende-generation-waechs t-nach-ld.1449223#swglogin (accessed July 24, 2019).

Nachtwei, Winfried. "Lehren aus 10 Jahren Aktionsplan Zivile Krisenprävention – Wie weiter?", *Sicherheit und Frieden* 32, no. 3 (2014): 201–5.

Nachtwei, Winfried. "Stellungnahme zur Öffentlichen Sitzung des Unterausschuss- es Zivile Krisenprävention, Konfliktbearbeitung und vernetztes Handeln", May 5, 2014. http://nachtwei.de/index.php?module=articles&func=display&catid=77 &aid=1286 (accessed August 31, 2019).

Nachtwei, Winfried. "Meine Stellungnahme zu den Leitlinien Friedensförderung der Bundesregierung: Deutlicher Fortschritt, aber mit Handicaps", June 29, 2017. http://nachtwei.de/index.php?module=articles&func=display&catid=77&a id=1482 (accessed July 24, 2019).

Nachtwei, Winfried. "Zivile Krisenprävention – grüner Markenkern in der Friedenspolitik?", March 16, 2019. http://nachtwei.de/index.php?module=article s&func=display&catid=77&aid=1585 (accessed August 31, 2019).

OWEN – Mobile Akademie für Geschlechterdemokratie und Friedensförderung e.V. "Women's Initiatives for Peace in Donbas(s)". www.owen-berlin.de/projekt e/wipd.php (accessed July 24, 2019).

PeaceLab2016-Redaktionsteam. "Reaktionen auf die Leitlinien", June 15, 2017. https://peacelab.blog/2017/06/reaktionen-auf-die-leitlinien (accessed January 25, 2021).

Plattform Zivile Konfliktbearbeitung. *Stillschweigender Abschied vom Aktionsplan Zivile Krisenprävention?* Stellungnahme zum 3. Umsetzungsbericht "Zivile Krisenprävention, Konfliktbewältigung und Friedenskonsolidierung" der Bun- desregierung vom 23. Juni 2010 zum Aktionsplan "Zivile Krisenprävention, Konfliktbewältigung und Friedenskonsolidierung". Berlin/Köln: Plattform Zivile Konfliktbearbeitung, 2010.

Rotmann, Philipp, and Léa Steinacker. "Stabilization, Doctrine, Organization and Practice. Lessons from Canada, the Netherlands, the United Kingdom and the United States", *Global Public Policy Institute*, December 2013. www.gppi.net/med ia/rotmann-Steinacker_2013_stabilization_new-brand.pdf (accessed July 21, 2019).

Schulze, Tobias. "Deutsche Regierung als Streitschlichter. Frieden schaffen ohne Waffen?", *taz.de*, June 15, 2017. https://taz.de/Deutsche-Regierung-als-Streitschli chter/!5418355/ (accessed September 14, 2019).

SPD parliamentary group. "Priorität für eine Politik der zivilen Krisenprävention und Konfliktregelung", *Bundestag document* 13/6999, February 19, 1997.

SPD/Bündnis 90/Die Grünen. *Aufbruch und Erneuerung – Deutschlands Weg ins 21. Jahrhundert*. Coalition agreement. Bonn, 1998. www.spd.de/fileadmin/Dokume nte/Beschluesse/Bundesparteitag/koalitionsvertrag_bundesparteitag_bonn_1998. pdf (accessed June 22, 2020).

SPD/Bündnis 90/Die Grünen. *ERNEUERUNG – GERECHTIGKEIT – NACH-HALTIGKEIT. Für ein wirtschaftlich starkes, soziales und ökologisches Deutschland. Für eine lebendige Demokratie.* Coalition agreement. Berlin, 2002. www.staedtebu nd.gv.at/index.php?eID=tx_securedownloads&p=8536&u=0&g=0&t=158287825 5&hash=dd7e34d8e1312a5fd130b290a85341437726db1c&file=fileadmin/archiv/ oestb_dateien/1042206327.pdf (accessed September 1, 2019).

"Stabilitätspakt für Südosteuropa" June 10, 1999. *Sicherheit und Frieden (S+F) / Security and Peace* 17, no. 3, Der Krieg im Kosovo (1999): 214–16.

Steinmeier, Frank-Walter. "Rede bei der Abschlussveranstaltung zu Review 2014 – Außenpolitik weiter denken", February 25, 2015. www.auswaertiges-amt.de/de/ newsroom/150225-bm-review-abschlussveranstaltung/269638 (accessed September 1, 2019).

Zapf, Marina. "Leitlinien Friedensförderung. Ungenau, unkritisch, ziellos", *WELT-SICHTEN*, June 20, 2017. www.welt-sichten.org/artikel/32964/leitlinien-friedens foerderung-ungenau-unkritisch-ziellos (accessed September 14, 2019).

Exploiting Potential: Peace Mediation in German Foreign Policy

Almut Wieland-Karimi

Introduction

This article begins in the middle of a foreign policy complexity for which a realistic mediation strategy must have answers. The goal is to illuminate the potential of Germany's contributions to both peace mediation and mediation support and to delineate possible specific approaches that it could take. A sharpened profile of Germany as a middle power and comparatively honest broker could arise, for example, by linking political initiatives on Track 1 to mediation support on levels 2 and 3. In addition, the expansion of innovative partnerships and long-term financing could constitute important building blocks for Germany's taking on a stronger mediating role.

Complexity of wars and conflicts

From A as in Abkhazia to Z as in Zimbabwe, conflicts abound around the world and have become more complicated in recent years. The length of conflicts serves as an indicator of this complexity: In 1970, conflicts ended after an average of 9.6 years, whereas in 2015 the average had increased to 15 years. The number of actors involved, including non-state armed groups, and the connection with transnational crime also have increased.[1] In addition, armed and militant factions, whether state or non-state actors, almost always operate in the same territory today. They are involved in domestic or interregional conflicts and behave in an asymmetrical manner, by hiding within the civilian population or conducting suicide bombings.

Furthermore, many fighters and warlords frequently change sides: They can be "rented" like modern temporary workers. Classic wars between two states or two coalitions or superpowers with their proxies, as we knew

---

1 William Robert Avis, *Current Trends in Violent Conflict* (Brighton: Institute of Development Studies, 2019): 2–9.

them from the two world wars or the time of the Cold War, are largely a thing of the past. Hence the complexity or interconnectedness of the conflicts is demonstrably intensifying (see David Lanz's contribution to this volume), which makes conflict transformation and peace mediation more challenging than ever.

Making peace with enemies, not with friends

"To make peace, you have to shake hands with the devil", said former United Nations (UN) Secretary General Kofi Annan (d. 2018) at the Oslo Peace Forum, the most important meeting of international mediators, in June of 2017. Most recently, Annan's advice was followed with the FARC in Colombia, for negotiations with the Taleban in Afghanistan and presumably in the future for discussions with the Islamic State and other still "taboo" actors in the Middle East and elsewhere.

Initially, it is almost always unthinkable to negotiate with parties to a conflict who have killed thousands of people, in particular civilians, and committed serious human rights violations. A rethinking often takes place when the international community, the government and the population of an affected country or region realize that the conflict cannot be won or transformed militarily. In the case of a political or military stalemate, these conflicts end up at the negotiating table, whether it be the IRA in Northern Ireland 20 years ago or the ETA 10 years ago in Spain.

One of the most respected books among international mediators is Jonathan Powell's *Talking to Terrorists*.[2] Powell explains why the moral barrier of not being able to talk to "terrorists" must be broken: Peace can only be negotiated with one's enemies. The dilemma is that neither a compromise with a violent, unscrupulous counterpart nor endless war presents a good option. Only a long-term, sustained negotiating process can arrive at an agreement, though it is mostly hard to carry through. In practice, this transformation is almost always accompanied by external mediation or support for peace mediation.

---

2 Jonathan Powell, *Talking to Terrorists: How to End Armed Conflicts* (London: The Bodley Head, 2014).

Peace mediation: The key to sustainable peace

Preventive and sustainable political and civilian conflict management is the key to lasting ceasefires, peace agreements and positive peace. Especially during the current crisis of multilateralism and both fundamental and severe clashes between great powers, mediation sends a strong signal against the militarization of conflicts and for a political conflict management.

Purely military interventions can certainly be a building block to ensure the protection of the civilian population or the Responsibility to Protect (R2P) in exceptional situations. In the context of the UN, it also has been shown that military interventions sometimes prevent a warring party from settling a conflict at the expense of the other side. At the same time, however, the diplomatic engagement of the UN and its member states is the most effective and ultimately the only way to convincingly signal to the warring parties and the local population that a compromise makes sense and can be achieved together.[3]

Hence peace mediation and mediation support are increasingly becoming a must for states and multilateral organizations – a wise investment, since peace agreements last significantly longer when they are achieved through a mediation process.[4] Today, 80 percent of peace processes are mediated by a third party.[5] Nevertheless, there are still many conflicts in which mediation support and mediation are either missing or should be significantly professionalized or optimized.

The development of tailored structures for peace mediation is a huge foreign policy task, which must encompass the entire spectrum of questions and answers – from the exploration of possible mediation engagements to the deployment of mediators who are both suitable to the task and acceptable to all parties in a conflict. In this context, the importance of mediation support is often underestimated. Professional expertise is crucial in a mediation process, for example, when it comes to constitutional questions, the distribution of natural resources and process design. This should constitute an initial starting point for raising Germany's mediation profile.

------

3 Kyle Beardsley, "UN Intervention and the Duration of International Crises", *Journal of Peace Research* 49, no. 2 (March 2012): 347.
4 Marie Olson Lounsbery and Karl DeRouen, "The Viability of Civil War Peace Agreements", *Civil Wars* 18, no. 3 (July 2016): 323.
5 Escola de Cultura de Pau and Universitat Autònoma de Barcelona, *Peace Talks in Focus 2019. Report on Trends and Scenarios* (Barcelona: Icaria editorial, 2019): 20.

Almut Wieland-Karimi

Neither small nor big: Germany's strength

There are a number of good examples of long-term and sustainable engagement by small countries in the field of peace mediation. Norway has made a name for itself particularly in the area of providing the capacities to conduct peace negotiations, making use of its position as a non-member of the European Union (EU). For example, it was easier for Norway to enter negotiations with non-state armed groups – such as it did when supporting the Colombian peace process – because it was not bound by the so-called list of terrorist organizations of the EU[6] or the United States. Switzerland's neutrality is also an important aspect of its success as a mediator. Mediation is a foreign policy priority of the Swiss government, which has established close cooperation with civil society and academia. Finland and Sweden are also involved intensely, especially in empowering women in peace processes.

Germany should adopt a focused and strategically planned profile as a mediator. On the one hand, because it enjoys excellent relationships with the experienced smaller mediation states, it is predestined to complement their approaches and strengthen them with its political clout. On the other hand, the middle power Germany is more trusted in many regions than the five permanent members of the UN Security Council (P5), which, as heavyweights with their distinctive histories and geopolitical ambition, either polarize or, because of political and economic interests, are disqualified to act as mediators in their zones of influence.

The definition and positioning of Germany's mediator role could be as follows: more power-conscious and politically and economically important than the classic mediators but more cautious and less geopolitically ambitious than the P5 states. Germany would then project its role as a middle power, which it already fills in Europe, to a broader field, thus meeting its own as well as international expectations regarding its assumption of responsibility. Germany's position as a "middle-weight" political power constitutes an explicit advantage, giving it the ability to shape the dynamics in peace negotiations.

Moreover, Germany is seen in many places as an honest broker, also because of our limited colonial history – even though this perception can be called into question because of our strong economic interests and integration into Western alliances. We should state our intentions clearly: We in-

---

6 See https://www.consilium.europa.eu/de/policies/fight-against-terrorism/terrorist-li st/ (accessed June 29, 2020).

volve ourselves in mediation not solely for altruistic reasons but also because it is in our own interest to contribute to the management of international crises and conflicts.

The fact that we confront our own war history and national processes of reconciliation so intensively provides us with experiences and insights that can represent great added value in a mediation process. Good international networking through diplomacy, long-term multilateral engagement and development cooperation are additional pluses. In a highly diverse mediation playing field consisting of many actors, Germany can offer something that others involved in mediation cannot.

Germany is especially suited to mediate geopolitically deadlocked or proxy conflicts, because of its international position. Germany's engagement in Ukraine is a good example of this. Last but not least, Germany is also one of the few actors that is in the position to bring about a rapprochement with Russia in order to make progress in conflicts such as those in Syria and Libya. Germany's balance between geopolitical and economic influence on the one hand, and foreign policy caution on the other, provides a decisive advantage in such conflict situations.

Women at the negotiating table

In the course of positioning itself as a mediator, Germany could strengthen a number of linked issues that are of special importance to German foreign policy. For example, Germany and its partners should work towards ensuring that women are more involved in mediation processes in accordance with Resolution 1325 of the UN Security Council. One of the resolution's goals was to empower women as mediators, since only 2.4 percent of the chief mediators were women, between 1992 and 2011. In the meantime, the Scandinavian countries have founded the Nordic Women Mediators Network, which also serves as a model for other regions and networks, such as the Pan-African Network of Women Mediators.[7] Just as important is the participation and support of women at the negotiating table. One good example of this is the peace process in Afghanistan. Only when women are strongly represented in talks with the Taleban can democratic achievements be maintained even after a likely international withdrawal.

---

7 United Nations Entity for Gender Equality and the Empowerment of Women, *Women's Participation in Peace Negotiations: Connections Between Presence and Influence*, 2nd ed. (New York: United Nations, 2012).

Incidentally, peace treaties in which women have participated as negotiators last longer on average. The probability that agreements will last for at least 15 years is 35 percent higher if women have played a major role in their creation.[8] The former Swedish foreign minister Margot Wallström names three crucial questions: Do women have the same rights? Are they present at the negotiating table? And do they have the same access to resources?[9] These questions should be asked more than once during every peace process.

Civilian conflict management as a priority

In Germany, civilian crisis management has developed greatly over the past 20 years. According to surveys by the Deutsche Gesellschaft für Internationale Zusammenarbeit (GIZ), a majority, especially of international observers, supports a stronger German involvement in international cooperation, especially in the soft-power area.[10] Since 2014, the Federal Foreign Office (FFO) has had its own Directorate-General for Humanitarian Assistance, Crisis Prevention, Stabilisation and Post-Conflict Reconstruction (see Julia von Dobeneck's article in this volume).

Mediation is only one of the many different instruments in the conflict management tool box. In order to sharpen Germany's profile in peace mediation for the reasons cited above, this instrument should be prioritized and not just remain on an equal footing with other tools, such as early warning and conflict analysis, which are intensively addressed by other states and organizations, such as the International Crisis Group. An important next step would be to visibly anchor mediation and mediation support on the list of foreign policy priorities.

With the founding of the Center for International Peace Operations (ZIF) in 2002, an additional step in the direction of a stronger German civilian contribution to peace operations was achieved. The German Bun-

---

8   Marie O'Reilly, Andrea Ó Súilleabháin, and Thania Paffenholz, *Reimagining Peacemaking: Women's Roles in Peace Processes* (New York: International Peace Institute, 2015): 12.

9   Kai Strittmatter, "Neuer Exportschlager. Nach der Außenpolitik soll auch der Handel feministisch werden", *sueddeutsche.de*, August 5, 2019, www.sueddeutsche .de/politik/schweden-neuer-exportschlager-1.4553507 (accessed June 29, 2020).

10 Deutsche Gesellschaft für Internationale Zusammenarbeit (GIZ), *Deutschland in den Augen der Welt*, 3rd study, results of the GIZ survey 2017/2018 (Bonn, Eschborn: Deutsche Gesellschaft für Internationale Zusammenarbeit – GIZ, 2017).

destag further affirmed this intention with the Secondment Act of 2017. By training and sending German personnel to take part in multilateral peace operations and also through operational, conceptual and analytical contributions as well as networking with bilateral and multilateral partners, Germany is strengthening its visibility in this area. The ZIF expert pool includes many experts with mediation experience.

Mediation is both an art and a skill

Germany should continue to invest in the training of diplomats and government representatives for the Track 1 level. Peace mediation is not only a diplomatic art but also a learnable skill. There are good capacity development opportunities that are geared towards leadership personnel, such as the UN Mediation Support Unit's mediation courses or the ZIF Mediation Peer Coaching for senior diplomats at the FFO and the European External Action Service (EEAS).[11] In addition, mediation modules are integrated into the training of attachés and the advanced training of so-called "midcareer" professionals in the FFO. These are good starting points, but their capacities have not yet been exploited systematically in peace mediation.

An internal pool of mediators in the FFO – in other words, methodologically excellent, experienced mediators with specific professional expertise who can be dispatched when needed to mediation deployments – would be desirable. A similar system already exists for diplomats with experience in crisis and conflict areas. To date, the number of Germans in leadership positions in international organizations, peace operations and political mediation is very limited. There is no need to create tension between strengthening structures and strengthening individuals. What is needed are structures that produce strong individuals as mediators as well as a systematic commitment to peace mediation.

---

11 Center for International Peace Operations (ZIF), "Austausch auf Augenhöhe. Peer Coaching Mediation", August 23, 2016, www.zif-berlin.org/de/ueber-zif/nac hrichten-aus-dem-zif/detailansicht/article/austausch-auf-augenhoehe-peer-coachin g-mediation.html (accessed June 22, 2020).

Almut Wieland-Karimi

Expand networks and link tracks

Germany has already established proven expertise in the field of peace mediation. In the course of several conferences, networks such as the Initiative Mediation Support Deutschland (IMSD) have spelled out a role for Germany in this area. Civil society organizations pursue important Track 2 and Track 3 activities (see above). Academia has built up in-depth and practical know-how. The Federal Ministry for Economic Cooperation and Development (BMZ) supports numerous local organizations worldwide in peacebuilding, of which mediation is a crucial element.

Nevertheless, the various activities initiated and promoted by Germany are only partially connected to one another. In the area of Track 2 and Track 3 mediation – thus, the support of local civil society leaders – Germany has long been an important donor but has taken a far less active role as mediator. The FFO's key partners include the Berghof Foundation and the Centre for Humanitarian Dialogue (HD) in Geneva.[12] At this point, it is important to forge synergies and set priorities for a multi-track approach. By linking and synchronizing Track 2 and Track 3 activities in a targeted way with our Track 1 diplomatic and political engagement and by underpinning those activities with scientific analysis and coordinating them with international partners, the chances for concrete mediation successes would certainly be improved. In addition, this procedure would create a visible signature for German mediation commitments, an important component of which would be a cooperative, cross-track and methodologically sound approach.

Forger of coherent coalitions

Conflicts move at their own pace and do not wait for the member states of the EU, the Organization for Security and Co-operation in Europe (OSCE) or the African Union (AU) to agree on a common approach. In certain conflict situations, more and more ad-hoc coalitions will be required to courageously reflect the anatomy of a specific case and find customized solutions (one example of this can be found in the article by Marike Blunck and Carsten Wieland in this volume). Germany should join in this effort when it can bring its comparative strengths to the table, such as the weight

---

12 Berghof Foundation, *Annual Report 2018. Creating Space for Conflict Transformation* (Berlin: Berghof Foundation, 2019).

it carries as a middle power in Central Europe or its close relationships with an affected conflict country. In appropriate situations, Germany should act as an "enabler" that makes agreements possible, inquires about readiness and institutionalizes structures. Not only the "usual suspects" should be requested for such coalitions but also new partnerships should be established, especially in the Global South. Ideally, instead of rivalries, new synergies could be created that would revitalize the fragile multilateral system by spelling out joint responsibility on the action level.

Necessary: Stamina and long-term financing

Most peace negotiation processes last for years, if not decades. Mediation takes place behind the scenes and not in the public spotlight, which is challenging in light of the short attention span in politics and the existing financial instruments. Germany must be prepared to risk an occasional failure and to price it in politically. In this respect, it is all the more important to establish politically sustainable structures, expertise and networks. Multi-year, long-term financing is indispensable, even if budgetary requirements appear to make it difficult to achieve. Peace negotiations are not determined by fiscal years but are extremely unpredictable and require a high degree of continuity and patience – also when it comes to finances. In order to use the funds that have been made available as effectively as possible, foreign policy engagement and foreign policy funds should be linked to other areas such as development cooperation, in which structures have evolved over decades. This is also one of the central proposals of the ground-breaking *Pathways for Peace* report by the World Bank and the UN.[13]

Conclusion

Mediation and the use of civilian tools to resolve conflicts should be high on Germany's foreign policy agenda. *Courageous, forward-looking* and *cooperative* are the keywords here.

And the right time for this is precisely now. With the secondary effects of the Covid-19 pandemic, such as poverty, inequality and humanitarian

---

13 World Bank Group and United Nations, eds., *Pathways for Peace: Inclusive Approaches to Preventing Violent Conflict* (Washington, D. C.: World Bank, 2018).

needs looming in the near future and the foreseeable consequences for crises and conflicts worldwide, the time has finally come for Germany to take on more responsibility – also in peace mediation.

Germany has the horsepower for this task – it must now be put on the road.

References

Avis, William Robert. *Current Trends in Violent Conflict.* Brighton: Institute of Development Studies, 2019.

Beardsley, Kyle. "UN Intervention and the Duration of International Crises", *Journal of Peace Research* 49, no. 2 (March 2012): 335–49.

Berghof Foundation. *Annual Report 2018. Creating Space for Conflict Transformation.* Berlin: Berghof Foundation, 2019.

Center for International Peace Operations (ZIF). "Austausch auf Augenhöhe. Peer Coaching Mediation", August 23, 2016. www.zif-berlin.org/de/ueber-zif/nachrichten-aus-dem-zif/detailansicht/article/austausch-auf-augenhoehe-peer-coaching-mediation.html (accessed June 22, 2020).

Deutsche Gesellschaft für Internationale Zusammenarbeit (GIZ). *Deutschland in den Augen der Welt.* Third study. Results of the GIZ survey 2017/2018. Bonn, Eschborn: Deutsche Gesellschaft für Internationale Zusammenarbeit (GIZ), 2017.

Escola de Cultura de Pau and Universitat Autònoma de Barcelona. *Peace Talks in Focus 2019. Report on Trends and Scenarios.* Barcelona: Icaria editorial, 2019.

Lounsbery, M.O., and Karl DeRouen, Jr. "The Viability of Civil War Peace Agreements", *Civil Wars* 18, no. 3 (July 2016): 311–37.

O'Reilly, M., Andrea Ó Súilleabháin, and Thania Paffenholz. *Reimagining Peacemaking: Women's Roles in Peace Processes.* New York: International Peace Institute, 2015.

Powell, Jonathan. *Talking to Terrorists: How to End Armed Conflicts.* London: The Bodley Head, 2014.

Strittmatter, Kai. "Neuer Exportschlager. Nach der Außenpolitik soll auch der Handel feministisch werden", *sueddeutsche.de*, August 5, 2019. www.sueddeutsche.de/politik/schweden-neuer-exportschlager-1.4553507 (accessed June 29, 2020).

United Nations Entity for Gender Equality and the Empowerment of Women. *Women's Participation in Peace Negotiations: Connections Between Presence and Influence.* Second edition. New York: United Nations, 2012.

World Bank Group and United Nations, eds. *Pathways for Peace: Inclusive Approaches to Preventing Violent Conflict.* Washington, D.C.: World Bank, 2018.

Complexity and Asymmetry: Challenges of UN Mediation in Syria and the Role of Germany

Marike Blunck & Carsten Wieland

Introduction

The landscape of Syria's conflict has developed more rapidly than the international efforts to resolve it. Mediation efforts often have lagged behind the realities of the conflict, and their proponents have been forced to reactively accept them and hope for new impulses from the outside. An escalation of the situation has had ripple effects far beyond the Syrian context. The conflict, which began in 2011, initially pitted the Syrian regime against a peaceful uprising of a large part of its own population. It has become increasingly violent and complex with each passing year.

During those years, the inner-Syrian fragmentation of actors and territory went hand in hand with the fragmentation and polarization of regional interests and a general bilateralization of international relations. The conflict increasingly became a proxy war for a growing number of regional and international actors, who used the destabilized country as a playing field for their own ambitions. This has resulted in a self-sustaining conflict system in which overlapping national and geostrategic interests mean that – ten years into the conflict – there is no indication either of an accommodation of interests or of war fatigue on the part of the main actors in the conflict. The only exceptions are the militarily exhausted moderate Syrian opposition and the suffering population, who are further away than ever from achieving the goals they expressed in the Arab Spring.

The hypothesis in this article[1] is twofold: First, we suggest that the inner-Syrian fragmentation is reflected on the level of the supporters' land-

1 This article covers the UN mediation efforts since their start in 2012 through December 2019. It draws on a series of methodically structured interviews between the authors in August 2019 and January 2020 as well as supporting research. It is based on the analyses and experiences of Carsten Wieland as diplomat and political advisor in the peace process under three UN special envoys for Syria (Brahimi, De Mistura and Pedersen). Our thanks go to Anne Holper (European University Viadrina) for the helpful conversations on the composition of this text.

scape – or, that the latter have helped to cause the former. Mediation efforts become more and more compartmentalized and (must) take into account an ever-growing mosaic of actors and interests. Second, this situation creates new (mediation) needs on the level of supporters, which gives potential bridge states like Germany an important and meaningful role as "mediator between mediators".

The Syrian conflict is often used to symbolize the increasing complexity of conflicts in general (see the contributions of Almut Wieland-Karimi and David Lanz in this volume). A look at UN mediation efforts makes it possible, *pars pro toto*, to shed light on the associated effects on current attempts at mediation, with relevance far beyond Syria. Despite the uniqueness of the constellation in and around Syria, its genesis and dynamics prove to be an essential reference frame for discussing Germany's possible profiles and activities in peace mediation.

The UN-Process: From Classic Process Design to a Strategy of Small Steps

From the very start of UN mediation efforts, the UN Security Council was divided on the Syrian conflict, thus largely paralyzed. As a result, the UN's early efforts appeared to be toothless and disparate. Hence it was only natural for the UN to rely on the so-called "Table 2", i.e., on the imaginary negotiating table of supporters outside Geneva.

All phases of the UN process were two-pronged: Alongside the efforts to build trust and readiness to negotiate between the national parties to the conflict, there were talks on the regional and international levels. Moments of concerted international dynamics, which could have formed the basis for a comprehensive approach to mediation, were usually short-lived, lacking in depth or disrupted by international developments. During favorable moments ("windows of opportunity"), UN mediation efforts were revived[2] and in some cases able to generate momentum. But in the long term, they never managed to become a center of gravity that could lock the relevant actors into the process at a national and international level and thus develop a certain momentum of its own.

---

2 Muriel Asseburg, Wolfram Lacher, and Mareike Transfeld, *Mission Impossible? UN Mediation in Libya, Syria and Yemen* (Berlin: Institute for International and Security Affairs, 2018).

When UN Secretary-General Ban Ki-Moon appointed Kofi Annan as the first UN Special Envoy to Syria (February–August 2012),[3] the conflict in that country was already escalating since almost one year. Annan's six-point plan provided for an "inclusive Syrian-led political process" and measures to curb violence.[4] His efforts within Syria failed. The regime's lack of willingness to negotiate meant that a political process could not be achieved, and the civilian observer mission (UN Supervision Mission in Syria – UNSMIS) was powerless in the face of the violence, which escalated again after a brief ceasefire.

Annan's parallel efforts on the international level also failed to bring any sustained new momentum to the process. However, Annan did succeed in inviting the Action Group for Syria to Geneva in a rare alliance, in which all relevant regional and international actors[5] (except for Iran, which was not present) supported the principle of a political transition process in an official statement known as the Geneva Communiqué.[6] But it was never clear what this process should look like. Given the Syrian government's unwillingness to negotiate and the lack of concerted international support, Annan resigned his mandate after only six months.

Subsequently, Joint Special Envoy of the UN and the Arab League Lakhdar Brahimi (August 2012–May 2014), carried out classic state diplomacy: He leaned heavily on the conventional superpowers – the USA and Russia – as guarantors of the process and initiated the Second Geneva Peace Conference. Its opening meeting in Montreux in the presence of the Syrian parties and without Iran (due to a US veto) paved the way for Brahimi, the first and until early 2020 only UN Special Envoy, to convene direct talks between the government and the opposition delegations.[7] The Syrian government only participated because of great pressure from Russia.

---

3 United Nations General Assembly, *Resolution Adopted by the General Assembly 66/253 – The Situation in the Syrian Arab Republic* (New York: United Nations, 2012).

4 Reuters, "Text of Annan's Six-Point Peace Plan for Syria", April 4, 2012, www.reuters.com/article/us-syria-ceasefire-idUSBRE8330HJ20120404 (accessed June 2, 2020).

5 The participants were the Secretary-Generals of the UN and the Arab League, the foreign ministers of China, France, Russia, the United Kingdom, the USA, Turkey, Iraq, Kuwait, Qatar and the then–High Representative of the European Union for Foreign Affairs and Security Policy, Catherine Ashton.

6 UN Report, "Action Group for Syria: Final Communiqué", June 30, 2012, https://un-report.blogspot.com/2012/06/action-group-for-syria-final-communique.html (accessed June 29, 2020).

7 The opposition consisted of the broadest platform at the time, the National Syrian Coalition in exile in Istanbul.

From the outset, however, the talks had little chance of success. An important actor, Iran, was missing at the table and the Syrian government delegation had only come to Geneva under pressure from Russia and not out of a desire to negotiate. The fact that Brahimi invited the relevant actors to take part in talks at all was due to strong pressure from international players and from inside the UN to initiate some form of engagement with the biggest conflict of this century.

However, the process architecture – with the USA and Russia as the main pillars – collapsed when the conflict between Ukraine and Russia broke out in February 2014. As a result, the USA and Russia stopped holding any discussions with one another, let alone on the topic of Syria. This external event shifted the international tectonics in the peace process landscape.[8] Ever the realist, Brahimi no longer saw any basis for continuing his mediation attempts.

The escalation of violence and fragmentation of the Syrian conflict landscape, intensified by the bilateral interests of regional and international actors, meant that a comprehensive political transition process, as laid out in the Geneva Communiqué, was increasingly unlikely. This was also reflected in the UN's mediation efforts under Staffan De Mistura (September 2014–December 2018), who initially pursued a strategy of small steps.

A resumption of talks between the Syrian government and the opposition only became possible again when new dynamics arose at the international level. After ratification of the nuclear agreement with Iran in 2015, the USA and the other Western states accepted Iran as a dialogue partner.[9]

At the end of 2015, the International Syria Support Group (ISSG) was established in Vienna. This loose association of 20 countries (including Iran) and international organizations under the leadership of the USA and Russia represented one of the few instances of concerted effort in the Syrian conflict and gave the UN process a short-term boost: The Vienna negotiations culminated in UN Resolution 2254, which repeated (in a somewhat weakened tone) the demands of the Geneva Communiqué for a political transition process and renewed the mandate of the UN mediation efforts.[10]

---

8 On this point, see also: Carsten Wieland, "Teufelskreis der Gewalt: Die Syrien-Konferenz als Beispiel für die Herausforderungen internationaler Konfliktlösung", *Die Politische Meinung* 63, no. 553 (November 2018): 42–9.

9 On this point see also: Wieland, *Teufelskreis der Gewalt*.

10 UN Security Council, *Security Council Resolution* 2254 (New York: United Nations, 2015).

Against this backdrop, De Mistura invited the Syrian government and the meanwhile expanded number of opposition groups to Geneva at the end of January 2016, to take part in indirect talks ("proximity talks"). As a precaution, De Mistura had dubbed his effort "Geneva Talks" from the outset; in fact, the indirect talks never advanced beyond "talks about negotiations".[11]

During De Mistura's tenure as UN Special Envoy, the UN was confronted increasingly with the dilemma of how to remain relevant in Syria without turning the process into a mere "fig leaf".[12] However, within the framework of the Geneva Talks, the UN also had created its own civil-society structures, such as the Civil Society Support Room and the Women's Advisory Board. But these could only attain marginal significance, since the main process noticeably lost its binding force for the subsidiary processes as well.

The Fragmentation of the Peace Process: Tug-of-War between the UN and the Astana Trio

With the Astana process in early 2017, Russia joined with Iran and a new partner, Turkey – the so-called "Astana Trio" – in an attempt to fill the vacuum and to have a stronger influence on the political process in Syria. This attempt included the propagandistically motivated inner-Syrian "reconciliation conference" in Sochi in January 2018, which was on the verge of setting up a constitutional committee under Russian leadership and without a clear role for the UN. This could have brought a bilateral bias into the process in favor of the key countries involved in the war. Although the UN was able to prevent this through intensive negotiations, one thing was clear: The UN process was confronted with openly competing understandings of and approaches to conflict resolution. De Mistura took up the Russian proposal to first try to establish a Syrian constitutional committee and to postpone the core issue of political transition. Although that turned the roadmap of UN Resolution 2254 upside down, the proposal fit with political realities. Nevertheless, the negotiations dragged on for so long that De Mistura had to hand over the project unfinished when he stepped down from his position in late December 2018.

---

11 Wieland, *Teufelskreis der Gewalt*: 44.
12 Asseburg, Lacher, and Transfeld, *Mission Impossible? UN Mediation in Libya, Syria and Yemen*: 42.

The Astana process and the conference it generated in Sochi posed a dilemma for the UN mediation efforts: Either the UN boycotted the process with the risk of splitting mediation efforts into two parallel processes, which, given a lack of Russian support, risked rendering the UN's efforts meaningless, or the UN would be legitimizing – through its support – a process conducted under Russian leadership and in Russia's interests as a party to the war. In other words, Russia and the other Astana powers had great potential to shape and influence the conflict but weak international legitimacy, while the UN was a weak political actor with a high degree of international legitimacy.

Although Russia was aware of this discrepancy and therefore sought to steer the process more in its own direction – for example, with the constitutional committee – it remained interested, at least pro forma, in an international legitimacy of the process through the UN. The political tug-of-war was conducted at the highest level: Ultimately, it was UN Secretary-General Guterres and Russian Foreign Minister Lavrov himself who found a compromise that allowed the UN to participate in the Sochi conference without losing face. At the same time, the Sochi congress commissioned the UN in Geneva to establish a Syrian-Syrian constitutional committee under UN auspices. However, in the months following the conference, what originally represented a good result for the UN was increasingly weakened under political pressure from the Astana Trio. The composition, mandate and procedural conditions of the constitutional committee would be the subject of intensive negotiations for another year and a half, until the body met for the first time in Geneva at the end of October 2019.

In the struggle surrounding the Syrian peace process, neither the UN nor the Astana process managed to become a gravitational center for substantial intra-Syrian negotiations and political change in the country. But they came to an arrangement: The Astana states managed to keep the UN involved as a participant in their format, and, in order to restart the deadlocked process, the UN accepted to frontload the constitutional discussion as well as qualitative compromises in the composition of the constitutional committee. Thus the shift at the level of mediation efforts opened up new windows of opportunity, just as it closed others.

After nine years of war, the very fact that the constitutional committee convened at all could be seen as a success. But at the same time, the peace process was (initially) limited to a constitutional process, which could be both a "door opener" (which both the UN and the opposition wanted) and a way of delaying substantial political changes within Syria, because the regime in Damascus continued to fear changes of any kind. In November 2019 it became clear just how difficult this path would be. The constitutional committee, despite a promising opening meeting, was unable to manage a second one, because the parties could not agree on the agenda for the subsequent sessions.

Even with a constitutional committee under UN auspices, the arena for mediation efforts remains contested. That makes the question of who shapes the mediation using which target definition even more relevant (see the article by Simon J. A. Mason in this volume), along with the associated danger of a "fig-leaf process" in a conflict that may have been largely resolved militarily but is far from a sustainable peace.

"Where next?" – Dealing with Complexity and a Possible Role for Germany

The complex mix of interests and the interlinking of national conflicts with the geostrategic interests of various regional and international actors have prevented a clear stalemate (a necessary, so-called "ripeness" for promising peace initiatives) on the national and international levels. They also have intensified the asymmetrical character of the national conflict and engendered a deeply divided and polarized supporters' landscape. This led to camps being formed between the Astana Trio and the so-called "Small Group", made up of the USA, Great Britain, France, Germany, Saudi Arabia, Egypt and Jordan, which was founded as a counter-reaction to the Astana Trio and which in turn – even within the respective formats – is divided due to partially irreconcilable interests. A common format, such as the ISSG of 2015 (which still exists formally, but for all intents and purposes is dysfunctional), has become highly unlikely. This was further exacerbated by the USA's termination of its nuclear agreement with Iran, which underscores the incompatibility between two central actors.

In this context, newer advances are of growing importance – advances such as a quadrilateral format consisting of Germany, France, Russia and Turkey, which act as bridge-builders in certain situations and create opportunities.

Following talks with the government in Damascus and the opposition in Riyadh, the Norwegian diplomat Geir O. Pedersen (UN Special Envoy to Syria since January 2019) decided to continue working towards a constitutional committee, despite initial doubts. But he made it clear that he would again broaden the scope of his mediation efforts. This was also evident from the five-point approach[13] that he introduced to the UN Security Council, which included exploring greater cooperation at the international level – especially between the Astana Trio and the Small Group – in order to create a new support geometry. But there has been no significant progress towards implementing the five points.

Germany could make strategic use of the gaps that have opened up in the mediation efforts between the various actors and levels – and give them its own methodological signature. These gaps suggest that mediation should be used where small but important steps can be taken towards sustainable conflict resolution. In concrete terms, this means:

- Germany should increasingly assume the role of a "mediator between mediators". There are diverse starting points for this role within the fragmented support landscape – above all, the polarization between the Astana Trio and the Small Group. One reason why the quadrilateral format has received so much attention is that it has been able to fulfill a temporary bridging function at this important juncture. Within and without such ad-hoc formats, Germany, as a strong advocate of multilateral approaches,[14] should identify, create and make use of specific areas of opportunity.

- Germany should focus on its role as a bridge-builder in the UN Security Council, in order to create momentum for a new geometry of international support. This could possibly lead to a renewal of the UN mandate. To that end, one must ask whether a new UN resolution would make sense, and, if so, which content could achieve consensus and also lead to resolving the conflict.

- A plan should be worked out at the European level to acknowledge the efforts of the government in Damascus to achieve recognition, reconstruction and a normalization of relations. This acknowledgment should be coupled with demands that Damascus participates constructively in the peace process and that measures be taken and substantial progress be visible on the ground in terms of respecting human rights, allowing the return of refugees, initiating political reforms and holding fair elections in accordance with UN Resolution 2254. This long and

---

13 Geir O. Pedersen, "Security Council Briefing on Syria, Special Envoy Geir O. Pedersen", *Political and Peacebuilding Affairs*, February 28, 2019, https://dppa.un.org/en/security-council-briefing-syria-special-envoy-geir-o-pedersen (accessed June 29, 2020).

14 Federal Foreign Office, *Peace Mediation Framework* (Berlin: Federal Foreign Office, 2019).

rough path can be accompanied by a give and take, by incentives and by firmness – such as the adherence to or reformulation of sanctions primarily aimed at individuals. But these steps must be prepared and coordinated in a concrete roadmap.

- In addition to the multilateral formats, Germany should attempt to hold more regular and intensive bilateral talks on a higher level with Russia about the importance of a functioning constitutional committee in Geneva and a broader political process.

Conclusion

Without a political process that initiates a minimum of reforms in the country, Syria is a long way from seeing any sustainable stabilization. Instead, the existing power relationships that led to the popular uprising against arbitrary rule and the escalation of violence, and that dragged the country further down the path towards ruin and desolation, will become more entrenched. The regime can no longer keep its head above water without constant intervention and economic support from Russia and Iran. These states are trying to cement the political power structure in Syria at tremendous costs to themselves. But their efforts are not sustainable over the long term. The UN process has never been able to produce a political alternative, but it has managed to provide selective relief – for example, through ceasefire agreements or through the Humanitarian Task Force and the increase of public pressure to facilitate humanitarian access. With the support of certain Western states, it has at least been able to maintain a certain political influence on the process. The Syrian conflict shows that the tools needed for achieving change have become more specialized and the levels of negotiation more numerous.

Even though the complexity of peace mediation in the current international arena may be reflected in a particularly dramatic way in Syria, it is precisely this systemic complexity and the questions it raises to which modern mediation initiatives must find answers. For the peace mediation landscape, this means thinking more deeply about the approach of "comprehensive peace processes" and developing methodological acumen in dealing with such complexity. Here Germany also could make important contributions as a mediation actor.

References

Asseburg, Muriel, Wolfram Lacher, and Mareike Transfeld. *Mission Impossible? UN Mediation in Libya, Syria and Yemen.* Berlin: Institute for International and Security Affairs (SWP), 2018.

Federal Foreign Office. *Peace Mediation Framework.* Berlin: Federal Foreign Office, 2019.

Pedersen, Geir O. "Security Council Briefing on Syria, Special Envoy Geir O. Pedersen", *Political and Peacebuilding Affairs*, February 28, 2019. https://dppa.un.org/en/security-council-briefing-syria-special-envoy-geir-o-pedersen (accessed June 29, 2020).

Reuters. "Text of Annan's Six-Point Peace Plan for Syria", April 4, 2012. www.reuters.com/article/us-syria-ceasefire-idUSBRE8330HJ20120404 (accessed June 29, 2020).

UN Report. "Action Group for Syria: Final Communiqué", June 30, 2012. https://un-report.blogspot.com/2012/06/action-group-for-syria-final-communique.html (accessed June 29, 2020).

UN Security Council. *Security Council Resolution 2254.* New York: United Nations, 2015.

United Nations General Assembly. *Resolution Adopted by the General Assembly 66/253 – The Situation in the Syrian Arab Republic.* New York: United Nations, 2012.

Wieland, Carsten. "Teufelskreis der Gewalt: Die Syrien-Konferenz als Beispiel für die Herausforderungen internationaler Konfliktlösung", *Die Politische Meinung* 63, no. 553 (November 2018): 42–9.

Part II:
The Fact Sheet Series "Peace Mediation and Peace Mediation Support" – Methodological Professionalization

Overview Part II

Anne Holper & Lars Kirchhoff

This section compiles five central documents from the Fact Sheet Series "Peace Mediation and Mediation Support" compiled by the FFO and IMSD.[1] From a scientific and practical standpoint, these Fact Sheets are an achievement, a balancing act and a compromise. For this very reason, they are also remarkable from a political point of view, as an expression of lived cooperation between politics, civil society organizations and academia.

They are a compromise because in several cases it was impossible to adequately represent the ongoing scholarly discourse (for example, regarding the reference frame for inclusion, specific questions of contemporary conflict analysis or the exact validity claim of normative orders); attempting to do so might have meant missing the primary target group, who above all need a quick and clear orientation as a basis for their practical work.

At the same time, we felt that it was our mandate and requirement not to over-simplify, hence distinguishing the volume from superficial information brochures. One glance at the models of conflict analysis or the categories and inherently conflicting objectives in the normative dimensions of peace mediation, for example, reveals that the Fact Sheets deliberately perform a balancing act at what otherwise can be dangerously simplistic points, in order to apply the necessary detailed knowledge in a tangible way, even though – from a scientific standpoint – the deeper discourse is only alluded to.

But not only do the Fact Sheets consolidate knowledge and approaches; the series' true achievement could well be their establishment of a confidence-building precedent for participatory resource development between ministries, civil society and academia – something that would make sense in many political and social arenas, but which few have yet dared to try. For this reason, and also because of the time-consuming development and coordination processes, we would like to emphasize that all five organizations of the IMSD and the relevant persons and units of the Federal Foreign Office were intensively involved in preparing all the Fact Sheets.

---

1 The Fact Sheets are printed in their original versions. Their formats may differ in some aspects (e.g., the references) from the standard in the rest of this volume.

With that in mind, the authors of each Fact Sheet would like to thank the other individuals from the IMSD for their comprehensive feedback and contributions to the development of the Fact Sheets, contributions that may not have been visible in the resulting text, but that often proved central to the creative process. A special thanks goes to the respective coordinators of the IMSD – Philippe Taflinski, Christoph Werthmann, Jana Schildt, Laura Hunder, Nina Strumpf and Karoline Eickhoff – who pulled together the logistical strands of the project. When it comes to content and editing, we wish to highlight the role of Julia von Dobeneck, now at Center for International Peace Operations (ZIF), who, for most of the process, assumed overall responsibility for the development of the Fact Sheet series.

The following Fact Sheets are published in this volume:[2]

- Basics of Mediation: Concepts and Definitions (Sebastian Dworack, Christoph Lüttmann, Brigitta von Messling and Luxshi Vimalarajah)
- The Roles and Contributions of Multilateral and Non-State Actors in Peace Mediation (Sebastian Dworack, Christoph Lüttmann, Brigitta von Messling and Luxshi Vimalarajah)
- Conflict Analysis and Mediation Entry Points (Julia von Dobeneck, Anne Holper and Dirk Splinter)
- The Normative Framework and the International Legal Basis of Peace Mediation (Lars Kirchhoff, Anne Holper and Felix Würkert)
- Methodology and Communication Tools in Peace Mediation (Lars Kirchhoff and Dirk Splinter)

---

2 In addition to the Fact Sheets printed in this volume, the Fact Sheet "The Roles and Contributions of States in Peace Mediation" is available for download on the homepage of the German Federal Foreign Office (https://www.auswaertiges-amt.de /blob/1993530/c07f37ac854fe08e8f9c79960a0c7648/roles-of-states-in-peace-mediatio n-data.pdf) and the IMSD (https://www.friedensmediation-deutschland.de/ressourc en.html), respectively.

Basics of Mediation: Concepts and Definitions

Sebastian Dworack & Christoph Lüttmann & Brigitta von Messling & Luxshi Vimalarajah

 Federal Foreign Office

 PEACE MEDIATION
GERMANY

Basics of Mediation: Concepts and Definitions

Peace mediation is a term that covers a range of instruments used to deal with intra- and inter-state conflicts. It includes mediation, mediation support and mediation-based dialogue processes. Such mediation and dialogue processes can be actively supported by third parties with the relevant mandates and mediation frameworks. States play a key role and often make effective contributions. At the Federal Foreign Office, the Directorate-General for Humanitarian Assistance, Crisis Prevention, Stabilisation and Post-Conflict Reconstruction, set up in March 2015, acts as a focal point for matters relating to mediation and mediation support. Moreover, in this area the Federal Foreign Office is in contact with a number of German civil society organisations which have come together under the umbrella of the Initiative Mediation Support Deutschland (IMSD).[1]

This fact sheet is part of a fact sheet series on peace mediation that provides a structured overview of approaches, stakeholders, challenges and possibilities for action in the field of peace mediation.
Published in January 2016; revised edition in January 2017.

Mediation

The United Nations (UN) Guidance for Effective Mediation describes mediation as a voluntary process "whereby a third party assists two or more parties, with their consent, to prevent, manage or resolve a conflict by helping them to develop mutually acceptable agreements".[2] The term peace mediation comprises the entire structured process of supporting negotiations, from initial contact between mediators and conflict parties to ceasefire negotiations and the implementation of peace agreements. Mediation is thus an instrument that can be used throughout the whole conflict cycle.

Just like diplomacy in general, peace mediation aims to address and resolve conflicts in a constructive and non-violent manner. Yet a significant difference between mediation and diplomacy lies in the fact that diplomacy predominantly focuses on a country's own foreign policy goals and interests, whereas mediation is a consensus-based method to further all parties' interests. This leads to differing concepts of the roles of diplomats and mediators and, consequently, different approaches. Moreover, diplomats are more restricted when it comes to cooperating with certain conflict parties (above all violent non-state actors), whereas mediators are fully able to include any conflict party in mediation processes in appropriate constellations. This is why coordination of diplomacy and mediation offers great potential.[3]

Mediation, a case study: Kenya

The efforts of Kofi Annan's mediation team in Kenya in the spring of 2008 are often cited as an example of the successful deployment of an expert mediation team. The former UN Secretary-General was asked to mediate on behalf of the African Union between the two main political factions in the conflict that broke out following the 2007 presidential elections. During the unrest, many people were displaced and at least 1,500 lives were lost. In order to de-escalate the conflict, the Kenya National Dialogue and Reconciliation Team, which comprised the Panel of Eminent African Personalities, attempted to bring about cooperative governance and power sharing between the two conflicting parties. Seeking expertise in the field of governmental cooperation between divergent political factions, it asked Germany to share its experience of coalition governments. Dr Gernot Erler, at the time Minister of State at the Federal Foreign Office, was asked to offer expertise as the only representative of a non-African country. After months of negotiations, Africa's first grand coalition was sworn in on 14 April 2008. It helped to de-escalate the situation in both the short and medium term. The reformed constitution, adopted in 2010, served as the basis for the peaceful elections that took place in 2013. The case study of Kenya shows that mediation teams – both professional mediators and eminent figures – can strongly influence the success of peace initiatives. Furthermore, Germany's particular expertise contributed to finding a solution and resolving the conflict.

Approaches to mediation[4]

In both theory and practice, there are different views regarding the mediator's role and style. The following three approaches are relevant for peace mediation:

Facilitative mediation focuses on organising and facilitating communication between the parties in a non-directive manner, eliciting the underlying interests and needs behind the stated demands and positions. In order not to jeopardise multi-partiality[5], the mediator refrains from making substantial recommendations or suggestions.

In **formulative mediation**, the mediator takes a more directive role. In addition to structuring the process and gathering proposed solutions, the mediator offers different options, e.g. by formulating option papers or drafting agreements. As in facilitative mediation the consent of the parties is seen as essential.

The focus of **power-based mediation** lies in using the mediator's leverage in order to reach an agreement. A strong mediator deploys his power and uses strategic tactics. The conflict parties are encouraged to agree through threats of punishment and promises of reward (carrot and stick approach).

In practice, there is not always a clear-cut difference between these methods, and different mediation actors can use these approaches or combinations thereof at different stages of the mediation process. While the UN Guidance for Effective Mediation emphasises consent of the conflict parties, impartiality of the mediator and inclusivity of the process as mediation fundamentals[6], these elements are not always met in all the approaches.

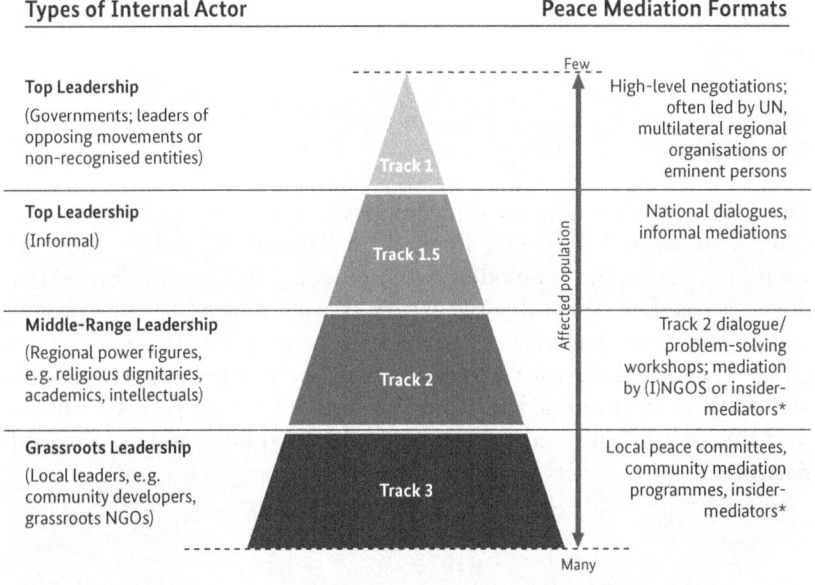

Types of Internal Actor	Peace Mediation Formats
Top Leadership (Governments; leaders of opposing movements or non-recognised entities) — Track 1	High-level negotiations; often led by UN, multilateral regional organisations or eminent persons
Top Leadership (Informal) — Track 1.5	National dialogues, informal mediations
Middle-Range Leadership (Regional power figures, e.g. religious dignitaries, academics, intellectuals) — Track 2	Track 2 dialogue/ problem-solving workshops; mediation by (I)NGOS or insider-mediators*
Grassroots Leadership (Local leaders, e.g. community developers, grassroots NGOs) — Track 3	Local peace committees, community mediation programmes, insider-mediators*

Based on Lederach, John Paul (1997). Building Peace. Sustainable Reconciliation in Divided Societies. Washington D.C.: USIP, p. 39, adapted by IMSD.
* Insider Mediators are "trusted and respected insiders at all levels of a conflicted society who have a deep knowledge of the dynamics and context of the conflict and a sensitivity in their contribution to finding solutions that are recognized and valued by the parties themselves". (Hislaire/Smith/Wachira (2011). Insider Mediators in Africa. Prangis: PeaceNexusFoundation, p. 2.)

Multiple tracks of engagement

Peace processes take place at different societal levels (tracks) and are in often supported by external third parties. The first level (track 1) comprises the leadership of a country (e.g. political and/or military). The second level (track 2) covers leading figures in society such as religious dignitaries, intellectuals, political parties and regional power figures. Track 3 comprises leading civil society figures at the local level and grassroots initiatives. Work on the ground highlighted the need to expand this three-level structure to include a further component: the track 1.5 level, which refers to top-level political decision-makers, yet in informal, non-official settings. These track 1.5 mediation/dialogue processes often serve to sort out and prepare for track 1 talks, develop options and help bring about better comprehension and understanding between conflict parties. The potential offered by peace mediation can only be fully unlocked through coordinated interaction between these tracks. A lasting peace process thus often requires a multi-track approach, which does not only mean conducting activities on all tracks but also interlinking these activities in ways that increase their effectiveness.

What does a mediator need?

Method-based communication techniques ("mediation micro-skills") can make a substantial difference in peace mediation: the ability to reframe strong statements into non-offensive comments, eliciting and formulating the true interests of conflicting parties as well as constructively dealing with the typical dynamics of perception in conflicts can lead to real progress. In addition, structured conflict analysis and process design can be used to generate multiple and at times unorthodox entry points for mediation approaches. This needs to be methodically trained and continuously developed.

Mediation Process Design

Using the results of comprehensive conflict analysis and building on identified entry points, peace mediation interventions have to be designed carefully before processes start. In the Process Design phase, decisions on objectives, appropriate measures, procedures, formats, strategies, methods and logistics are taken while equally considering relevant norms and operationalising the mediation principles. The resulting design (Process Design) lays out the structure of the process and can serve as a roadmap for third parties. Due to changes within the conflict setting, the Process Design may require continuous and dynamic adaptation.

During Process Design, the following aspects are among the most relevant and should be clarified and structured before the beginning of a process (uncategorised interchangeable order; exemplary questions).

- **Objective:** What is the overall objective of the process? What does the mandate include and is it aligned with the objective and context of the process?

- **Tracks:** Which track(s) should be used to fulfil the objective? If multi-track, which approach is to be applied on which track and how should tracks be interlinked?

- **Participation:** Which actors have to be included with regard to objective and in which manner: active participation/representation/consultation/information (including media/information to the public)?

- **Format(s):** Which format(s) reflect(s) the objective (direct talks, proximity, shuttle diplomacy, bilateral meetings, working groups, plenary)?

- **Procedures (Decision-Making):** How should decisions be taken: by majority, by consensus? Is confidentiality necessary?

- **Agenda and Sequencing:** Who sets the agenda (mediator, conflicting parties, both)? How is the agenda to be structured?
  a) Easy-to-hard (incremental approach, most common approach);
  b) Hard-to-easy (most difficult issue first, easier ones later);
  c) Committee approach (all issues at the same time: "nothing is agreed until everything is agreed");
  d) Framework mediation (general agreement first (early in process), details later)

- **Timing and Frequency:** When are negotiations held in terms of ripeness?[7] How often are they held (regularly, on demand)?

- **Third Party Composition:** How should the third party be composed in terms of mandate, leverage, perception, expertise? How can coordination be effective?

- **Funding and Donors:** Who is funding the process and for how long? Do donor interests have to be respected? Might they affect the process?

- **Venue(s):** Where does mediation (and potential accompanying activities) take place (e.g. in-country, out-of-country)?

- **Normative framework:** What norms should be considered?[8]

Mediation support

The term "mediation support" refers to methodical, technical, logistical, regional knowledge support provided by experts to mediation processes guided by mediators. The aim of mediation support is to improve and create the conditions needed for mediations/negotiations or long-term peace processes. Target groups and beneficiaries of mediation support include not only mediating third parties, but also conflict parties, interest groups, donor institutions and other supportive actors. Mediation support also covers support in developing mediation structures as well as promoting local mediators. Mediation support can be provided in the following areas:

a) Implementation and operational support for mediation processes

Implementing or supporting mediation processes, planning and preparing logistical and organisational elements, methodological, thematic, strategic, psychological or legal advice and collaboration, dovetailing of key stakeholders and processes, monitoring and evaluation, funding.

b) Compiling and disseminating expertise

Evaluating mediation processes (lessons learned), and further developing concepts and instruments, developing analysis on conflicts, stakeholders and relevant topics such as religion, ethnicity, human rights, gender, drafting laws and constitutions, etc., as well as developing guidelines, good practice standards and codes of conduct for mediation.

c) Capacity building

Training on acquiring methodological, thematic and normative knowledge and practical mediation skills, workshops on boosting human and institutional skills and expertise, coaching and mentoring of mediators/ diplomats to enhance their skills, e.g. in the fields of communication, negotiation and designing processes, preparing conflict parties for mediation processes.

d) Developing/expanding mediation structures

Providing support and advice in establishing mediation at the political level, in legislative processes related to mediation, in integrating mediation support departments in ministries and international organisations, in developing and managing expertise on mediation, in the design and setup of fixed standby teams and external pools of experts (rosters) as well as in developing conflict management systems and mediation infrastructure, i.e. mediation centres, contact points for mediation, and embedding them in their respective legal/political/social context.

Mediation support, a case study: Sudan

Against the background of different, decades-long armed and political conflicts, in January 2014, Sudan's President Omar al-Bashir announced an inclusive national dialogue. In order to support the official dialogue process at the track 1.5 level, the Federal Foreign Office (FFO), the Berghof Foundation and the German Institute for International and Security Affairs (SWP) are working together to implement Project Sudan: Support to National Dialogue and Reconciliation. The project seeks to support trust and consensus building within the opposition groups and enable the two parties to discuss arrangements for joint meetings at numerous talks.

The project conducts mediation between the parties as well as facilitating unified positions within the opposition. The mediation format links the Berghof Foundation, the FFO and the African Union High Implementation Panel (AUHIP), which agreed a strategic partnership with Germany. The mediation activities ranged from informal meetings between the opposition and government hosted by the FFO and Berghof Foundation, to co-chairing with the AUHIP the formal negotiations between the Government of Sudan and the Sudan People's Liberation Movement North in Berlin, Germany. Meditation support activities conducted by the Berghof Foundation aimed to support the parties in preparing, carrying out and evaluating informal and formal meetings in Addis Ababa and various other venues.

Following a long preparation phase, ongoing consultations with the Sudanese Government and opposition groups, intensive, trust building communication with other relevant stakeholders and close collaboration with the African Union High Implementation Panel (AUHIP) and the international community, in February 2015 the German initiative managed to bring together the main opposition groups in Berlin for a national dialogue. At the meeting, the groups represented signed the Berlin Declaration, agreeing to take part in a preparatory meeting for the national dialogue in Addis Ababa.

Dialogue facilitation

The facilitation of dialogues through third parties is subsumed under the term "peace mediation", because it has a vast overlap with mediation, particularly the facilitative style of mediation. While mediation attempts to reach substantial agreements that solve issues at the heart of a conflict, the primary aim of dialogue is to learn more and understand better the views and needs of the opponent and thereby transform the relationship, create trust and in many cases lay the ground for substantive agreements at a later stage. Dialogues on track 1.5, track 2 or 3 are often initiated in order to explore readiness for official negotiations, when formal peace talks are stalled, in order to broaden public participation and support for existing official peace processes or to secure sustainable implementation of peace agreements. They are thus an essential component of an effective multi-track approach.

Dialogues are usually facilitated by a third party whose role, methods and skills are very similar to those of a facilitative mediator: Dialogue facilitators help the stakeholders involved to communicate their own positions and interests, to understand those of the other side, to de-escalate contentious topics by phrasing them differently and foster mutual understanding.[9]

Support to national dialogue

National dialogues are nationally owned political processes aimed at generating consensus among a broad range of national stakeholders in times of deep political crisis, in postwar situations or during far-reaching political transitions. National dialogues offer the opportunity to work on a comprehensive range of topics. Moreover, while often only a limited number of stakeholders are involved in mediation processes, national dialogue processes seek to involve a broad spectrum of predominantly local stakeholders. Despite the fact that in a national dialogue there is no official mediator, there are regular chairs for plenary sessions and working groups who moderate with a mediation-based approach. The process is often supported technically by third party actors and can thus be seen as being part of peace mediation.

When Yemen was on the brink of civil war in 2011, the GCC initiative (Gulf Cooperation Council) presented a roadmap for a political transition process. Its main elements included a transfer of power to an interim president, the establishment of a government of national unity and the organisation of a National Dialogue Conference (NDC) to lay the foundations for a new constitution in Yemen. The NDC convened over ten months with a total of 565 delegates from the various political and social components of Yemeni society (the main political parties, parts of the Southern Movement, the Houthis, independent women and young people's groups as well as other civil-society actors. The conference's agenda covered a broad range of issues of national concern and concluded with more than 1,700 recommendations.

On invitation of the main political parties and President Abdul Rabo Mansour Hadi, the Berghof Foundation and its Yemeni partner organisation, the Political Development Forum (PDF), established the National Dialogue Support Programme (NDSP) in 2012 with financial and political support from the German Federal Foreign Office. The main aim of the programme was to support an inclusive Yemeni-led national dialogue process. Activities in the framework of the NDSP comprised capacity-building measures, process advice and support through thematic expertise. The programme provided facilitation support, negotiation and dialogue trainings, thematic mappings, as well as analysis papers, coaching and public education materials.

Since the escalation of the crisis in Yemen at the end of 2014, the NDSP organised a series of inclusive multiparty consultations (with the conflict stakeholders and political parties) in- and outside the country to support consensus-building among the Yemeni actors. These high-level meetings are organized in close cooperation with the Office of the UN Special Envoy to Yemen and seek to complement and strengthen the official UN-led track-I negotiations through an informal track-II dialogue process. The programme further provides thematic support to help the Yemeni parties to develop concrete problem-solving mechanisms and to identify pathways out of the crisis. In this context, crucial issues such as interim security measures and confidence-building mechanisms, the restoration of state institutions, elements of a transition roadmap, mechanisms of inclusion and the division of powers, the organization of a future political dialogue in Yemen, as well as ways to strengthen local governance structures were tackled by the different groups.

The experiences made in Yemen have highlighted that, at times, it is important (if not imperative) to readjust ongoing efforts of peace support in order to adapt to fast-changing conflict environments. Building long-term relationships of trust and reliability is often key for sustaining this support also in times of escalated conflict and societal polarization. While the conceptual distinction between mediation, mediation support and national dialogues is theoretically useful and crucial to understand and develop tailor-made approaches, the change (or escalation) of conflict dynamics often requires parties to find new ways of paving the path to peace. In light of this, the potential and purpose of international third party support in peace processes has to be understood as a dynamic and interdependent endeavour.

References

1 The members of the IMSD are: the Berghof Foundation, the Center for Peace Mediation (CPM) at the European University Viadrina, the CSSP – Berlin Center for Integrative Mediation, inmedio berlin – institut für mediation. consulting. development and the Center for International Peace Operations (ZIF).
2 United Nations (2012). Guidance for Effective Mediation, p. 4.
3 Federal Foreign Office and Initiative Mediation Support Deutschland (2015). Germany as Mediator – Peace Mediation and Mediation Support in German Foreign Policy (conference report). Berlin: Federal Foreign Office and Initiative Mediation Support Deutschland, p. 12.
4 Wilkenfeld, Jonathan, Young, Kathleen, Asal, Victor, Quinn, David (2003). "Mediating International Crises", in: Journal of Conflict Resolution (2003), p. 279 – 301; Lanz, David, Wählisch, Martin, Kirchhoff, Lars and Siegfried, Martin (2008). Evaluating Peace Mediation. Brussels: Initiative for Peacebuilding, p. 10.
5 Besides impartiality, definitions such as omni-partiality or multi-partiality are used by practitioners, putting a stronger emphasis on the ability of mediators to understand the interests and concerns of all the key actors involved.
6 Other mediation fundamentals outlined in the UN Guidance are Preparedness, National ownership, International law and Normative frameworks, Coherence/Coordination and Complementary of the mediation effort.
7 The concept of a ripe moment assumes that parties resolve their conflict only when they are ready to do so, which they are under certain

conditions: Zartman, I. W., (2000). "Ripeness: The Hurting Stalemate and Beyond", in: Stern, P. and Druckman, D., eds. (2000), International Conflict Resolution after the Cold War. Washington: National Academy Press.

8   For further details see Fact Sheet "The normative framework and the international legal basis of peace mediation", 2019.

9   Berghof Foundation (2012) Berghof Glossary on Conflict Transformation. Berlin: Berghof Foundation, p. 28f.

PEACE MEDIATION
GERMANY

Initiative Mediation Support Deutschland (IMSD) comprises:

Berghof Foundation

 Center for Peace Mediation
EUROPA-UNIVERSITÄT VIADRINA

Berlin Center for
Integrative Mediation

 inmedio
peace consult ggmbh

 Center for
International
Peace Operations

The Roles and Contributions of Multilateral and Non-State Actors in Peace Mediation

Sebastian Dworack & Christoph Lüttmann & Brigitta von Messling & Luxshi Vimalarajah

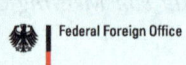

The Roles and Contributions of Multilateral and Non-State Actors in Peace Mediation

Different third parties – different roles

Not only states but also other third parties are active in peace mediation. Over the past ten years, international organisations and non-governmental organisations in particular have assumed an increasingly important role in the field of peace mediation, stepping up their cooperation with states. This fact sheet provides an overview of the characteristics and strengths of these actors.

This fact sheet is part of a series of fact sheets on peace mediation. It provides a structured overview of methods, actors, challenges and options in the field of peace mediation.
This fact sheet examines the different roles that multilateral and non-state actors can play in the field of peace mediation as well as the contributions they can make.
Published in January 2016; revised edition December 2017.

International organisations

The majority of international organisations are active at the international level in the field of peace mediation and mediation support (see also Fact Sheet: Basics of Mediation: Concepts and Definitions).[1] The main global actor is the United Nations (UN), but regional multilateral organisations such as the Organisation for Security and Co-operation in Europe (OSCE), the European Union (EU), the African Union (AU), the Organization of American States (OAS) and the Association of Southeast Asian Nations (ASEAN), as well as sub-regional organisations like the Economic Community of West African States (ECOWAS), the East African Community (EAC) and the Southern African Development Community (SADC), have taken on a greater role in peace mediation over the past few years. These regional and international organisations provide the added value of a multilateral approach to peace mediation by wielding potentially larger political clout in complex or regionalised conflicts where states are often not accepted as mediators.

Many of these organisations have set up special units and structures for peace mediation.

- The UN has a Mediation Support Unit (MSU) within the Department of Political Affairs. The MSU provides specialist expertise for peace processes, develops the UN's mediation capacities and supports UN Special Envoys. In 2012, the MSU issued the United Nations Guidance for Effective Mediation.[2] Since 2008, there has also been a Standby Team of Mediation Experts with particular expertise in a wide range of issues and regions who can be deployed at very short notice to provide technical advice to mediators or conflict parties. The team is on permanent standby. Germany supports this instrument, Frank-Walter Steinmeier, at the time Federal Foreign Minister, emphasised in October 2015: "Another example is mediation, an area where we will be enhancing the UN's capacities. We want to establish a sort of rapid response unit – not a military force but a rapid-response team for the negotiating table!"[3].
- The EU is active politically in peace processes as well as a major funder of others' peace mediation work, from grassroots mediation initiatives to international NGOs, regional organisations and the United Nations. The EU's own diplomatic mediation work is led by the European External Action Service (EEAS), and can involve its Senior Management, EU Heads of Delegations, as well as a number of EU Special Representatives and Special Envoys. Inside the EEAS, technical support is provided by a Mediation Support Team that is integrated into the Division for Prevention of Conflicts, Rule of Law and SSR, Integrated Approach, Stabilisation and Mediation (PRISM). Its work includes advice on EU involvement in peace processes; deployment of experts; and institutional capacity building. The EU system has put in place a number of instruments to rapidly support peace mediation efforts, for instance through logistically supporting the holding of talks.
- The Mediation Support Team (MST) within the OSCE Conflict Prevention Centre/Operations Service (CPC/OS), consisting of three seconded Mediation Support Officers has been established in 2011 based on a Ministerial Council Decision by its 57 participating States. It serves as the main resource for mediation support within the OSCE. The MST offers methodological support to OSCE's peace processes, in particular to the Chairmanship's Special Representatives, Head of Missions, institutions, the OSCE Parliamentary Assembly, and other executive structures. The mediation support provided by the MST is request-based and includes conflict analysis and advice on process design, strategy planning workshops, tailor-made coachings, and operational guidance on specific thematic issues of dialogue facilitation or mediation processes.
- At the AU, the Peace and Security Department of the African Union Commission is responsible for handling conflict interventions, includ-

ing mediation projects. The ECOWAS Mediation and Security Council mandates the organisation's activities in the field of peace and security, including mediation. Both organisations are currently in the process of forming pools of experts.

Non-governmental organisations

Besides multilateral organisations, various non-state organisations are active in international peace mediation. A large number of them have many years of experience in specific countries, regions and conflict contexts and thereby combine mediation and process skills with regional expertise and specialist knowledge, e.g. on how to integrate women into peace processes, strengthen local mediators' competences or approach conflicts over resources. Non-governmental organisations (NGOs) can often react quickly and with a minimum of red tape. In addition, in many cases they have different, easier, access to civil-society, regional and local actors (tracks 2 and 3). This enables NGOs to work with stakeholders who are excluded from official processes or whose involvement could lead to diplomatic disruptions, e.g. armed rebel groups. In some cases, however, even government parties to a conflict prefer support from an NGO in an intra-state conflict, rejecting intervention by another government in its domestic affairs. This was the case, for instance, in the peace negotiations in 2015 between the Indonesian Government and the Free Aceh Movement (GAM), which received substantial support from the NGO Crisis Management Initiative.[4] For these reasons, NGOs can be important cooperation partners for embassies.

The most renowned NGOs active internationally and working in the field of peace mediation include: ACCORD (South Africa), Berghof Foundation (Germany), Centre for Humanitarian Dialogue (Switzerland), Conciliation Resources (UK), Crisis Management Initiative (Finland), Muhammadiyah (Indonesia), Serapaz (Mexico), swisspeace (Switzerland), the Asia Foundation (USA), the Carter Center (USA), US Institute of Peace (USA) and West Africa Network for Peacebuilding (Ghana). Religious non-governmental organisations like the Community of Sant'Egidio or religious leaders can also play an important role in mediation processes.

Insider mediators[5] differ from regional or international third parties in a number of ways which enable them to make a major contribution to unofficial negotiating processes. In general, insider mediators can be defined as "trusted and respected insiders at all levels of a conflicted society who have a deep knowledge of the dynamics and context of the conflict and a sensitivity in their contribution to finding solutions that are recognized and valued by all parties"[6].

Unlike external mediators, insider mediators are personally rooted in the conflict context and have a vested interest in ending it. For this reason, they usually bring long-term commitment to the mediation process. Having deep roots in the society, insider mediators enjoy the respect, legitimation and trust of the population and the conflict parties, but they need to be particularly careful to maintain their impartiality and to ensure that third parties perceive them as impartial, by working with networks and by being transparent about their goals and interests.[7] As part of the society in conflict, they also have a profound knowledge of cultural norms, of the country's history and political landscape, and of the conflict, as well as of the interests and strategies being pursued by the conflict parties. This often gives them easier access to relevant stakeholders, allowing them to play an important role in building up trust and confidence. In addition, insider mediators have a number of resources which can motivate them to keep up their commitment: support from the society which is giving them an informal mandate; teamwork with and in networks which provides a way to counter any (perceived) bias on the part of the local mediator; religion and cultural practices, communication methods and interpretations can provide local mediators with inspiration and orientation as well as personal experience and recognition.

Insider mediators are important actors in negotiating processes for the following reasons:*

→ **Insider Mediators** can act where external mediators cannot: in situations where external third parties are not wanted, or cannot be involved for other reasons, insider mediators can play a key role towards resolving the conflict.

→ **Insider Mediators** complement external mediators: in particular, they are able to move between the various stakeholder levels and to facilitate interaction between processes on tracks 1, 2 and 3 (insider mediators are themselves usually on track 1.5 or track 2).

→ **Insider Mediators** are particularly relevant during transformation processes and in fragile contexts often characterised by the lack of any conflict management approach by a formal government structure. So insider mediators can act as facilitators at official level and play an important part in preventing and containing conflicts.

* Gourlay, Catriona and Ropers, Norbert (2012). Support for 'Insider' Mediators: A Gap in EU Ambitions for Mediation? In: Strengthening the EU's Peace Mediation Capacities: Leveraging for Peace through New Ideas and Thinking, edited by Tanja Tamminen, Finnish Institute of International Affairs (FIIA), pp. 93-97.

Coordination and cooperation of third parties

The number of different actors in the field of mediation brings many opportunities for a mediation process if good use is made of their various potentials, opportunities for access and networks. At the same time, the large number of actors means that coherence, coordination and complementarity are indispensable. However, coordinated cooperation between organisations with differing financial resources, ideas on standards, administrative rules and political decision-making cultures also brings many challenges. It is important to ensure a clear division of responsibilities in line with the comparative strengths of the individual stakeholders. A joint management of mediation interventions affords one possibility for coordination between regional and international organisations. However, practice has shown that it is preferable to have one organisation leading the process and coordinating the cooperation with other organisations in a strategic way rather than a joint leadership by several organisations.[8] At best, cooperation between the organisations is based on a joint mediation strategy and agreements on transparency and information-sharing.[9] Coordinated support for local mediators from international organisations and a coordinated approach to dealing with the parties to a conflict can also ensure a coherent mediation process. One innovative model for cooperation is the International Contact Group for the Mindanao peace process, which was set up in 2009 and comprises the UK, Japan, Turkey and Saudi Arabia as well as four international NGOs (Centre for Humanitarian Dialogue, Conciliation Resources, Muhammadiyah and the Asia Foundation). The Contact Group helped broker a comprehensive peace agreement between the Philippine Government and the Moro Islamic Liberation Front (MILF) in 2014.

References

1 Lüttmann, Christoph and Splinter, Dirk (2014). Friedensmediation organisiert sich – Ein Überblick zu Institutionalisierung und wachsenden Strukturen. In: Konfliktdynamik 4/2014. Stuttgart: Klett-Cotta Verlag.
2 United Nations (2012). UN Guidance for Effective Mediation. New York: United Nations.
3 Speech by Foreign Minister Frank-Walter Steinmeier to the German Bundestag on the 70th anniversary of the United Nations, 14 October 2015.
4 Mason, Simon and Sguaitamatti, Damiano (2011). Mapping Mediators. A comparison of third parties and implications for Switzerland. Zurich: Center for Security Studies (CSS), ETH Zurich, p. 22 et seq.
5 In a 2009 study entitled "Insider Mediators – Exploring Their Key Role in Informal Peace Processes" (Berlin: Berghof Foundation for Peace Support), the Berghof Foundation was one of the first organisations to coin and explore the term "insider mediators".
6 Hislaire, Peter and Smith, Richard and Wachira, George (2011). Insider Mediators in Africa. Understanding and enhancing the contribution of Insider Mediators to the peaceful resolution of conflicts in Africa. Prangins: PeaceNexus Foundation, p. 2.
7 Gourlay, Catriona and Ropers, Norbert (2012). Support for 'Insider' Mediators: A Gap in EU Ambitions for Mediation? In: Strengthening the EU's Peace Mediation Capacities: Leveraging for Peace through New Ideas and Thinking, edited by Tanja Tamminen, Finnish Institute of International Affairs (FIIA), pp. 90–102.
8 United Nations (2012). UN Guidance for Effective Mediation. New York: United Nations, p. 18.
9 Alvarez, Miguel et al. (2012). Translating Mediation Guidance into Practice: Commentary on the UN Guidance for Effective Mediation by the Mediation Support Network.

PEACE MEDIATION
GERMANY

Initiative Mediation Support Deutschland (IMSD) comprises:

Conflict Analysis and Mediation Entry Points

Julia von Dobeneck & Anne Holper & Dirk Splinter

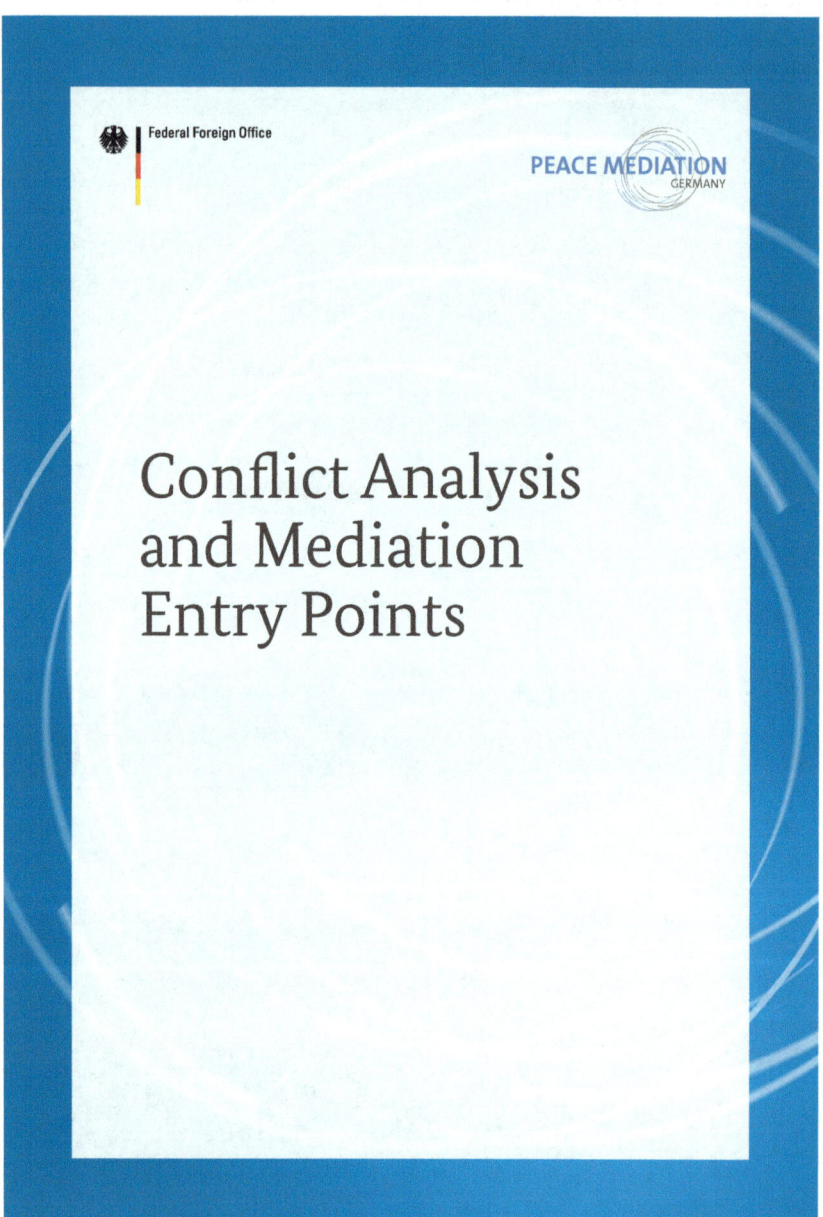

Federal Foreign Office

PEACE MEDIATION
GERMANY

Conflict Analysis and Mediation Entry Points

The importance of conflict analysis

Conflict analysis is of crucial importance in planning and designing mediation processes for conflict prevention, management, resolution and transformation. Both researchers and practitioners confirm that inadequate analyses are one of the most common reasons why mediation interventions are not effective enough or even fail.

This fact sheet is part of a series of fact sheets on peace mediation. It provides a structured overview of methods, actors, challenges and options in the field of peace mediation.
This fact sheet addresses the importance of conflict analysis for identifying mediation entry points and devising mediation interventions.
Published in January 2016; revised edition August 2017.

There are many reasons why conflict analyses may be inadequate, for example if they are not constantly updated in line with the process or if the focus is only on one's own intervention, thus possibly ignoring key aspects of the overall dynamic and the conflict environment. The non-inclusion of analysis findings in the strategic planning of a mediation process can also lead to suboptimal results[1].

International collaboration on producing conflict analyses, the inclusion of regional perspectives and the sharing of key findings among the organisations and institutions involved can and should be improved, as also stated in the UN Secretary-General's report, "The Future of United Nations Peace Operations", published in September 2015[2].

Conflict analysis: Fields of application

The term "conflict analysis" encompasses a very wide range of formats and approaches, whose respective features result both from the contexts in which they are produced and from the different objectives involved. In each case, the purpose of the analysis defines the most effective approach.

- **Context analysis: generating knowledge as the basis for policy action**

  The aim of comprehensive context analyses is to establish a sound basis for policy decisions. To this end, standard scientific information-gathering procedures (research, interviews with stakeholders, press reviews) are used and the findings are presented in the form of reports and recommendations for policymakers (e.g. by the International Crisis Group or Stiftung Wissenschaft und Politik – German Institute for International and Security Affairs).

- **Process guidance: intervention planning by or with third parties**

  On the basis of the policy analyses described above, certain aspects of the conflict are examined in a methodologically structured way, with the aim of identifying or weighing up options for bringing in third parties or further work to be carried out by them. This also involves identifying mediation entry points, i.e. concrete starting points for mediation activities. This type of guidance can be based both on specific aspects (such as preparing talks with a conflict party) and on the overall process. The analytical models and instruments used generally focus on individual aspects of the conflict, such as the power and influence of conflict parties as well as relations between them, the parties' interests and needs, the interaction between the various factors influencing the conflict or on methodological process-oriented questions.

- **Analysing the conflict jointly with the actors involved: a component of dialogue and mediation work by NGOs**

  Joint conflict analyses, produced during workshops with the parties, can even form part of an intervention in the conflict. The aims here can be to create greater understanding of the situation and for the actors involved, to explore backgrounds to the conflict and/or to research the effects of the conflict dynamics. Analysing the conflict together with the conflict actors helps to build trust and is a first step in dealing constructively with other actors' viewpoints. In this way, the analysis can become an integral part of the conflict transformation process.

Various institutions have developed their own preferred types of conflict analysis in line with the specific application field and goal[3]. For example, the Federal Ministry for Economic Cooperation and Development and the Deutsche Gesellschaft für Internationale Zusammenarbeit (GIZ) GmbH use Peace and Conflict Assessment (PCA)[4] in order to ensure conflict-sensitive programme planning. The OSCE Conflict Prevention Centre and the European External Action Service's Mediation Support Team hold internal workshops on conflict analysis for particular crisis regions. Local stakeholders are sometimes involved in these workshops and/or the analyses are carried out in cooperation with partner organisations.

Conflict analysis: Foci and instruments

The analysis instrument is chosen on the basis of the desired added value and intervention goals. The Conflict Wheel (Fig. 1) developed by the Swiss Agency for Development and Cooperation (SDC) in the Swiss Federal Department of Foreign Affairs provides a useful overview of the instruments available for various situations. It should be seen as a meta-analytical tool that presents a selection of standard analytical instruments and can also be used to sum up the various aspects of a conflict coherently. The individual instruments in the Conflict Wheel are explained in greater detail in the SDC's Conflict Analysis Tools Tip Sheet[5].

Conflict Wheel

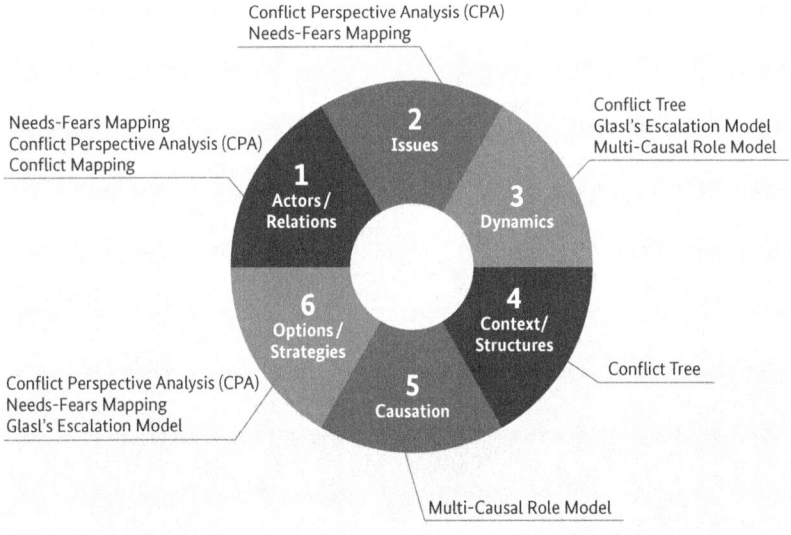

Fig. 1: Conflict Wheel

In the following pages, you will find a selection of the analytical instruments most commonly used in peace mediation, as well as aspects that may be of relevance with regard to mediation interventions in particular.

→ *Actor-Relationship Mapping*

Actor-Relationship Mapping[6] is a method that presents the main actors, their power relations and the various relationships among them (alliances, conflicts, dominances, dependencies) in visual form. Mediators and their teams use this instrument at the start of a mediation process with the aim of acquiring a better understanding of the conflict scenario and of identifying mediation entry points. Actor-Relationship Mapping provides information on which actors could be radicalised by certain interventions and should be included to a greater extent; who has contacts to these actors and thus scope to influence them; which actors can be seen as neutral or partisan; and which actors from civil society and other spheres might support official peace processes. Apart from mediators, conflict parties also use this instrument in order to refine their own strategies and to identify blind spots.

Afghanistan, October 1999

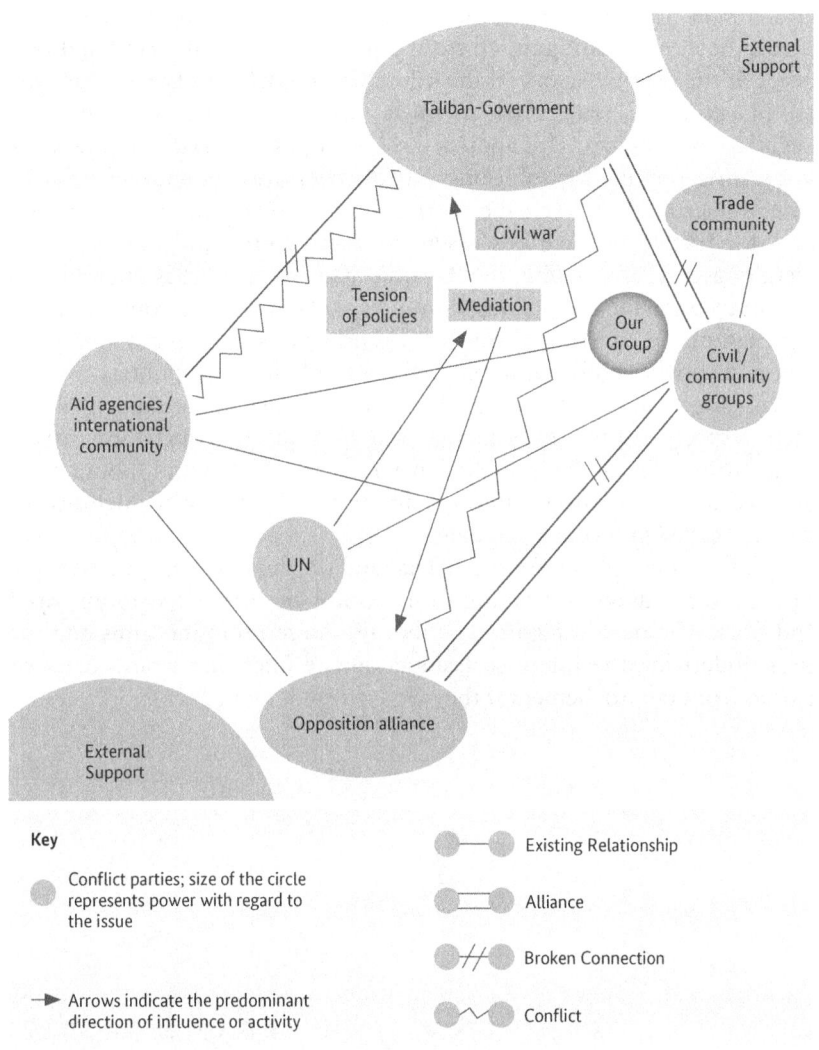

Fig. 2: Actor-Relationship Mapping, Afghanistan, 1999[7]

→ *Interest Analysis*

In an Interest Analysis[8], the interest profiles of all relevant parties to the conflict (including parties that may be excluded, actors affected geopolitically and (potential) third parties) are drawn up. The aim is to elicit the interests that may also lie behind the officially stated positions. Interests should be clearly distinguished from positions on the one hand and basic needs of the conflict actors on the other. Clearly defining the various interests in a conflict is particularly useful as regards preparing mediation-based negotiation processes. This approach makes it possible to develop new, value-creating options for solutions and discover areas of mutual gain and common ground between the parties. At the same time, it becomes evident for further negotiations where zero-sum games and non-negotiable identity aspects are shaping the dynamic. This knowledge is often of great importance for the negotiating conduct displayed by the conflict parties. For example, in a territorial conflict it is only possible to assess to what extent and to what ends economic, religious, ethnic or geopolitical motives explain the various demands by the conflict parties by carefully analysing their respective interests. The practical uses for the mediation process range from defining the most effective order in which topics should be negotiated to gaining insight into the amount and scope of regulations that will be needed in future agreements.

As in the example of Southern Thailand on the next page, interest profiles are often drawn up taking into account the actors' positions, needs and fears. The need category describes the more profound aims and motives underlying the interests. Fears designate lines that would deter the parties from rapprochement if they were crossed.

Category	Thai State	Liberation Movement	CSO Sector
Position	O Sovereignty and territorial integrity: Thailand is one indivisible Kingdom	O Independence from the Thai state, own Nation state	O Peace and justice O People's empowerment and self-determination
Interest	O Ensure law and order through necessary measures to prevent and suppress violence O Centralisation and upholding "Nation, Religion and Monarchy" that constitute national security	O Safeguarding autonomy, political freedom O Personal autonomy with regard to way of life and distribution of resources	O Sending a signal for equality; against discrimination O Creating harmony within a pluralistic society O Increasing decision-making authority in local affairs
Need	O Protection of Thai identity and dignity of Thai state O Political stability	O Freedom to conduct one's life in accordance with one's own faith and culture	O Political participation and recognition
Fear	O Losing authority and territory	O Being assimilated, ethnically, religiously and culturally to the extent of losing Malay-Patani identity	O Losing life or physical integrity

Fig. 3: Example of an Interest Analysis on Southern Thailand[9]

→ *Systemic Feedback Loop Mapping*

Systemic Feedback Loop Mapping explores the entire spectrum of factors (economic, socio-cultural, political, historical, etc.) affecting the conflict, as well as the dynamics that lead to changes in these factors.

This makes it possible to examine the relevance and effectiveness of planned or existing interventions. The aim is to find out which key factors can be influenced and how this should be achieved. This approach also explores which leverage points or unintended effects can be foreseen. For example, an evaluation of peace projects in Kosovo in the pre-2006 period revealed how international funding for inter-ethnic projects had inadvertently boosted nationalism. A large number of the projects were aimed at fostering greater practical inter-ethnic cooperation in various spheres of life (business, young people, health, etc.) on the assumption that this would improve inter-ethnic communication and build trust, thus reducing nationalism and animosity. However, it emerged that other influential factors had not been sufficiently taken into account. For example, the peer pressure encouraged by local political elites to adhere to social boundaries, i.e. the prevailing social norms that limit contact with other ethnic groups and sanction such contact, had not been addressed.

Systemic Feedback Loop Mapping, using Kosovo as an example

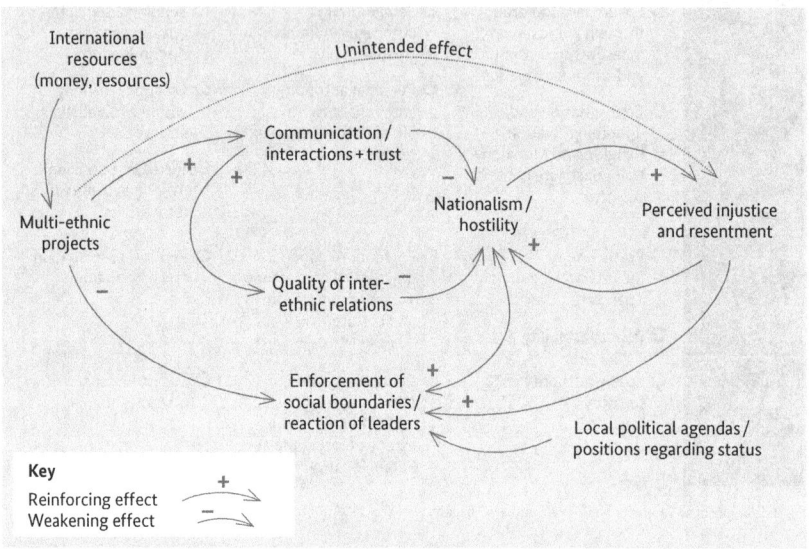

Fig. 4: Example of the findings of Systemic Feedback Loop Mapping on Kosovo[10]

Furthermore, the feeling that one's own ethnic group has been discriminated against (in the past and/or present) proved to be a key factor that was not addressed by the above-mentioned peace projects. In some cases, international funding for inter-ethnic projects was even seen as a continuation of this discrimination. In this way, the peace projects indirectly strengthened nationalist attitudes and the peer pressure mentioned above (see Fig. 4). This type of systemic analysis can provide wide-ranging and important information for the planning of mediation and dialogue initiatives. In this example, a possible finding would be to use dialogue and sometimes mediation to a greater extent in inter-ethnic cooperation projects in order to address the feeling of injustice and the peer pressure exerted by the elite in one's own ethnic group.

→ *Mediation-based Process Analysis*

Mediation-based Process Analysis is an instrument that uses the key phases and the essential methodology of mediation to analyse mediation processes. In this approach, information on conflicts and on past or potential interventions in the course of a conflict is analysed so that action options for an ongoing or upcoming mediation process can be defined. The findings may serve as a basis for deciding whether or not it makes sense to launch a mediation process in the first place, as a list of methodologically promising future steps within a current process or as a means of exploring what elements of the (interim) result of a completed mediation process might require adjustment.

Mediation-based Process Analysis highlights other aspects than a purely descriptive and analytical depiction of a conflict, and should be seen as complementary to the classic types of conflict analysis. It does not focus on the conflict as a whole or its causes, nor does it deal with the conflict dynamics or specific characteristics of the actors involved. Instead, it concentrates on the appropriate mediation approach, the tasks and limitations of the mediation mandate, ways and means of including the actors, and the use of mediation methods to define and merge interests into solutions on which consensus can be reached.

Mediation-based Process Analysis: examples of questions based on the different stages of mediation

Phases of the mediation process	Examples of questions in mediation-based process analysis	Examples: practical relevance of the findings
Mandate, format and actors	O Is there already a viable (partial) mandate for a mediation process? What are its limitations? O Have the decision-making processes and possible agreement formats and scope been agreed by everyone involved and communicated clearly? O Are all significant interests represented? If not, how can they be included (at a later stage)?	O Adjusting and issuing mandates; excluding topics O Decision on agreement formats; consensus on decision-making processes O Producing a participation design for the entire process
Conflict issues and agenda-setting	O Which (conflicting) positions exist? Which claims are made by the parties? Can these claims be fed into an agenda of issues on which consensus can be reached and for which regulations can be drawn up? If so, how? O How can entrenched positions, preconditions and taboos be addressed so that they do not block the negotiations?	O Practical work on conflict narratives O Rephrasing in non-confrontational language, while maintaining content
Managing conflicts and exploring interests	O Have the respective interests of the parties to the conflict been fully elicited? O Which links, dependencies and/or points in common exist with regard to these interests?	O Eliciting and integrating hidden interests; rephrasing biased demands O Recognising and/or explicitly stating non-competing common interests
Generating and evaluating options	O Have all options been explored in an unlimited fashion? O Which of the listed options are not possible for normative reasons?	O Feeding in value-creating methods and options O Exploring normative limits, but also scope/flexibility (possibly with actors such as the UN or courts)
Agreements and conclusion	O Is the planned agreement format appropriate? Do all sides accept and respect it? O Can the agreements be fully implemented by the institutions, bodies or persons involved?	O Detecting methodologically indicated adjustments in the agreement format O Detailed layering and monitoring of timescales, responsibilities and roles in the implementation

This instrument, which is primarily based on negotiation methods, thus serves both to explore mediation entry points and to plan the overall design of mediation processes. It is a particularly productive approach in frozen or protracted conflicts (such as the situation in Transnistria and

Georgia), in which extensive experience and data on the established conflict dynamics are already available.

From analysis to the identification of mediation entry points

The common objective of the various conflict analysis instruments is to identify mediation entry points for mediation interventions[11]. A multi-step approach is advisable here. Conflict analysis can be used to define at which point mediation-based interventions make sense as a means of reducing tensions or helping to resolve a conflict. The findings help to decide with which actors, with regard to which issues, and against the background of which conflict dynamics the mediation could take place. A review of the international intervention environment shows at which levels and with which actors other third parties are already working, and thus where efforts by one's own country could serve to complement existing endeavours[12]. In a further step, it should be decided at the political level if, when and how an existing mediation entry point should in fact be used. This requires comparison with the aims and strategic interests of the intervening third party and with its role in the system of multilateral organisations (political consistency). It also requires an assessment of whether sufficient specific expertise and infrastructure resources can be provided in order to become involved in mediating in the conflict (feasibility).

Summary of the Fact Sheet

In order to address conflicts, it is advisable to include people who are familiar with the specific conflict context on the ground, as well as people who have experience of using conflict analysis methods and the mediation entry points arising from them. The inclusion of different viewpoints, ranging from local actors to government officials, enriches the analysis and creates the potential to reveal new action options. In addition, it is essential to integrate conflict analyses even more consciously into existing decision-making processes and to update them on a regular basis.

References

1 Anderson, Mary B. and Lara Olson, with Kristin Doughty (2003). Confronting War: Critical Lessons for Peace Practitioners. CDA: Cambridge, MA.

2 UN General Assembly and UN Security Council (2015). The Future of United Nations Peace Operations: Implementation of the Recommendations of the High-Level Independent Panel on Peace Operations | Report of the Secretary-General (A /70/357–S /2015/682).

3 Conflict Sensitivity Consortium. Conflict Analysis Tools, http://www.c onflictsensitivity.org/conflict-analysis-tools/, Last download: 8 June 2017.

4 GIZ on behalf of the Federal Ministry for Economic Cooperation and Development (BMZ). Factsheet on the "Peace and Conflict Assessment (PCA)" methodological framework, https://www.bmz.de/en/zentrales_ downloadarchiv/themen_und_schwerpunkte/frieden/Peace_and_Confl ict_Assessment_Factsheet.pdf, Last download: 8 June 2017.

5 Adapted Conflict Wheel. Original: Swiss Agency for Development and Cooperation (2005). Conflict Analysis Tools, Tip Sheet http://www.css. ethz.ch/content/dam/ethz/special-interest/gess/cis/center-for-securities-st udies/pdfs/Conflict-Analysis-Tools.pdf. Last download: 18 April 2017.

6 Please note that the SDC tip sheet refers to this instrument as "Conflict Mapping".

7 Adapted from the original. Original: Fisher, Simon et al. (2000). Working with Conflict. Skills and Strategies for Action: London and New York, p. 23 et seq. The Actor-Relationship Mapping is drawn from the perspective of a small locally based NGO, mentioned as "our Group" in the map. Key has been added.

8 This instrument is also known as Interest-Needs or Needs-Fears Mapping (see SDC's Conflict Analysis Tools Tip Sheet).

9 Adapted from the original. Original: Ropers, Norbert and Anuvatudom, Mathus (2014). A Joint Learning Process for Stakeholders and Insider Peacebuilders: A Case Study from Southern Thailand, in Asian Journal of Peacebuilding, Vol. 2 No. 2 (2014), p. 286.

10 Slightly modified chart. Original: Woodrow, Peter, et al. (2011). Connecting the Dots: Evaluating Whether and How Programmes Address Conflict Systems, in: The Non-Linearity of Peace Processes: Theory and Practice of Systemic Conflict Transformation, edited by Ropers, Norbert et al. Barbara Budrich Verlag, p. 217.

11 For a definition of mediation, mediation support and mediation-based dialogue processes, please see Fact Sheet 'Basics of Mediation: Concepts and Definitions'.
12 Please see Fact Sheet 'The Roles and Contributions of Multilateral and Non-State Actors in Peace Mediation'.

PEACE MEDIATION
GERMANY

Initiative Mediation Support Deutschland (IMSD) comprises:

The Normative Framework and the International Legal Basis of Peace Mediation

Lars Kirchhoff & Anne Holper & Felix Würkert

The normative framework and the international legal basis of peace mediation

This fact sheet provides an overview on the various normative frameworks that mediating third parties and surrounding actors should bear in mind. The aim of the fact sheet is to offer sound and clear guidance pertaining to which norms are relevant to peace mediation, the extent to which each of them is binding, and the actual and potential implications of whether or not mediators observe them, as well as on parties and the sustainability of mediated agreements. One area of priority is listing the provisions of international law that relate to the mediation process. These have not been available in this kind of format before, despite their great practical relevance to processes and outcomes. After a brief contextualisation of the role and categories of norms in the realm of peace mediation, the fact sheet will present answers to the following focus questions:

I.   Which (process-related) norms are relevant to the design of a peace mediation process?
II. Which content-related norms of substantive (international) law must be paid attention to?
III. How relevant is the constellation of actors to the normative framework?
IV. What normative tensions exist within frameworks of transitional justice?
V.   What is the normative relevance of courts or tribunals to peace mediation?

With the aid of examples, the final section outlines how actors in the field of mediation can deal constructively with normative restrictions, conflicts between aims and dilemmas that arise, and thus ultimately reach good and well-thought-out decisions.

Norms for peace mediation: straitjacket or backbone?

Norms describe collectively established assumptions concerning "correct" behaviour in a given situation. Since numerous decisions regarding behaviour must be made according to procedure and to the negotiation agenda in the context of peace mediation, norms naturally play a major role in mediators' practical work. Mediation processes are informed by diverse normative reference systems, including **methodological** guidelines for successful mediation procedures, **ethical** principles that raise acceptance levels and prevent harm, rules governing the third party's specific **political** mandate and, of course, national and international **legal** frameworks.

> This fact sheet is part of a series of fact sheets on peace mediation that provides policymakers in the Federal Foreign Office and German Embassies with a structured overview of the approaches, stakeholders, challenges and possibilities for action in the field of peace mediation. Further fact sheets from the series are available on Division S 03's intranet page.

The role of norms in peace mediation has expanded in recent years, with regard to both procedure and negotiation topics. The aforementioned normative frameworks have been more precisely defined and delineated, even if there are still no uniformly consolidated norms for peace mediation. This trend has coincided with an intensification of the fundamental debate on the nature of the role that norms in general and international legal aspects in particular should or must play in peace mediation processes and the agreements that result from them: In order to be able to successfully mediate in conflicts comprising political and military power struggles, must mediators be free to act without normative constraints, or must they, even or indeed particularly in such conflicts, strive to actively ensure compliance with certain norms? Are there norms (and, if so, what are they?) that require mediators to restrict their flexibility, as the consequences of disregarding them would be intolerable for the parties and for those affected by the conflict?

However, the normative regulatory framework for peace mediation presented here is by no means to be understood – or misunderstood – as a "straitjacket" in which mediation activities must fit. On the contrary, individual norms or, as the case may be, a well-balanced combination of norms, can be used as a framework for normatively sound decisions on the procedural and substantive structure of mediation processes and agreements. There are no simple formulas for such decisions. In order to describe the impact of norms in specific cases and to be able to analyse the norms relevant to a given case responsibly and pragmatically, it is necessary to begin with an overview of the various dimensions of norms and the tensions surrounding them.

> *The inclusion of norms in mediation is less about trade-offs and more about careful navigation within a specific context.*[1]

Mediation-related dimensions of norms

It is important to distinguish between **general norms** that are relevant to mediation, such as **methodological, ethical or political norms**, on the one hand, and **legal norms** on the other. They differ in their binding effect, their binding intent, and the consequences of them being observed or not. While **general norms** always describe behavioural *expectations*, the category of **legal norms** encompasses behavioural *rules*, whose intent regarding the extent to which they are binding may include legally binding force. There are various consequences when norms are not observed, which can range from mere irritation to criminal penalties. The acceptance, implementation and sustainability of peace agreements may be impaired in many respects if relevant norms have been disregarded.

For a thorough understanding and practical contextualisation of the contents of this fact sheet, it is useful to clearly distinguish between the **procedural norms** of peace mediation (norms *for* peace mediation) and **substantive norms**, which affect the core content of negotiations and peace agreements (norms *in* peace mediation). Peace agreements themselves may be perceived as norms that are an **outcome of peace mediation** – one that influences and is influenced by norms – and which may reshape the context of the relevant conflict. Sometimes, however, the boundaries are not as clear-cut as they are in the national context. Substantive law frameworks also influence mediation processes, and procedural norms may be an integral part of the substantive negotiations in peace mediation. Consideration must also be given to the special features that find their way into peace mediation (see focus question III) as a result of norms **specific to particular actors** or legal requirements that apply only to individual actors (see next page). One model encompassing various categories grades norms according to their respective **positions in the mediation context**.[2]

How can norms be categorised?

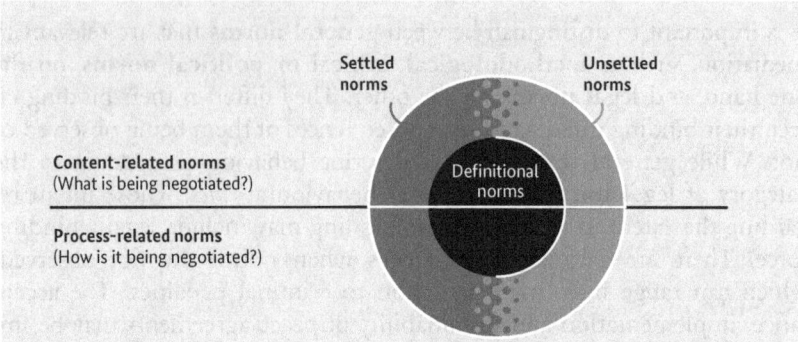

The norms that are relevant to mediation can be classified on the basis of the following categorisation criteria, making it easier to define them hierarchically where necessary – for example, if a conflict of norms is foreseeable. The first distinction that can be made is between *content-related norms* and *process-related norms*. The former relate to the content of mediation, that is, what can and cannot be negotiated during the mediation process. The latter relate to the manner in which the negotiations are conducted. Cutting across this division is a distinction between *settled* and *unsettled* norms. A norm is considered to be settled if it is not possible to deviate from it without a statement of grounds to justify such a deviation. This means that there are four general types of norms, e.g. *settled process-related norms*. One special type of settled norms concerns those derived from the definition of mediation. These *definitional norms* define the qualities without which the respective process can no longer be labelled as a mediation.

Examples

Settled process-related	→	Consent of the parties, involvement of all key parties to the conflict
Unsettled process-related	→	Neutrality of the third party (as opposed to omnipartiality, which is to be regarded as settled)
Settled content-related	→	Prohibition of general amnesties and protection of life
Unsettled content-related	→	Principles of democracy and equal economic rights

Fig. 1: Categories of norms (based on Hellmüller et al., 2015)

As a result, the regulatory framework that applies to peace mediation is largely characterised by the presence of a considerable number of normative levels: besides international and domestic law and mediation methodology and ethics, norms specific to particular actors, such as the normative dimensions of foreign policy, the internal rules of international organisations and the relevant culturally influenced normative attitudes of the parties to a conflict can also be important. Since the consequence is a shift in the regulatory framework that applies in any given case, depending on the subject matter of the conflict and the situation of the parties and third parties, the notion of a uniform regulatory framework for peace mediation is untenable. Instead, it makes sense to define categories on the basis of the focus questions, which must be drawn upon in practice for each individual case and provide specific calibration processes.

Focus questions:[3]

Focus question I: Which (process-related) norms are relevant to the design of a peace mediation process?

Many norms that are relevant to mediation relate to procedure, such as rules governing the conduct of mediation and the role of the mediator or dealings with non-state armed actors.

The **Charter of the United Nations** of 1945 contains statements that are not particularly specific, but highly relevant in political terms. In Article 33(1), mediation is listed as one of several means for settling disputes peacefully. As for key criteria for demarcating procedures, UN commentators agree that mediation, like resort to good offices, requires the consent of the parties at the outset and conclusion of the process if it is to be technically classifiable as a proper mediation procedure in the first place. The Charter does not go into detail regarding the nature of the actual mediation process.

The United Nations Guidance for Effective Mediation, which was published in 2012, provides information on designing mediation processes. This document is the most important and,[4] in terms of norms, most comprehensive codification of mediation in international peace processes at present. The relatively high degree of normative differentiation in the principles set out in this document leads to a remarkable paradigm shift in the field of peace mediation, with its traditional reliance on flexibility. The *United Nations Guidance for Effective Mediation* contains methodological and ethical guidelines for the peace mediation process based on shared experiences and assumptions regarding professional mediation management. Its content straddles the borderline between instructions regarding the practical formalities of peace mediation and recommendations based on best practices in the realm of mediation support. The *UN Guidance* document is sometimes described as the "procedural soft law" of peace mediation, in that it is not legally binding. While UN mediators are naturally bound by the ethics of the United Nations, other organisations, such as the

OSCE, have aligned themselves closely with the *UN Guidance*, fleshing out the content of the document and thus incorporating it into their own normative regulatory framework.[5] One concession to practical necessity has been the **undefined degree of binding intent and effect** of the various principles. The *UN Guidance* does not prescribe, for example, which of the principles, if any, safeguard constitutive minimum requirements for mediation and must therefore be prioritised when weighing up the applicable norms.[6]

In spite of the UN's expressed support for these principles, there often seem to be no significant repercussions if they are disregarded, even by UN mediators, let alone governmental and non-governmental mediators. Any visible breach, however, certainly creates a need for justification in practical discourse and public perception and may hamper cooperation. If constitutive principles of a mediation procedure, such as the consent of the parties, are ignored, the "only" consequence is that the procedure being followed does not represent mediation – or at least "state-of-the-art" mediation – but rather a different diplomatic instrument. There may well be good reasons for such procedural adaptations. If, however, the best practices accumulated over decades with regard to these procedural norms are disregarded without good reason, the potential methodological benefits of modern peace meditation are forfeited, as is the ensuing legitimisation of the procedure. This is particularly true if a process is explicitly labelled as mediation, thus supported by the parties to the conflict and members of the international community, and therefore subject to their respective expectations. In the case of the Geneva II talks, for instance, observers carefully analysed the extent to which civil society's envisaged participation actually materialised. The "good reasons" that may prompt compromises on procedural norms should not, in other words, be hastily pressed into service as justification simply because a non-consensual or non-inclusive approach seems more promising in the short term against a backdrop of time pressure and continuing violence.

United Nations Guidance for Effective Mediation in brief

Preparedness, which is listed as the first principle, refers to the thorough preparation of a mediation process as regards the individual, collective and structural resources of the mediator, mediation team and active stakeholders as the prerequisite for responsible intervention. **Consent** means that the parties must agree to the implementation of the mediation process, including its ground rules and intended format. **Impartiality** relates to the absence of partiality of the mediator, but the guidance document explicitly states that impartiality is not synonymous with neutrality. The norm of **inclusivity** defines the objective of the participation and representation of all relevant actors in the mediation process and overlaps with the requirement of **national ownership**. On the one hand, this principle relates to an inclusive process, involving all stakeholders in the conflict-ridden country and extending to the implementation of a peace agreement. On the other hand, it raises the substantive issue of the relevance of legal systems affiliated with particular parties. Under the heading of **international law and normative frameworks**, the guidance document provides information on the core subject of this fact sheet. The inclusion of information on procedural and substantive law is regarded as evidence that the realm of peace mediation is gradually developing towards positioning itself within the (international) legal system. In addition, mediators are expressly urged to make their guiding norms clear to the parties to the conflict. The principle of **coherence, coordination and complementarity of the mediation effort** entails formulating requirements that are conducive to better exchanges between the stakeholders in the field, and has prompted numerous countries and organisations to refine their mediation support and cooperation networks. The final principle, **quality peace agreements**, concerns issues relating to the content and implementation of the mediated agreement and must therefore be classed in normative terms within the legal dimension as the outcome of peace mediation.

One of the most frequently discussed procedural issues concerns the **normative limits and scope for conducting talks with terrorists**. Security Council Resolution 1373 (S/RES/1373 (2001) of 28 September 2001), citing chapter VIII of the Charter of the United Nations, prohibits the provision of any form of active or passive support to entities or persons involved in terrorist acts (point 2(a)). The initiation and conduct by governmental entities of mediation with terrorist groups do not constitute support within the meaning of the Resolution, even in its broadest possible interpretation, since the Resolution cites the recruitment of members of terrorist groups and the supply of weapons to terrorists as an example. It should also be noted that neither the Resolution nor any other norms of international law contain a binding definition of terrorism on which consensus might be reached. National anti-terrorist legislation contains highly diverse interpretations, some with a decidedly low threshold, of what may be regarded as support for terrorists. The United States, for instance, possesses a wide range of legal sanctions, and the prohibitions and restrictions set out in the pertinent instruments generally have implications with regard to criminal law, too. While it is therefore conceivable that private entities may face criminal charges under some national legal systems for mediation activities involving groups classed as terrorists, the same does not apply to governmental entities, since national codes of criminal law do not, in principle, apply to state entities. National law, then, is the only means of determining the admissibility of mediation in which terrorist groups are active participants. Such mediation is admissible in international law, and states must therefore reach a political decision based on the current sensitivity and relevance of the issue.

Summary conclusion on focus question I

At first glance, the normative expectations for peace mediation processes seem to be high. The degree to which the relevant norms are binding varies widely and is not infrequently controversial. The requirements set out in the UN Guidance are to be understood as methodological and ethical guidelines and condensed best practice that constitute and legitimise the mediation process. Their observance is not compulsory, but as a rule, it is extremely advisable.

Focus II: Which content-related norms of substantive (international) law must be paid attention to?

Numerous international legal norms become relevant in a peace mediation process. These may be divided into peremptory norms and other (ordinary) law. **Peremptory norms of international law** are the small but, in the context of mediation, significant group of norms that are non-negotiable in principle for all parties and other stakeholders. Their existence is laid out in Article 53 of the Vienna Convention on the Law of Treaties (VCLT) and largely enjoys general acceptance. Peremptory norms of international law are particularly deeply rooted in legal consciousness; in the hierarchy of norms, they take precedence over contractual and customary law. From a political and ethical perspective, peremptory norms of international law are essential to the cohesion of the international community, as they serve as a minimum standard that bridges the global diversity of norms and the multipolar power structure in the world. The **other norms of international law** are those which, though they may well be universally applicable, can be voided of their binding nature by the subsequent emergence of different norms or the termination or suspension of a treaty, at least if they are not norms of customary international law. If in the course of peace mediation legal norms are created for the national legal order, or if their creation is planned, such national norms must not conflict with those of international law. Even constitutional norms must not ultimately be inconsistent with international law.

a) Peremptory norms of international law relevant to mediation

The post-conflict legal and constitutional order

The legal and constitutional order that results or is supposed to result from the mediation process must not on any account permit racial discrimination (Article 4(1) ICCPR),[7] especially not in the form of apartheid (Article 7(2)(h) Rome Statute). Slavery must be abolished in law and in practice (Article 8(1) and (2) ICCPR), as must torture (Article 7 ICCPR and Article 2 of the UN Convention against Torture).

Amnesty bans and legislative and sentencing obligations

Several agreements require the Contracting Parties to criminalise certain offences in their national legal orders and to ensure that offenders are prosecuted. In addition, the Rome Statute of the International Criminal Court enumerates what it deems the most serious crimes of concern to the international community as a whole, which it states must be prosecuted. These include genocide (Article 6 Rome Statute; see also Article III of the UN Genocide Convention and, on the obligation to enact criminal legislation, Article IV of the same Convention), crimes against humanity (Article 7 Rome Statute), war crimes (Article 8 Rome Statute) and crimes of aggression (Article 8 bis Statute). Torture is also to be made a criminal offence, and perpetrators are to be prosecuted (Articles 4, 5 and 7 of the UN Convention against Torture). Accordingly, a general amnesty can never be the result of a mediation process conducted in the light of international law. Leaders who have committed such crimes must face criminal sanctions. This may be done in cooperation with a truth and reconciliation commission.

Principle of non-refoulement

In the course of a mediated peace process, people must not be expelled to places where they will be exposed to the risk of torture (Article 3 of the UN Convention against Torture) or where their lives or freedom would be threatened on account of their race, religion, nationality, membership of a particular social group or political opinion (Article 33(1) of the Convention relating to the Status of Refugees).

b) Other norms of international law potentially relevant to mediation

Political participation

Various provisions of international law guarantee political participation. These norms must therefore be taken into account when political reorganisation, the allocation of public offices, and a possible new or reformed constitution are on the agenda. Article 25 ICCPR guarantees every citizen the right and opportunity to take part in the conduct of public affairs through periodic universal elections based on equal suffrage and to have access, on general terms of equality, to public service in their country. This article does not, however, encompass a wider "human right to democracy" in the sense of liberal multi-party democracies. The UN Convention on Women's Rights (Convention on the Elimination of all Forms of Discrimination against Women) defines women's right to participate in political life on equal terms with men in Article 7, while Article 7(c) focuses particularly on participation in non-governmental organisations and Article 8 accords the same rights in the context of international representation. In addition, States Parties pledge in Article 2(e) to take all appropriate measures to eliminate discriminatory practices in their societies.

Judicial rights

Issues of ownership and compensation, which often have to be resolved in the aftermath of armed conflicts, may fall under civil or public law; when they arise in connection with the investigation of past crimes, they regularly also involve criminal proceedings. These issues and the related procedures require judicial clarification. They become even more relevant in cases where the creation of new judicial and quasi-judicial institutions is being negotiated in a mediation process. Emphasis must be placed in this context on the right to proper defence (Article 14(3)(b), (d) and (e) ICCPR), the prohibition of double jeopardy (Article 14(7)), the prohibition of forced self-incrimination (Article 14(3)(g)), the prohibition of retrospective criminal liability (Article 15), the presumption of innocence (Article 14(2)), equality before the law (first sentence of Article

14(1)) and the right of appeal (Article 14(5)). Furthermore, consideration must be given to the right to a fair hearing (second sentence of Article 14(1) ICCPR), as well as to the special rights of children and young people in judicial proceedings (Article 14(4) ICCPR and Articles 37 and 40 of the UN Convention on the Rights of the Child).

Rights of prisoners of war

After both internal and international armed conflicts, mediation must take the rights of imprisoned conflict participants, as defined by the Geneva Conventions, into account. Prisoners of war within the meaning of Article 4 of the Third Geneva Convention are guaranteed humane treatment in line with the requirements of the Convention. Imprisoned combatants must not face criminal prosecution for their participation in an armed conflict, provided their actions were not in breach of international humanitarian law. After the cessation of active hostilities, all prisoners of war are to be released (Article 118 of the Third Geneva Convention). Persons actively involved in the conflict should, as far as possible, be exempt from prosecution (Article 6 of Protocol II to the Geneva Conventions). The limits to this immunity are the most serious crimes listed in Article 5 of the Rome Statute (cf. peremptory norms of international law, sentencing obligations and amnesty bans).

Displacement and statelessness

Normative issues relating to managing the consequences of displacement and forced migration have become topical, for example in the negotiations in the EU and with Turkey. Article 12(4) ICCPR guarantees people the right to enter their own country. People who have fled their country in the wake of a conflict therefore have the right to return. This is complemented by the right to leave one's country (Article 12(2) ICCPR), although that right may be restricted in any of the significant extenuating circumstances listed in Article 12(3). Freedom to choose one's residence within a state (Article 12(1) ICCPR) is relevant both for internally displaced persons and those who have fled abroad. This may likewise be restricted under Article 12(3). Under Article 22 of the UN Convention on the Rights of the Child, displaced and refugee children and young people are entitled to special protection.

Article 27 ICCPR gives ethnic, religious and linguistic minorities the right to enjoy their own culture, to profess and practise their own religion, and to use their own language – and to do so with the support of the state as far as possible. Accordingly, demands for the prohibition of a particular language, religion or culture, which are often made unilaterally in mediation processes, are precluded.

Summary conclusion on focus question II

The framework of substantive law will naturally vary from case to case, but the main universally valid sources and frameworks are clearly visible. In the framework of peace mediation, the informed inclusion of peremptory norms of international law is particularly relevant. In practice, these amount to no more than a modest number of norms.

Focus question III: How relevant is the constellation of actors to the normative framework?

In the preceding sections, the norms relating to international law were presented on their own, without reference to the actors involved. At any stage of a peace mediation process, however, one relevant practical question may arise: namely, which norms are binding to which actor – and to which extent they are binding. **States** are fundamentally bound to any treaty they have ratified, as well as to the norms of customary international law. Regardless of its origins, some of which are to be found in specific treaties, the body of law defined above as peremptory norms of international law, also known as *ius cogens*, possesses the characteristics of customary law and is binding on all states. Substantive legal norms from a **party's** norm system may set clear limits on the jointly negotiable subject matter and thus become part of the regulatory framework that applies to the mediation process. If, for instance, a State Party has committed itself, within the framework of an international treaty, to greater protection of particular human rights, it must not fall short of that level of protection in the mediation process and the intended peace agreement if it wishes to avoid violating international law.

Mediation can be challenging in normative terms if it involves **non-state armed actors**. There is broad consensus that violent actors are also bound by the fundamental norms of international humanitarian law, that is, the Hague and Geneva Conventions. Peremptory norms of international law also apply to these actors. Moreover, some violent nonstate actors unilaterally observe certain norms, which also makes these norms part of the regulatory framework of the mediation process. Commitments to human rights and international obligations in other spheres do not bind violent non-state actors *per se*, although international law is showing clear signs of moving in that direction.

Where non-governmental organisations (**NGOs**) are involved in peace mediation processes, an extremely relevant practical question arises as to whether and to which extent they are bound by norms of international law and as to the part they play in the dissemination and application of norms. Whether, considering their increasing rights to participation in the international arena, NGOs may be accorded the status of partial subjects of international law is a question that has yet to be answered. As in the case of violent non-state actors, it stands to reason that the minimum standard set by peremptory norms of international law must also apply to NGOs.

Furthermore, NGOs are always additionally bound by the national legal norms of the country in which they are headquartered. The **third party** also brings, at the very least, procedural legal norms, as well as substantive norms into the process. In other words, it certainly makes a difference whether the mediators are working for the UN, the EU or another intergovernmental organisation, or for a state or an NGO. UN mediators, for example, operate within the legal framework of the Charter of the United Nations, the resolutions of the Security Council and General Assembly, and the UN's internal rules. State mediators, for their part, are bound by the Charter of the United Nations and Security Council resolutions, as well as the entire set of obligations under international law described above and the applicable norms of their national legal systems. Finally, **all participants**, be they individuals at the negotiating table or the groups and societies they represent, come with their own culturally influenced normative ideas of what is fair and proper in conflict resolution processes and agreements. For these cultural reasons, but also for political reasons, some protagonists cannot identify with the international system of norms and reject its claim to be universally binding.

How is the regulatory framework of a mediation process composed?

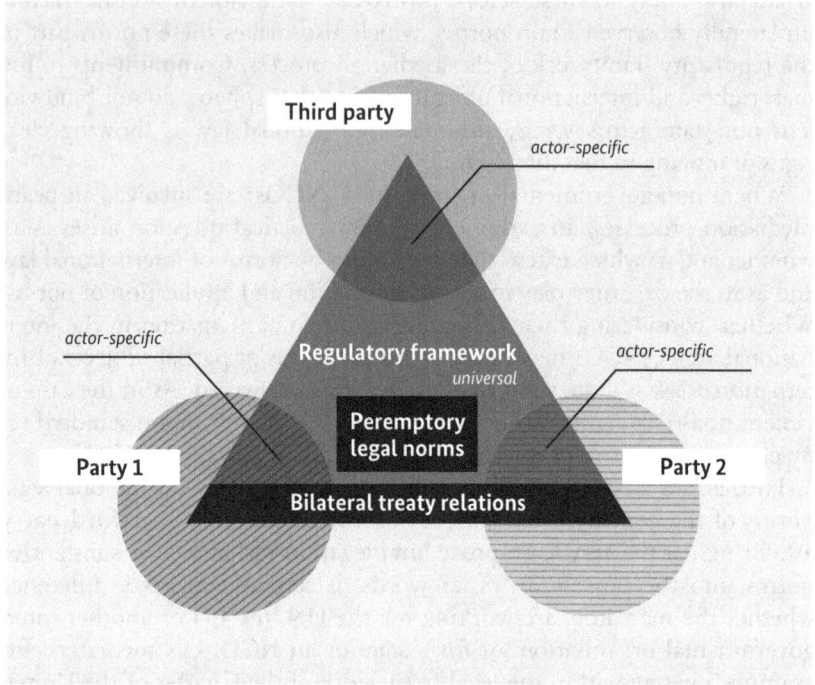

Fig. 2: Elements of the regulatory framework (based on Leffmann, 2016)[8]

The interaction between these diverse participants in peace mediation depicted in the above diagram not only occurs within the described regulatory framework but also influences this framework for future peace processes. In conflicts and mediation processes in particular, state practice and legal convictions, which form the fundamental building blocks of customary international law, manifest themselves on a regular basis. Whether and to what extent non-governmental organisations and violent non-state actors are bound by international law or, to put it another way, to what extent violations of international law have consequences, is one of the questions that are answered in these very scenarios; in that respect, mediators also act as developers of norms. The developments regarding the protection of women in armed conflicts and their participation in peace processes that were initiated through Security Council Resolution 1325 can be seen as one illustration of this phenomenon.

Which of the relevant norms are binding on which actor – and to what extent – is a question that requires careful examination in each individual case. Besides the parties to the conflict, the third party itself brings a significant normative momentum into play, one that is often underestimated but can be relevant in the early stages of designing the process.

Focus question IV: What normative tensions exist within frameworks of transitional justice?

> *"...the conception of justice in periods of political change is extraordinary and constructivist: It is alternately constituted by, and constitutive of, the transition."[9]*

The role of the law in peace mediation has not yet been exhausted in the functions described above. Legal norms not only limit the shape of the peace process but are themselves a means and a subject in the structuring of societies that occurs in the course and aftermath of a peace process. The term "transitional justice" is an attempt to convey this transformative function of the law. Transitional justice is one of the key concepts of peace consolidation in post-war societies that have been developed by the international community and global civil society since the mid-1990s with a view to ensuring lasting peace in post-conflict societies.[10] The term encompasses all of the measures with which violations of the law, human rights abuses and acts of violence are to be punished and addressed by society. These measures may comprise international and national criminal trials, but also non-judicial strategies for reconciling the perpetrators and victims of conflicts, reparations such as restitution and compensation, the demobilisation of perpetrators, and the quest for truth and fact-finding. The norms that apply in the realm of transitional justice are exerting a growing influence on peace negotiations, and peace agreements are ever more frequently and visibly laying down benchmarks for their application.[11] The objective of many peace processes, and hence of the mediation that takes place as part of those processes, is to establish stable societies based on an assured minimum level of legal certainty and the rule of law. In each of these processes, the law must re-establish its legitimacy as an instrument for guiding and shaping society.

In such cases, transitional justice is regularly reduced to a conflict of aims between peace and justice, yet on closer inspection these are not competing but rather interdependent aims, for unless there is an end to violence (peace), individuals cannot benefit from measures to address the past, compensation and human rights (justice), and *vice versa*. In this context, transitional justice must address normatively complex phenomena such as formally legal injustices, including those committed by the state, and individual victims' compensation entitlements. The key normative principles in the realm of transitional justice are based on the principles developed by Louis Joinet for the UN Commission on Human Rights. The purpose of these principles was to combat impunity in cases of massive violations of human rights and international humanitarian law. The four focal points are the right to justice, the right to reparations, the right to know and the guarantee of non-recurrence. These four principles recognise victims' rights and define the state's obligations. The UN and EU[12] expressly strive for adherence to the increasingly refined principles of transitional justice in the peace mediation efforts they conduct or support; some other stakeholders involved in mediation regard this as normative overloading of the mediation process and lament a further loss of mediators' substantive freedom of action and flexibility as regards outcomes. There is therefore a need to avoid artificial antitheses in peace mediation practice, and the complementary approach of "peace in justice and justice in peace" can meet that need.

Summary conclusion on focus question IV

Norms have been situated within the field of transitional justice in a careful and practical manner. The extent to which these norms are actually taken into account in a peace mediation process ultimately proves to be a political decision; developments in the UN and EU, however, clearly indicate a trend towards an increasing relevance of normative requirements from this field.

Focus question V: What is the normative relevance of courts or tribunals to peace mediation?

In spite of its nature as an extrajudicial dispute resolution mechanism, peace mediation has close ties with international, hybrid and national courts and tribunals. Particular attention has been placed in this context on the **International Criminal Court (ICC)**. One pertinent example of its relevance is to be found in the Colombian peace process, in which the ICC was closely involved through preliminary investigations, when its prosecutor determined whether there were grounds for initiating investigations under Article 15 of the Rome Statute that might ultimately lead to arrest warrants being issued. In principle, however, the ICC has no jurisdiction during a peace process as long as the state concerned is willing and able to conduct scrupulous investigations and criminal proceedings. One of the purposes of preliminary investigations and subsequent reports issued by the state in question is to verify this willingness and capability. During the peace process in Colombia, this approach helped to keep the focus on the certainty of prosecution for the most serious crimes. The ICC was thus instrumental in the creation of an autonomous mechanism in Colombia for dealing with the past that includes criminal prosecution. On the one hand, the recent example of Colombia illustrates the beneficial influence of independent international criminal prosecution as a constant within a peace process. On the other hand, there may be a need for restraint at sensitive stages in the process, such as the postponement of normatively appropriate sanctions. One means to this end is the deferral, under Article 16 of the Rome Statute, of investigation or prosecution, although this requires a Security Council Chapter VII resolution. In view of this significant obstacle, the more promising option is Article 53(1)(c) and (2)(c) of the Rome Statute, which allow the prosecutor to refrain from investigation or prosecution if such action "would not serve the interests of justice". In this case too, determining whether there are any reasonable grounds for proceeding is the sole responsibility of the prosecutor, whose decision cannot therefore be influenced by any participants in the mediation process.

Hybrid criminal tribunals are based both on an international and national legal act. They are often created in cooperation with a state in the wake of internal conflicts or following the commission of serious crimes in that state. Examples include the Khmer Rouge Tribunal in Cambodia, the Special Panels for Serious Crimes in East Timor and the Special Tribunal for Lebanon. The importance of hybrid criminal tribunals may be illustrated by the example of the Special Court for Sierra Leone, which ruled that the amnesty clause that had previously been enshrined in the Lomé Peace Agreement was not an obstacle to criminal prosecution. A peace agreement concluded within an internal armed conflict, the court held, did not constitute an international agreement and therefore could not bind a hybrid tribunal, which was outside the national legal system; granting an amnesty for the most serious crimes was, in fact, a violation of international law.

The normative regulatory framework of peace mediation is also regularly influenced by the **case law of regional courts of human rights**. The Inter-American Court of Human Rights, for instance, declared early on that blanket amnesties were irreconcilable with the rights of victims and their relatives, thus paving the way for criminal investigation of past wrongdoings in Latin American dictatorships. This wide-ranging ruling strongly influenced the peace process in Colombia, and all parties took detailed note of it. Besides the amnesty issue, the case of *Sejdić and Finci v. Bosnia and Herzegovina* before the European Court of Human Rights (ECtHR) showed how close interaction can be between practical peace mediation and the normative dimension of its outcome. In this case, the ECtHR held that constitutional norms in Bosnia and Herzegovina, which provided for proportional representation of the main ethnic groups in political posts and entirely excluded minorities from political office, were illegal. As the Constitution of Bosnia and Herzegovina had resulted from the Dayton Peace Agreement of 1995, this example shows that even peace agreements are open to judicial review.

Finally, the role of **national courts** in the normative fabric of peace mediation can scarcely be overstated. National courts influence the process of dealing with the past and can likewise subject the foundations of a peace or transition process to judicial review. The Constitutional Court of South Africa, for example, ruled that the amnesties granted by the Truth and Reconciliation Commission were constitutional. For its part, the Federal Constitutional Court in Germany upheld the judgments in the *Mauerschützen* trials that had convicted those responsible for issuing and following shoot-to-kill orders at the Berlin Wall, rejecting the argument that the orders were legal under the law of the German Democratic Republic.

> **Summary conclusion on focus question V**
>
> The interaction between international, hybrid, regional and national courts is every bit as complex as it is crucial to the conduct of normatively sound peace mediation processes. The mere fact that peace agreements are open to judicial review alters and defines the process of negotiation between the parties and the mediator and implies first and foremost that the third party must possess accurate and normatively robust knowledge – particularly, but not only, as regards issues relating to criminal law.

Summing-up: methodological considerations on conflicting normative aims

It is neither possible nor necessary to take into account all of the norms that are relevant in the context of a peace process. Nevertheless, in order to make peace processes tenable in normative terms, it is necessary to undertake a **feasibility and tenability assessment** and to gauge what is useful in the given case. This is the best way to include the most relevant norms and their functions, such as ensuring procedural efficiency or safeguarding the rights of those affected by a conflict. The objective will often be a pragmatic appraisal of which divergences from normative requirements are acceptable and justifiable in light of their expected consequences.

Such an appraisal is most easily made if mediators begin by clarifying where the normative limits lie and where room for manoeuvre is available, in other words which norms *must* be respected and where flexibility can be exercised because the adverse effects would be minimal or tolerable. The important thing is to examine the consequences for *all* stakeholders who will potentially be affected by the decision, namely the conflicting parties, the populations affected by the conflict, the mediators and those who give them their mandate, and possibly also the national and international community. With regard to the methodological and ethical procedural principles, for example, the genuine – that is to say unforced – consent of the parties to the process and agreement is a minimum normative requirement if mediators want to ensure that the parties to the conflict will not scupper the negotiation and implementation of agreements. A different approach is needed **if conflicting normative aims escalate into a dilemma** in which mediators are compelled to take simultaneous account of diverse norms and practical or political imperatives, for example inclusivity and efficiency, which – at least to all appearances – are mutually exclusive.

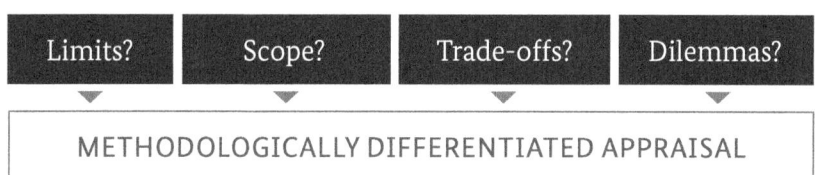

| Limits? | Scope? | Trade-offs? | Dilemmas? |

METHODOLOGICALLY DIFFERENTIATED APPRAISAL

Example: conflicting norms in mediation practice as illustrated by the cases of Uganda and Sudan

One controversial example of the potential for conflicts between methodological, strategic and legal norms of peace mediation are the warrants issued by the International Criminal Court (ICC) for the arrest of the President of Sudan, Omar al-Bashir, and leading members of the Ugandan rebel group, the Lord's Resistance Army (LRA). The arrest warrants issued in 2005 against leading LRA members made the group less willing to negotiate, as its leaders were insisting on impunity.

The Ugandan Government, which had previously referred the conflict with the LRA to the ICC, subsequently tried to have the arrest warrants suspended, but in vain. As in 2009 and again in 2010 in the case of the warrants issued for the arrest of Omar al-Bashir, the conflict of norms manifested itself in the fruitlessness of the arrest warrants for want of sufficient cooperation and enforcement mechanisms and in the jeopardising of the relevant parties' willingness to negotiate on a peaceful settlement to the conflict when confronted with the issue of the arrest warrants.

Prioritisation, sequencing and compartmentalisation: methods for dealing with dilemmas

Prioritisation means graded compliance with norms, so that the norm accorded the highest priority is applied in full, the norm ranking second is partially applied, but another norm, perhaps priority number three, is not applied. In the example referred to above, that might mean exceptionally subordinating prosecution, in view of the slim prospects of enforcement, to the strategic imperative of maintaining the parties' willingness to negotiate.

This could also take the form of **sequencing**, in which norms that cannot be applied simultaneously are considered in chronological order, although that order must be established in advance. It might, for example, be incremental sequencing ("easy to hard"), in which the simpler demands are addressed first, followed by those that are more difficult to meet, or else "agreement in principle" sequencing, in which an overarching agreement is sought at an early stage in the process, for instance by including "dealing with war crimes" as an item on the agenda, while the negotiation of details is left until a later, more strategically favourable time. Other options are to follow a "hard-to-easy" sequence, in which the most difficult hurdle is tackled first so that lesser challenges can then be more easily surmounted, or a committee sequence, in which parties to the conflict are put to work simultaneously in separate groups on normative requirements until their proposals have been adopted by the whole body ("nothing is agreed until everything is agreed").

Following an approach of **compartmentalisation**, roles and measures that cannot be performed and implemented simultaneously by a single actor without violating crucial norms are distributed among various actors.

Conflicting norms, trade-offs and dilemmas may be divided into **collisions within the same normative sphere**, such as competing international and national legal norms, and **collisions between norms from different spheres**, for example when ethical and methodical principles clash with legal or political priorities. What approach should one adopt when such conflicts occur? When dealing with the **first category**, that is, collisions within the same sphere, it is best to spell out and weigh up the implications of infringing each of the pertinent norms; the chosen path should be the option with the lowest compliance costs. These compliance costs must be examined within the relevant sphere – the legal system, for example – but also beyond that sphere, where consideration must be given to factors such as the burdens on stakeholders and stakeholder groups and the political cost of a conscious breach of legal provisions. As for the **second category**, a conflict of norms from different spheres, the following two case studies are presented by way of illustration.

Case study 1: Collision of norms in talks with actors classified as terrorists

Core issue of the conflict of aims	Can or should a non-governmental organisation funded by the Federal Foreign Office provide a listed organisation with mediation support, such as negotiation training, in order to better qualify its leaders to take part in ceasefire talks?
Relevant norms	**Pro** (methodological-ethical): The mediation principles of inclusivity, ownership and sustainability **Contra** (legal-ethical): The principle of not supporting "terrorist" organisations
Aspects to be taken into account: implications, cost/harm and benefits of applying norms as opposed to overriding them	**Inclusivity and ownership** O Enhancement (v. stagnation) of negotiating skills, integration (v. continued exclusion) of the interests of a conflict party with great disruptive potential, minimisation of hostilities (v. risk of escalation) O Enhancing the status of the listed organisation (v. leaving it without any status) O Third-party focus on (v. distancing itself from) sensitive areas of criminal responsibility **Anti-terrorism laws** O Avoidance (v. risk) of criminal liability of the third party O Exclusion (v. risk) of enhancement of the group's standing and instrumentalisation of the mediation process by the group O Dynamics: the more innocuous the support provided, the more ineffectual it is
Possible action (examples)	O Transparent provision of advice and guidance on measures by legal experts with a view to continuously examining and dispelling any accusations of aiding and abetting O Ensuring that potentially sensitive measures in terms of criminal law, such as funding, are implemented by cooperation partners to which the relevant legal provision does not apply O Ensuring maximum confidentiality and privacy of the talks O Support for mandating and training a non-listed person closely associated with the listed actor as a chief negotiator
Approaches to the balance of norms (examples)	» The principles of inclusivity and ownership may be taken into account as long as the risk of participants in the mediation process being involved in criminal activities is minimised by means of continuous legal advice and prudent risk-sharing (prioritisation) » Roles and action steps may be broadly spread out with transparent procedural stages (compartmentalisation) » The emphasis may be placed on the benefit to public morale derived from keeping talks going

As this first example shows, if a third party is aware that conflicts between legal, ethical and methodological aims are part and parcel of mediation at many stages in the process, it can tailor its approach accordingly.

The second case study extends this balancing matrix to include the (foreign) policy dimension and illustrates how sequencing and separation of roles may be an effective response to normative trade-offs and dilemmas.

Case study 2: Collision between political and legal norms in the case of an illegal annexation

Core issue of the conflict of aims	Can or should a mediator exclude a conflict party's violation of a fundamental principle of international law, such as territorial integrity, from the agenda of peace negotiations in order to preserve that party's willingness to negotiate?
Relevant norms	**Pro** (methodological, strategic and political): preserving willingness to negotiate **Contra** (legal-ethical): respect for international law and sovereignty; possibly omnipartiality
Aspects to be taken into account: implications, cost/harm and benefits of applying norms as opposed to overriding them	**Preservation of willingness to negotiate** O Ensuring (v. jeopardising) the party's willingness to continue negotiating and/or to reach an agreement O Impression of weakness (v. normative stringency/strength) on the part of the mediator through implicit unilateral concessions to the conflict party violating international law **Territorial integrity of states** O Maintenance (v. loss) of trust in the mediation process on the part of the actor affected by the violation of international law and/or awareness of the validity of legal limits on the part of the violator O Reinforcement (v. implicit undermining) of the international legal order
Possible action (examples)	O Mediation with transparent references to diverging legal positions between both parties to the conflict (this is an explicitly non-judgemental approach to mediation) O Exclusion of the issues relating to international law during the first stage (chronological sequencing) O Declaring recognition of the violation of international law to be a prerequisite for mediation O Delegation of the third-party role to an actor that is not bound by international law
Approaches to the balance of norms (examples)	» Engendering respect for both systems of norms, for example, by emphasising to the parties and the public at an early stage that the negotiations are not taking place in a legal vacuum » Allocation to various actors (mediator, ICC, UN) of the roles required for the purpose of penalising the violation of norms and possibly parallel initiation of legal investigation by the International Court of Justice (ICJ) (compartmentalisation) » Inclusion of the matter in interim agreements as an unresolved issue, possibly in the form of a memorandum, to counteract tacit recognition ("agreement in principle" sequencing)

References

1 Quote from an anonymous background interview on Hellmüller et al., The Role of Norms in International Peace Mediation, NOREF Policy Brief, May 2015.

2 The model forms the basis of a project conducted by swisspeace and ETH Zurich, as well as by the Norwegian Centre for Conflict Resolution (NOREF), and is presented here because relevant aspects of the current international discussion relate to this categorisation; see Hellmüller et al., 2015, p. 2.

3 Sources and background material on the focus questions can be found in the research studies conducted by Felix Würkert on the normative dimension of peace mediation.

4 The UN Guidance for Effective Mediation, commissioned as an appendix to Resolution A/65/283 (22 June 2011), was adopted unanimously by the General Assembly. The guide was published as an annex to a report of 25 June 2012 by the UN Secretary-General (report A/66/811, entitled Strengthening the role of mediation in the peaceful settlement of disputes, conflict prevention and resolution).

5 OSCE, Mediation and Dialogue Facilitation, Reference Guide, which can be downloaded from http://www.osce.org/secretariat/126646?download=true.

6 The Mediation Support Network, comprising international organisations from the field of peace mediation, produced a commentary on the UN Guidance for Effective Mediation in an attempt to interpret the UN guidance document and to define which principles must be adhered to so that the procedural requirements for mediation are met. The commentary, Mediation Support Network (MSN), Translating Mediation Guidance into Practice, 2012, can be downloaded from http://peacemaker.un.org/sites/peacemaker.un.org/files/TranslatingMediationGuidanceIntoPractice_MSN_2012.pdf.

7 The following abbreviations are used in this section: ICCPR = International Covenant on Civil and Political Rights and ICESCR = International Covenant on Economic Social and Cultural Rights (1966).

8 The original version of the graphics, along with a commentary, can be found in Leffmann, Der völkerrechtliche Ordnungsrahmen der Mediation in internationalen Friedensprozessen, European University Viadrina, 2016.

9 Teitel, Transitional Justice, Oxford University Press, 2009, p. 6.

10 https://www.uni-marburg.de/icwc/forschung/transitionaljustice; for an examination of the direct links between transitional justice and media-

tion, see Kirchhoff, "Linking Mediation and Transitional Justice. The Use of Interest-Based Mediation in Processes of Transition", in Ambos/Large/Wierda (eds.), Building a Future on Peace and Justice. Studies on Transitional Justice, Conflict Resolution and Development. The Nuremberg Declaration on Peace and Justice, Berlin, Heidelberg, 2009, p. 237-260.

11 See also, for example, European Union External Action Service, "Transitional Justice in the Context of Peace Mediation", in Factsheet – EEAS Mediation Support Project – Knowledge Product, European Union, 2012.

12 See, for instance, Council of the European Union, Concept on Strengthening EU Mediation and Dialogue Capacities, 2009.

PEACE MEDIATION
GERMANY

Initiative Mediation Support Deutschland (IMSD) comprises:

Berghof Foundation

cpm Center for Peace Mediation
EUROPA-UNIVERSITÄT VIADRINA

Berlin Center for
Integrative Mediation

inmedio
peace consult gmbh

zif Center for
International
Peace Operations

Methodology and Communication Tools in Peace Mediation

Lars Kirchhoff & Dirk Splinter

Methodology and communication tools in peace mediation

"So many people want to join mediation teams without having worked on the micro-techniques of mediation. These may seem far removed from bringing warring factions together. It relates more to the normal management of human interaction in conflict. These techniques have to do with the way you hold yourself; the way you listen; and the way you recognise where people have a common interest."

Nicolas ‚Fink' Haysom, South African mediator in countries including Burundi and the Sudan; former Special Representative of the UN Secretary-General for Afghanisthan.[1]

"The right temperament is manifested primarily in the innate ability to listen to negotiators, to understand, absorb and even feel what they say about themselves and what they want. Let us call these the empathetic skills. The reason this is so important is that for a party in conflict, moving to negotiation is a huge step; he must be confident that the mediator who accompanies him in this perilous transition, fully metabolizes his grievances and demands and the reasons for them. (…) But the mediator (…) must instil this same confidence in all parties – i.e. he must process bifocalism – the ability to see a given situation from different perspectives."

Alvaro de Soto, Peruvian diplomat; former UN Under-Secretary-General/mediator in a large number of peace processes.[2]

Quotations such as these that focus on methodology (as opposed to anecdotal evidence), current analyses of mediation processes, and systematic debriefings of mediators illustrate the particular value – and often crucial role – of good communication in peace mediation. The micro-techniques of mediation mentioned in the quotations above, combined with an empathetic attitude and the third party's experience and personality, play an important and increasingly recognised role in the success of negotiations. Active listening, the targeted use of empathy, a detailed presentation of interests and a constructive approach to conflicting viewpoints and narratives among the parties to a conflict can be systematically learned and streamlined. The aim of this fact sheet is to illustrate the relevance and forms of expressions of empathy, attitude, and robust methodologies toward the success of mediation, anchored in a practical and scientific approach.

This fact sheet is part of a fact sheet series on peace mediation that provides policymakers at the Federal Foreign Office and German Embassies with a structured overview of the approaches, stakeholders, challenges and possibilities for action in the field of peace mediation. Further fact sheets from the series are available on Division S 03's intranet page.

I. Empathy and attitude as the foundation of peace mediation

Along with Álvaro de Soto's words (*"to understand, absorb and even feel what they say about themselves and what they want"*), the following quotation shows both the relevance and the various functions of empathy in mediation processes.

"Empathy is a core skill of diplomacy, yet it is mostly unacknowledged and rarely admired. It helps diplomats enhance their understanding of other countries, especially powerful elites, but also the nation as a whole and groups within it."[3]

The communication methods presented in this fact sheet illustrate how mediation processes can foster mutual understanding, a change of perspective, and the potential for finding solutions. The goal here is to define the term "empathy" concretely and systematically, thus imbuing it with an analytical dimension in addition to its inherently emotional aspects. Aligning empathy with emotions such as sympathy and acceptance, as well as with concepts like altruism and compromise displays only *one* dimension of the term. The other dimension, which is equally relevant to mediation, corresponds to the active attempt to adopt another person's world view or situational perspective for the purposes of resolving a conflict, to *want* to do so (in terms of attitude), and to *be able* to do so (in terms of methodology).

The goal of an empathetic approach can indeed be analytical or even purely strategic, as it is (only) when one understands an interlocutor's argumentation and world view, that both opportunities for rapprochement and acceptable solutions can arise in situations in which insisting on one's own perception would only lead to escalation and dead ends.

Role and attitude in mediation

The impact and thus the effectiveness of mediators' professional conduct are influenced in part by the empathetic use of communication methods and by their attitude to the parties to the conflict as well. The term "attitude" generally refers to a mediator's stances and inner positions, which define how he or she communicates and processes information. This affects how the parties to a conflict experience the quality of the process, whether they find the mediator's actions "technical", "contrived," or even "invasive," or, on the other hand, "authentic", "congruent," and "respectful of boundaries". The following aspects of attitude are particularly relevant in mediation.

Multipartiality

In the context of mediation, the term "multipartiality" is progressively replacing the terms "neutrality" and "impartiality." "Neutrality" suggests that the mediator does not have his or her own opinion on the conflict and the parties to it, thus denying the inevitable and subjective attitudes and political stance every person possesses. "Impartiality" is often associated with a rather "cool" and distanced approach to those involved in a conflict. In contrast, the term "multipartiality" demonstrates that the mediator should show an active interest in and support for both or all parties to a conflict.

Acceptance and respect

Acceptance does not mean agreeing with the statements and attitudes of the parties to a conflict. It rather indicates that the mediator – even if he or she has other views and values – fundamentally accepts the parties to a conflict, as well as their views and positions, takes them seriously, and treats them with respect. This goes hand in hand with the lived conviction that the mediator is not mandated or in a position to change actors or their political agenda. Instead, his or her mandate is to create a communicative context in which change can occur through the parties to a conflict.

The requirement of respect can also be seen as the "operationalisation" of the fundamental notion of empathy presented above. However, a respectful attitude in conflict resolution is not to be (mis)understood as "professionally prescribed sympathy", but rather as the sustained willingness to perceive the (remaining) constructive aspects of an individual as well as the plausible elements of their conduct, and to pay tribute to them, sometimes explicitly. One important aim here is to create a counterweight to the often entirely negative perception the parties to a conflict have of one another.

Authenticity

The attitudinal aspect of authenticity, that is, a combination of credibility, genuineness, and congruence, is a necessary addition to these role requirements. Third parties come across as authentic "when rational and emotional, verbal and non-verbal, and visible and invisible signals and information correspond"[4]. The degree of authenticity determines the extent to which parties feel that multipartiality, acceptance, and respect are genuine or contrived. This, in turn, determines whether these attitudes and the methodology employed in the conflict resolution will be effective.

II. Communication tools for good mediation

The importance of the methodological dimension of mediation is reflected in many topics in this series of fact sheets. In the phase prior to mediation talks, required techniques include comprehensive analysis of the causes, topics and dynamics of the conflict (see Conflict Analysis and Mediation Entry Points Fact Sheet), complex context analyses (power relations, political logic, strategic calculation by third parties and the parties to the conflict), the definition of relevant mediation entry points (see Conflict Analysis and Mediation Entry Points Fact Sheet), and a process design that takes these factors into account (see, inter alia, the Basics of Mediation: Concepts and Definitions Fact Sheet).

In many of these steps, but especially later in the actual negotiations, the quality of the communication and of the openness, trust, and constructiveness that subsequently unfolds is often paramount, particularly at challenging and complex moments. No matter the degree to which style, charisma, diplomatic expertise, and experience are important, the qualitative difference that can be achieved through the skilled use of the following communication tools in such situations is both tangible and relevant.

1. Actively ensuring that a message has been understood

In confrontational and intercultural contexts in particular, the aim of subtle and seamless understanding rests at the heart of possible rapprochement. This can be facilitated by methods such as active listening[5], which can be summarised as follows:

- The receiver of a message listens attentively.
- If the interlocutor is emotional, the receiver "labels" the sender's emotional state (see point 2 on dealing with emotionality).
- The receiver then paraphrases the message in his or her own words, structuring and reducing the message to its key points.
- The receiver requests confirmation from the sender on whether this summary reflects what was meant (that is, asks for confirmation that he or she has understood correctly). Depending on the situation, the speaker then has the option to add something, correct anything that has been misunderstood, or confirm that the message has been understood.

Only by constantly "looping what was *heard* back with what was *meant*" is it possible to Interactively check whether all relevant messages have been understood, as depicted on the following page and subsequently illustrated by an example. A secession conflict proves to be a useful example for explaining the other methodological tools contained in this fact sheet (see next page) as well.

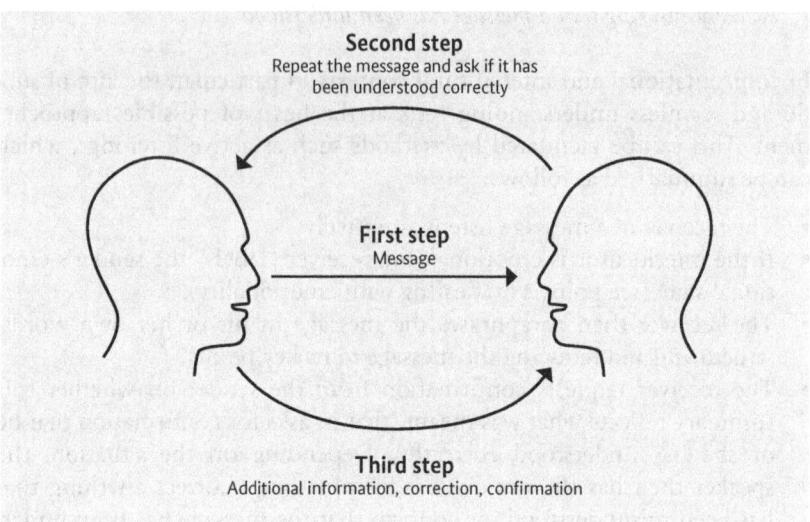

Second step
Repeat the message and ask if it has
been understood correctly

First step
Message

Third step
Additional information, correction, confirmation

Fig. 1: Active listening through the loop of ensuring a message has been understood (European University Viadrina)

Actively ensuring a message has been understood – example of a secession conflict

Representative of the secession movement: "You know, you should all understand that it's not just a matter of sensitivities here or of blind rage and aggression. It's about the necessary reactions to degrading events, things like the way the government has refused for decades to even discuss recognising our language as the second official language or the way our culture is deliberately repressed in state media. All of that gradually led to escalation. And most recently, it has unleashed a willingness to use violence, something I personally deplore. But this concerns the survival of an entire culture. That's the point, and a few people getting hurt doesn't count for much."

Instead of using a classically friendly and approachable response ("Please believe me when I say that everyone here in this room has profound respect for the value of culture and language."), moral admonishment ("Every person should count.") or immediately posing rational questions ("But what if your noble desire is simply unrealistic?"), the benefits of third parties actively ensuring they have understood the message are particularly apparent in such situations: "So – if I understood correctly – you're critical of the procedural level, that is, the government's long-standing refusal to discuss the language issue. At the same time, you see your regional culture as deliberately under-represented in state media, and regard your cultural identity as being at risk as a result. You explain the current violence in light of this historical background, but distance yourself personally from the scale of it. Is that right?"

Unlike the first responses mentioned above, the party to the conflict knows as a result of this reaction that his or her words have been understood in their entirety and that their legitimacy has neither been immediately denied nor confirmed by the mediator.

2. Dealing with emotionality

Even though people who conduct negotiations in international settings are usually politically experienced, talks on conflicts almost inevitably lead to emotional reactions. Actively seeking confirmation that one has understood a message thus often includes an emotional dimension. Firstly, emotions fulfil several important functions in mediation. They serve as an outlet, that is, their – sometimes unchecked – articulation often clears the way for more rational and ultimately more cooperative forms of exchange. At the same time, emotions in mediation talks are valuable indicators of where the parties' primary interests, needs and fears actually lie.

Dealing with emotions – the example of Camp David

Talks on the conflict in the Middle East were held in the year 2000 between President Bill Clinton, the President of the Palestinian Authority Yasser Arafat and Israeli Prime Minister Ehud Barak at Camp David, the US President's country residence. In the almost five-hour-long documentary film, "Elusive Peace" (available on YouTube; please see minutes 20 to 25), there is an impressive scene about the emotional dimension involved for both parties as regards any question concerning the sovereignty over and division of Jerusalem. Without such a precise assessment and description by Clinton, who expressed his immense respect for the importance of the city in both religions through his historically aware choice of words, tone of voice and body language, the breakthrough the negotiators aimed to achieve would have been inconceivable.

Secondly, emotions generally resist appeals. This means that the advice given in many contexts and situations that one should please concentrate on the facts in the interests of all sides inevitably fails to achieve results. In a constructive reaction to emotionality, a filter should first be used. Should an emotional statement prove to be more of a negotiating strategy or attempt to manipulate, it can and should remain in the background and there is no need for the third party to respond. However, if indicators such as the speaker's body language, voice or general level of involvement send clear signals that the emotion is genuine, it should be named as such in a respectful way. This method of "emotional tagging" requires labels for the emotions that are both precise and concise. This act of labelling comprises a statement by the third party showing that the emotional component has been seen and describing what it comprises:

> **Emotional tagging – example of the secession conflict II**
>
> Alongside the request for confirmation that a message has been understood in terms of content in the above example, and depending on the concrete situation, the following labelling by the mediator would make sense: "In view of what you have just said, it seems to me that you find the government's refusal to enter into dialogue unfair and hurtful. And the preservation of your cultural identity in particular currently seems to be causing a lot of anxiety. The government's conduct is leading to rage and indignation. Is that right?"

In order to be simultaneously understood as empathetic, respectful and face-saving, the exact words must take into account what is appropriate to the situation and culture.

3. Building trust and personal contact (rapport)

The successful use of the communication methods described above is based on – and further fosters – personal contact[6] between the parties to the conflict and the mediators that has been developed previously. Already in the very early stages of a mediation process, the level of trust (even if it is still very rudimentary) is crucial. The mediators are generally political actors themselves. It thus seems natural to suspect that they may have their own interests and hidden agendas. In fact, the ideal type of an independent, neutral mediator who is open to all solutions scarcely exists in international political conflicts. Limitations often arise as a result of ethical and moral considerations, economic interests, norms of international law or obligations arising from alliances. This can be challenging. However, it need not be counter to a multipartial stance (see above) as regards the process. Ultimately, it involves a normative assessment.[7]

Further, it is crucial to communicate these limitations actively and transparently in order to build and maintain trust among the parties to a conflict. Paradoxically, trust is created when the points that the parties to a conflict might not regard as completely trustworthy are revealed in a transparent fashion.[8]

Naturally, the conflict parties' *realpolitik* concerns play a crucial role in the assessment of other actors' trustworthiness. This is largely based on information about the other side's plans and options. However, there are always uncertainties in the context of mediation processes as regards assessing the other conflict party's intentions. A party will wonder if the other side is serious about negotiating or merely wants to gain time. The mediator's communication conduct and the building of personal contact play a vital role here.

Non-verbal communication

The most frequently quoted experiment-based study on non-verbal communication[9] concludes that how credible and trustworthy a person is seen depends 7 percent on what they say, 38 percent on their voice (tone, modulation) and 55 percent on body language. Naturally, in political mediation, body language – no matter how "good" it is – does not "beat" reliable information about the other side (see above). However, in face-to-face contact, people always look for congruence. They ask to what extent the message (e.g. statements by the mediator on his or her multipartiality) corresponds with signals sent by the mediator's body language. How is this multipartiality reflected in body language in meetings with both parties to a conflict? Particularly at times when talks are hanging in the balance, the mediator's sensitivity to the impact of his or her body language can play an important role.

Furthermore, a prompt reaction to messages sent by the conflict parties' body language can prevent some crises in the negotiations.

Research on non-verbal communication is currently dominated by constructivist approaches that do not assume certain gestures or postures have a fixed meaning. Apart from the fundamental expression of certain basic emotions (known as micro-expressions), it is assumed that body language differs widely among cultures and individuals and that its interpretation is subjective. Accordingly, there can be no good or bad or right or wrong body language.[10] This means that information on, for example, the impact of one's own body language on others, cannot be found in textbooks, but rather from the repeated comparison of one's own perception with that of others.

One example is the unofficial back channel between Robert Kennedy and then Russian Ambassador Anatoly F. Dobrynin during the Cuban Missile Crisis of 1962, when Kennedy's authentic emotional expression of huge concern during the confidential talks had a significant influence on the Soviet Union's assumption of the credibility of the US proposals on unofficially linking a withdrawal of Soviet missiles with a later withdrawal of US nuclear missiles from Turkey.[11] In many cases, circumstances that can be put down to coincidence[12] or intuitive interventions on a personal level (see the text on "a photo for the grandchildren") have a crucial impact on the building of trust. The lesson for designing mediation processes must be that mediators should actively look for ways to create a personal relationship and consciously create space for personal encounters between the parties to the conflict.

A photo for the grandchildren – example of Camp David

"I handed him the photographs. He took them and thanked me. Then he happened to look down and saw that his granddaughter's name was written on top of it. He spoke it aloud, and then looked at each photograph individually, repeating the name of the grandchild I had written on it. His lips trembled, and tears welled up in his eyes. (...) We were both emotional as we talked quietly for a few minutes about grandchildren and about war."[13] Former US President Jimmy Carter on a moment when the peace talks between Israel and Egypt in Camp David had in fact already collapsed, as Israeli President Menachem Begin had announced that he was leaving.

Prior to that, Begin had asked Carter to sign photos for his grandchildren. Carter had his team research the children's names so that he could autograph the photos in a more personal way. As a result, Begin decided to stay and the negotiations were concluded relatively successfully.

Relevant encounters between the participants also include, for example, the negotiating delegations' social activities outside the official talks. In the mediation between North and South Sudan that led to the Comprehensive Peace Agreement of 2005, as well as in the Colombian peace talks between 2012 and 2016, watching football matches together on television built trust between the delegations.[14] Furthermore, it is certainly possible to establish a personal dimension in the meetings in informal Track 2 and 3 dialogues (and sometimes in Track 1.5 as well). For instance, this can occur via a discussion on the impact of the conflict on the lives of the representatives of the parties.[15]

4. Creating a nuanced interest profile

The interests of the parties to the conflict play a key role both at the level of resolving the conflict and of designing the process of peace mediation. Their interests are identified through comprehensive preparation and review of relevant sources, actively seeking to ensure that one has understood what has been said (see above under point 1) in preparatory talks, at the negotiating table and through constant structured (re-)formulation of the parties' statements. An interests-based solution to complex political conflicts cannot be achieved without a complete and methodologically clear identification and consideration of the interests involved.[16]

Functions of a nuanced formulation of interests

O Fosters understanding between the parties and between the parties and the mediator

O Raises openness to new solution areas

O Reveals possible **non**-competing fields of interests

O Provides a reference frame for the evaluation of options

Ideally, **understanding has already been fostered** during the pause for thought necessitated by the definition of interests, that is, the interim period between exchanging antagonistic narratives of the conflict and an attempt to find a solution. As parties do not immediately move from presenting their positions to the stage of tough negotiations over a compromise or settlement, they may shift from an aggressive and reactive to a more constructive and creative modus.

The mediator's question about what constitutes the core for the parties in a specific conflict gives each party the space to define its own concerns clearly. At the same time, formulating one's interests expedites the cultivation of empathy and fosters a change of perspective (see section 5).

This effect is generally strengthened by the fact that the more a party encounters understanding for its own interests, the more likely it is to show understanding for the other side. **Greater openness** results from the reassurance that one's own interests have been thoroughly understood and are being taken into account in the search for a solution. This creates the prerequisite that the parties are able to move away from their entrenched positions and initial demands. If the different interests are explicitly formulated, **non-competing areas** and thus possible solutions that have been overlooked so far can often become apparent. These possible solutions constructively redefine the nature of the negotiations from a zero-sum game to a more integrative style ("expanding the pie").

In the evaluation of the options, the parties' interests subsequently function as a key **reference frame for the quality of a solution**. Systematically comparing options with interest profiles can demonstrate whether a solution is comprehensive and fair to the interests of all sides, and thus sustainable.

Criteria for formulating interests

Interests must be defined in a way that furthers understanding and fosters creativity, for example, by ending a fixation on particular opposing positions. At the same time, interests must be defined concretely enough to serve as a reference frame for evaluating solution options.

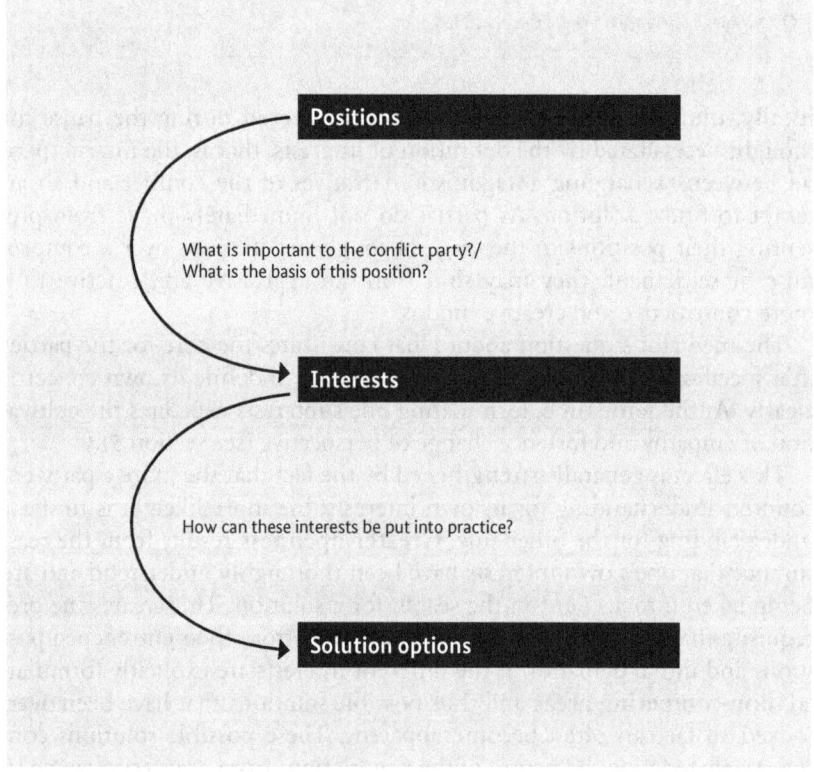

Fig. 2: Differentiating between positions, interests, and options (European University Viadrina)

Interests may be defined more clearly by working interactively with the parties to the conflict. Interests that are formulated at the end of this frequently intensive process should be based on the following criteria in or-

180

der to ensure that they can be applied in the best possible way in the later stages of mediation:

- **Openness to several implementation options**
  There must be *several* ways to put an interest into practice. An overly concrete formulation, such as one that only includes a single option for action (for example, the introduction of a second official language on 1 January 2020), does not provide scope for solutions, thereby re-igniting the dispute on positions.

- **Concreteness**
  Interests must be equally concrete and capable of being implemented in order to form a basis for evaluating solution options. Those that are formulated very generally (such as "the relevance of cultures" in the above example) or aspects based on needs[17] ("security") should be defined in more concrete terms.

- **Positive formulation**
  Formulating an interest in a positive way primarily means avoiding a definition of what a party does *not* want ("under no circumstances may..."). This leads to stagnation. Searching for what each actor is seeking – formulated in a positive way – often necessitates meeting several times to define the interests clearly.

- **Generating resonance**
  Resonance means an affirmative reaction by each party on an interest's relevance to the concrete resolution of a conflict. From the mediator's perspective, it is a prerequisite for including an aspect in the interests profile, because in order to arrive at sustainable and realistic solution options at a later stage, the focus should only be on points that are of genuine importance to the parties (be this for emotional or strategic reasons). There should be as few aspects as possible that are merely being used as ploys or tactics in the negotiations.

Creating interest profiles – example of a secession conflict III

The mediator's task is to explore the interests behind the position of the delegation striving for secession (in concrete terms, the position that its language be recognised as the second official language). This ideally happens in the presence of the other party (in this case, the state delegation). While the ethnic group's main *needs* (recognition, security, self-determination) can be stated fairly clearly in a situation of this type, its *interests* must be identified in more concrete terms in order to be of use as a sufficiently clear frame of reference for mediation talks. The following are – by necessity, hypothetical – examples of possible interests of the party striving for secession, explaining its positional demand for the introduction of a second official language:

- Long-term preservation of its own language as part of cultural identity.
- Automatic representation in day-to-day state affairs.
- Equal access to public authorities and educational institutions.

5. Fostering a change of perspective

In mediation, the phrase "change of perspective" is used to describe moments in which the parties to a conflict succeed in recognising the *other* party's viewpoints and interests and in understanding them, at least to a certain extent. The ability to put oneself in someone else's position has been the subject of extensive research in the fields of developmental psychology and neurophysiology. Experiments have recently confirmed the conflict-theory assumption that natural empathetic reactions are highly impaired in conflicts.[18] (Re-)enabling a change of perspective is thus regarded as an important task of mediation and thus as applied empathy (see above).

During official negotiations (track 1 mediation), a change of perspective as regards the fundamental conflict, that is, participants saying that they suddenly understand another group's suffering, cannot usually be expected, as political representatives are often too closely tied to their mandate and fixed negotiation positions. Furthermore, fundamental interests generally do not become apparent only during the mediation session itself (and then possibly bring about a spontaneous change of perspective). They are largely known in advance and in some cases are discussed and analysed by the public, in publications and among expert groups while mediation is taking place.

This means that the crucial change of perspective does not primarily occur in the official plenum. In many cases, it often transpires during unofficial parallel formats. Through internal discussions, this subsequently has an indirect impact on the official talks. As these parallel processes in the form of track 1.5 or track 2 dialogues and bilateral consultations with individual parties to the conflict are often guided by mediators, an opportunity presents itself here to deliberately work towards changing people's perspectives. Communication techniques such as circular questions (see box) can be used here. From a mediation viewpoint, it is essential to note that conflict parties are only willing to change their perspective if they experience understanding for themselves from the mediating third party (see section 1). Otherwise, interventions aimed at changing people's perspective are perceived as manipulative and biased.

While a change of perspective regarding the substantial issues rarely occurs during the official mediation sessions (see above), it must be assumed that the parties' interests and fears as regards the negotiation process itself will certainly become apparent at the negotiating table and that a change of perspective on these issues can accordingly be fostered. This can, for example, create understanding about where and why the other party's hands are tied as regards possible concessions. Alongside the above-mentioned circular questions, one can ask open questions such as "Which of the points just mentioned by the other side can you understand to a certain extent? What parts of them do you understand?"[19] Prompt reciprocity must be ensured here, that is, if one side constructively expresses a certain understanding for the other side's concerns, without itself being understood in any way, this mainly leads to setbacks and a hardening of positions in the process. Encouraging the other conflict party to first respond in a positive way should therefore be a priority.

Creative methods aimed at changing people's perspectives are used in track 2 and track 3 mediation and dialogues in particular. This is also possible in a track 1.5 process, as the example below on a role play conducted in a fishbowl setting shows.

"On one occasion to help reframe the talks, facilitators invited the parties to conduct a role-play. Observed by the Abkhaz, the Georgians role-played the Abkhaz discussing what would be acceptable to them in order to facilitate progress and what factors obstructed progress. Participants on both sides were stunned by how well the Georgians played the Abkhaz, creating a powerful resonance for those involved. Both sides' eyes were opened to factors that explained the other's behavior. The insights derived from these discussions led to senior Georgian officials drafting a series of options for moving forward that were presented to the new Georgian President in 2004 and which informed negotiations under the auspices of the UN for the next two years."
Centre for Empathy in International Affairs (2016)[20] on a track 1.5-moderated dialogue.[21]

Circular questions

Circular questions are an effective instrument that enable mediators or consultants to encourage a party to a conflict to put themselves in the other side's position, without coming across as moralising or manipulative (and thus biased). Such questions can be posed in bilateral consultations, but in some cases also in the presence of both parties. Circular questions are based on the following pattern:

→   What do you think is the biggest problem as regards this topic from the point of view of ... (the other side)?

→   What is particularly important for ... in this matter? Why?

→   What are the key interests of ... as regards this topic?

→   What makes it difficult for ... to agree to this?

→   What does ... fear as regards this topic?

→   How would ... react to this suggestion? Why?

Although the view[22] that the following interview by a US lawyer with then Egyptian President Gamal Abdel Nasser in 1970 helped to bring about a ceasefire in Egypt the following day may seem somewhat exaggerated, the following is a good example of the use of a circular question in an international conflict context:

Journalist: *What do you want [Israel's Prime Minister] Golda Meir to do?*

Nasser: *Withdraw!*

Journalist: *Withdraw?*

Nasser: *Withdraw from every inch of Arab territory!*

Journalist: *Without a deal? With nothing from you?*

Nasser: *Nothing. It's our territory. She should promise to withdraw.*

Journalist: *What would happen to Golda Meir if tomorrow morning she appeared on Israeli radio and television and said, "On behalf of the people of Israel, I hereby promise to withdraw from every inch of territory occupied in 1967 (...) And I want you to know, I have no commitment of any kind from any Arab whatsoever."*

Nasser: *(laughing) Oh, would **she** have trouble at home!*

6. Methodology for finding options and solutions

Good solutions require good ideas. In practice, a large number of difficulties can arise on the path to finding a solution, ranging from blind spots, entrenched thinking or a refusal to cooperate to concerns about fairness or a lack of resources to achieve certain proposed options. In order to do justice to mediation's complex goal of finding a (partial) answer to disputed issues that includes as many interests as possible – thus providing a lasting solution – a good combination of creativity, a systematic approach and a sense of reality is particularly important when exploring options.[23] A range of intuitive or systematic techniques that foster individuals or groups' creative potential in deadlocked settings can be helpful here.[24]

By specifically asking for analogies or example-based answers to complex problems in completely unfamiliar contexts ("How would the corporate world deal with competition for such a scarce asset?") or by deliberately simplifying overly complex problems ("How can a city be divided in the first place?"), the parties are encouraged to think outside the box.

Thinking outside the box merely appears incompatible with the established image of a tense conflict situation. In many situations, the negotiating parties are in fact aware that a shift can only realistically be achieved through unconventional interventions. However, it is important that the mediator does not suddenly confront the participants with (personally or culturally) unfamiliar experiments. The parties must be able to understand the approach on the basis of the interests that have been identified. In many cases, one of the following ways of thinking – illustrated here by examples – is used:

Strategies for thinking outside the box

From "either/or" to "both ... and ..."

In many secession conflicts, the interests behind the mutually exclusive positions of "breaking away" versus "national unity", namely the desire for either internal self-determination or external sovereignty, can be met via legislation on autonomy, decentralisation or a federal structure. Instead of thinking in terms of "either/or", the extent of self-determination can then gradually be negotiated.

Making use of ambiguity

Following an incident involving a US intelligence aircraft in Chinese airspace in which the pilot of a Chinese interceptor fighter jet was killed, China detained the crew of the US aircraft for eleven days and demanded an apology (that is, an admission of guilt). The crew was finally released after the US authorities wrote a letter saying they were "very sorry", thus enabling the Chinese authorities to interpret this phrase as an apology, while the US did not regard it as an explicit apology.[25]

... or neither/nor[26]

In the mediation between Russia and Georgia on the former's accession to the WTO, the conflict on the status of South Ossetia was circumvented through consensus that the Russia-Georgian trade corridor through South Ossetia would be monitored by private-sector companies, in other words, neither by Russian nor by Georgian customs officials, which in each case would have implied implicit recognition of the status.[27]

Creating a fair process

If no way can be found to take the main interests into account to the satisfaction of all, creating a fair process can form the key element of a face-saving solution. One example was the agreement to hold a referendum on South Sudan's independence as part of the Comprehensive Peace Agreement of 2005 between the Sudanese Government and SPLM/SPLA.[28] (Please also see the Madrid Principles on resolving the Nagorno-Karabakh conflict; these principles include a referendum.)

The options on the table must be systematically evaluated. Following the first phase of creative thinking, this ensures that limitations (norms, technical feasibility, political will) are shown realistically and taken into account (no wishful thinking). This is followed by a phase in which the proposals that prove successful are combined as a possible draft agreement. Particularly in complex cases in which a large number of possible combinations remains even after the options have been systematically evaluated, it can be useful to develop several alternative solution packages in the form of scenarios.[29] These are discussed at regular intervals in the delegations (or fed back to political decision-makers who are not present) before the first solid (partial) agreements become possible.

Gathering/evaluating options – example of a secession conflict IV

Based on confirmation that a message has been understood and on the emerging interest profile, the following additional options to the parties' starting positions are available as regards the second official language:

- Requirement that a defined number of official forms be made available in both languages
- Commitment to holding and scheduling a structured dialogue on the status of the language
- Introduction of a quota for songs in XY language in radio stations
- Licence for a state-funded television station in XY language
- Establishment of a number of schools/faculties/higher education institutions that offer advanced education in XY language
- Identification of further options by comparing the country with/finding inspiration in countries where bilingualism is put into practice (e.g. Belgium)

These options would then be evaluated on the basis of interests, the parties' preferences and feasibility. If the parties are in principle willing to strive for rapprochement, this would generate a number of nuanced scenarios for the future, integrating as many interests as possible. These scenarios' respective acceptability would then be a topic for further discussion.

Summary: a skilful combination of technique and art

When used in a logical order, all of these communication techniques combined constitute the overall internal structure of a mediation process which is reflected in the established phase model and process structure: namely, creating a process framework that builds trust, followed by an attempt to understand all perspectives, resulting from active listening and a precise exploration of the interests, followed by a value-creating search for options that include as many as possible of the key interests of the main actors and thus form the heart of a subsequent solution.

No matter how simplistic the methods may seem when one reads about them, even experienced mediators struggle to implement them consistently in practice. In such tense situations in particular, it is helpful when the mediators' communication methods comprise just a few yet clearly defined tools that can also be used under pressure and when time is short.

Peace mediation is not about using communication methods in a purely technical way, but rather about promoting possibilities for rapprochement or (partial) agreement by making use of all resources. It is important to note that these resources include intuition, personality and very individual negotiating "arts". When an ethically aware, respectful and strategically skilled individual applies the methods that have proved particularly helpful in theory-reflected practice over many years, this is an ideal situation.

In an effective peace mediation, (methodological) techniques and (individual) art are not in competition. Instead, it is the combination of both that creates success.

References

1   In: Letters to a Young Mediator. A Collection of 10 Letters from Some of the Great Mediators of our Time. Swisspeace and Federal Department of Foreign Affairs, 2015.
2   Ibid.
3   Waldman, Matt (2016): The Software of Geopolitics, p. 10; cf. www.centerforempathy.org.
4   http://www.die-akademie.de/glossarbegriff.html.
5   The terms "paraphrasing", "summarising" and "looping" are used interchangeably in specialist literature.
6   In communication psychology, rapport is described as interpersonal contact in a current situation based on trust and mutual empathetic attention.

7 See Fact Sheet on the Normative Framework and the International Legal Basis for Peace Mediation.

8 Cf. e.g. Watzlawick, Paul; Beavin Bavelas, Janet; De Avila Jackson, Don (1968): Pragmatics of Human Communication. A Study of Interactional Patterns, Pathologies, and Paradoxes.

9 Cf. Mehrabian, Albert (1972): Nonverbal Communication.

10 For mediation, cf. Hunder, Laura; Wüstehube, Ljubjana (2018): Körpersprache und Auftritt des Mediators. In: Kracht, Stefan; Niedostadek, André; Sensburg, Patrick Ernst (eds.): Praxishandbuch Professionelle Mediation.

11 Cf. Wong, Seanon (2016): Emotions and the Communication of Intentions in Face-to-Face Diplomacy. In: European Journal of International Relations, 22.1, pp. 144–167.

12 One example is the accident during a fishing trip in 1991, when a participant in the talks removed a fishing hook from an opponent's finger. This incident created a firm relationship between two high-ranking participants in the negotiations between the African National Congress and the National Party in South Africa and proved to be a lifeline during a crisis in the talks the following year. Cf. Powell, Jonathan (2014): Talking to Terrorists: How to End Armed Conflicts, p. 238.

13 Carter, Jimmy (1982): Keeping Faith. Memoirs of a President.

14 Cf. Mason, Simon A. (2006): Lehren aus den Schweizer Mediations- und Fazilitationsdiensten im Sudan. In: Wenger, Andreas; Maurer, Victor (eds.): Bulletin 2006 zur Schweizer Sicherheitspolitik, pp. 43–96; Mediation Support Network (2017): Encountering and Countering Temporary Impasses in Peace Mediation; Colombia Farc: The Norwegian who helped broker peace (2016): http://www.bbc.com/news/world-latin-america-37206714.

15 Cf. e.g. Bar On, Dan; Kassem, Fatma (2004): Storytelling as a Way to Work through Intractable Conflict. In: Journal of Social Issues, 60.2, pp. 289–306; Splinter, Dirk; Wüstehube, Ljubjana (2017): From Shared Narratives to Joint Responsibility. In: Adhikari, Pankaj; Ghimire, Subhash; Mallik, Vidyadhar (eds.): Nepal – Transition to Peace; Zemskov-Züge, Andrea; Wolleh, Oliver (eds.) (2018): Changing the Past in Our Heads. A Facilitator's Guide to Listening Workshops.

16 See Gläßer, Ulla; Kirchhoff, Lars (2005): Interessenermittlung – Spannungsfeld zwischen Emotion und Präzision. In: Zeitschrift für Konfliktmanagement, 4, pp. 130–133.

17 Some conflict-resolution concepts fundamentally focus more on needs than on interests (human needs theory; nonviolent communication). It is correct that interests always result from (basic) needs. However, these

are only discussed in mediation if one side is unable to understand the other side's interests.

18 Cf. Bauer, Joachim (2005): Warum ich fühle, was du fühlst; on international relations: Holmes, Marcus (2013): The Force of Face-to-Face Diplomacy, Mirror Neurons and the Problem of Intentions. In: International Organization, 67, pp. 829–861; on mediation: Splinter, Dirk; Wüstehube, Ljubjana (2005): Perspektivenwechsel – der Weg auf den Stufen der Anerkennung. In: Perspektive Mediation, 2, pp. 66–71.

19 A closed question would be: "Can you understand that?" These questions are often perceived as directive or manipulative.

20 Waldman, Matt (2016): The Software of Geopolitics, cf. www.centerforempathy.org.

21 Further techniques and methods that foster a change of perspective (but are most suited to workshop settings) include: scenario planning; systematic feedback-loop-mapping; empathy lists; systemic work on constellations; and drama exercises.

22 As explained in the source, the classic text "Getting to Yes" by the Harvard Project on Negotiation (Fisher, Roger; Ury, William/Patton, Bruce [2002]).

23 For comprehensive information on the creative part of mediation, cf. Kessen, Stefan; Troja, Markus (2016): Ablauf und Phasen einer Mediation. In: Fritjof Haft; Katharina Gräfin von Schlieffen (eds.): Handbuch Mediation, pp. 329–356.

24 Cf. Zebisch, Herrmann (2009): Die kreative Phase in der Mediation, pp. 180–182.

25 http://www.spiegel.de/politik/ausland/dokumentation-das-entschuldigungsschreiben-der-usa-a-127856.html.

26 The binary logic of "either/or" is sometimes extended by use of the tetralemma model from the philosophy of law of Theravada Buddhism. It adds the notions of "both" (both A and B) and "neither" (neither A nor B) to the logical options of "either/or".

27 Cf. Federal Foreign Office/IMSD: The OSCE as Mediator. Instruments – Challenges – Potentials. German OSCE Chairmanship 2016 Conference. Conference Report, p. 15.

28 Sudanese People's Liberation Movement/Army (SPLM/A).

29 For detailed information on the methodology used in the option-evaluation phase, cf. Gläßer, Ulla; Kirchhoff, Lars (2007): Lösungsfindung – Zusammenspiel von Kreativität und Systematik. Zeitschrift für Konfliktmanagement, pp. 157–160.

PEACE MEDIATION
GERMANY

Initiative Mediation Support Deutschland (IMSD) comprises:

Berghof Foundation

 cpm Center for Peace Mediation
EUROPA-UNIVERSITÄT VIADRINA

 Berlin Center for Integrative Mediation

 „inmedio"
peace consult ggmbh

 zif Center for International Peace Operations

Part III:
Peace Mediation as a Balancing Act Between Methodology, Power and Politics

Peace Mediation as a Balancing Act Between Methodology, Power and Politics

Anne Holper & Lars Kirchhoff

The articles in this publication on the theme of peace mediation cover a broad field, which is, however, only a segment of a much larger one: the field of crisis prevention, crisis intervention and stabilization. The attempt to synthesize these contributions is unavoidably fragmentary and dependent on subjective perspectives.

This is why we wish to clarify our own point of view, which informs our analysis in this final section: We are commenting on the basis of a genuinely transfer-oriented understanding of science, which aims to ensure that politics and science strengthen their different social functions through intensive exchange (instead of diluting them or sealing them off from each other). Our view derives from own observations as scholar-practitioners who have supported the tailor-made use of peace mediation in this context and have been actively involved in the developments in this field. This creates a particular perspective, to which we owe specific insights, and which simultaneously binds our conclusions to a certain frame of reference. Finally, we are commenting as scientists who are aware of their own position and involvement, and therefore take a step back to include other, opposing perspectives. In this regard, the critical examination of nameable successes can prove especially fruitful.

A brief broadening of the perspective is necessary in advance, towards what is happening simultaneously in the international landscape of peace mediation but will not be fully examined in this volume: The increase in the number of transnational non-state armed conflict actors,[1] the role of religion and tribalism in political conflicts, the multipolarity of ideological and political systems, and the activities of China[2] and Russia as conflict

---

1   Karin Göldner-Ebenthal and Veronique Dudouet, *Dialogue with Salafi Jihadi Armed Groups: Challenges and Opportunities for Conflict De-escalation. Research Report* (Berlin: Berghof Foundation, 2019).

2   Miwa Hirono, "China's Conflict Mediation and the Durability of the Principle of Non-Interference: The Case of Post-2014 Afghanistan", *The China Quarterly* 239 (2019): 614–34.

parties and mediators raise profound questions that cannot be addressed within the framework of this publication. The damage[3] caused by a lack of coordination between competing mediation actors, the regularly unfulfilled multi-track promises and the disconnect between local and international realities and expertises[4] point to areas where fundamental structural, conceptual, and political or systemic work is needed.

Moreover, the view of developments within Germany in this volume is strongly influenced by the perspective of the Federal Foreign Office. A description of the establishment of peace mediation from, say, the point of view of development cooperation might suggest a different story, with different decisive moments and optimization needs; without question, such a perspective would be just as worthwhile and meaningful for the configuration and calibration of Germany's role in tomorrow's foreign policy.

And so we present the following classifications in full awareness of their limitations, selectivity and subjectivity. After examining the central themes of this publication (professionalization, adaptivity, discrepancy between conceptual and methodological demands and political reality), we point out developmental axes for peace mediation in Germany that arise from these topics (effectiveness assessment and experience, standardization and regulation, adaptation of the political-structural embedding and functional concepts of peace mediation), in order to spell out the remaining open questions about Germany's profile as a mediator. Answering these questions would represent a decisive next step towards consolidating that profile.

1. Classifications and Explanatory Approaches

Professionalization and Cooperativity

Considered together, the contributions to this volume give the impression of a rapid and dynamic professionalization of peace mediation in Germany. Originally triggered by international impulses, the topic of peace mediation in Germany has since developed a logic of its own, and – in terms of conceptualization, structural development, provision of resources

---

3 David Lanz and Rachel Gasser, "A Crowded Field: Competition and Coordination in International Peace Mediation", *Mediation Arguments*, no. 2 (2013): 22.

4 Séverine Autesserre, *Peaceland: Conflict Resolution and the Everyday Politics of International Intervention* (New York: Cambridge University Press, 2014).

and commitment – long ago moved beyond its initial stage. Today, peace mediation in German foreign policy is going through a phase of growth, contouring, critical reflection and practical testing.

Over the course of this professionalization, many actors have become involved in the complex establishment process and have actively shaped the developments. Although it would be going too far to say that the current status quo is a product of "participatory foreign policy", the developments have been astonishingly transparent, permeable, open and ultimately cooperative. And that is pleasingly congruent, considering the subject matter at hand.

Adaptivity in Response to Volatility

A decisive increase in congruence can also be observed in another area: Everyone now understands that political conflicts involve highly dynamic and volatile matters, characterized by systemically complex interdependencies. The resulting recognition of the equally volatile nature of peace mediation and the challenges of evaluating its impact have paved the way for a systematic conceptual exploration of the subject. Today, it is widely acknowledged that mediation and dialogue processes rarely follow the original plan and therefore require an adaptable design and flexible implementation. It is also understood that their effects depend on numerous contextual factors, are produced indirectly and sometimes occur long after an intervention. In the past, the uniqueness of conflicts (and of processes for their resolution) often led to the (more interesting than relevant) realms of the anecdotal. Today, on the other hand, the dependence on context and the systemic dynamics of conflicts and negotiation processes are no longer seen as barriers to acquiring intersubjective knowledge. Instead, they are viewed as a premise and starting point for contextually grounded, partially generalized and situationally adaptive peace mediation concepts and procedures.[5]

One can see this shift currently, for example, in the fact that the revised monitoring and evaluation cycle for mediation and dialogue projects funded by the Federal Foreign Office is much better tailored to fit the volatility

---

5 Michael J. Butler, "Adaptive Peacemaking in Protracted Conflicts: Mediation in the Second Sudanese Civil War", *Global Policy* 10, no. 2 (2019): 93–100; Cedric de Coning and Stephen Gray, "Adaptive Mediation", *ACCORD*, September 18, 2018, www.accord.org.za/conflict-trends/adaptive-mediation/ (accessed June 29, 2020).

and modes of action of these procedures. Classic evaluation approaches in the field of mediation and dialogue, which compared planned activities at the end of the year or project with the original goals, tended to lead instead to a subsequent adjustment of the official project narratives, in order to fit objectives that had been overtaken by political realities. Today, the continuous adjustment of activities to changing realities is recognized and promoted as a feature of good process support. German peace mediation has seen the development of a new, transparent approach to flexibility and comprehensibility – two key requirements for mediation and dialogue processes in a volatile and sometimes unfathomable field. This approach is an outgrowth of trial-and-error experiences of both the Federal Foreign Office and the implementing organizations.

Discrepancy Between Conceptual and Methodological Demands and Political Reality

After noting these two congruences, a first diagnosis of discrepancy intrudes: Despite these developments – impressive in themselves – peace mediation is not an established part of general political practice in Germany. The political basis on which the current professionalization and consolidation process rests continues to be remarkably narrow and unstable.

Hence the question of whether the Federal Foreign Office's methodological expertise is applied to peace mediation in processes shaped by power politics still depends on the constellation and disposition of the decision makers involved in a given conflict. Particularly in such cases as Germany's gradually increased role in mediating the Ukraine crisis or the conflict in Libya (an engagement that became public in January 2020 in Berlin and that the Chancellery had actively co-designed), the question of whether and how peace mediation skills institutionalized in the Federal Government can influence the planning of such relevant and complex processes must still become clearer.

To put it more concretely: We believe that there is still a contrast between the conceptual and methodological demands formulated in the Federal Foreign Office's mediation concept and the German Federal Government's own practical political activities in peace mediation processes. While the methodological demands on funded projects of other actors and NGOs have grown noticeably and measurably, it is our observation that other dynamics continue to control especially politically relevant and visible mediation processes. To express it using the triad of terms in the book title: When the stakes are high, methodology obviously takes a back seat to (power) politics.

Following the American scholar of international law Michael Reisman[6], this means that although there is no deep *programmatic* divide between the "myth system" of peace mediation (i.e., the globally growing, occasionally idealized narrative regarding methodology, cooperation, inclusivity and a multi-track approach) and the regularly dominant "operational code" (i.e., the factual, politically shaped practical thinking and acting in conflict mediation), there is nevertheless a significant *practical gap*. This gap becomes bigger, depending on how politically relevant, visible and close to the government the mediation initiative is. In other words, peace mediation – both politically and methodologically defined – is still not an integrated part of Germany's visible foreign policy.

Competition Between Methodology and Policy?

This discrepancy is interesting from a scientific point of view, since it indicates overlooked starting points for change or possibly good reasons for sticking with tried-and-true practices. Here it is important to identify, non-judgmentally and with an open mind, the missing link between the German mediation concept and the lived political practice: Is the problem "merely" a lack of institutional anchoring and suboptimal communication flows that exist despite a fundamental willingness to act? Is it because there are no individual or political incentives to use mediation as a foreign-policy instrument? Is there still not enough political support for peace mediation? Are political negotiators not convinced by mediation methodology, or do the existing concepts fail to sufficiently address the actual need? Finally, are professionalized peace mediation methodology and diplomatic mediation policy deliberately kept apart, due to existing differences and perceived competition? While the proposed answer below is complex, the reality is likely even more so.

First, the government actors involved in the planning and execution of political processes on the one hand and the concretely institutionalized methodology of peace mediation in the Federal Foreign Office on the other hand still belong to *different institutional and operational spheres* (see the article by Julia von Dobeneck in this volume). These spheres are reflected

---

6 Michael Reisman, "Myth System and Operational Code", *Yale Journal of International Law* 3, no. 2 (1977): 23.

in various distinct areas of responsibility (departments and divisions), which are subject to different organizational rationales and cohesive and centrifugal forces. Where the Chancellery or political departments of the Federal Foreign Office are in charge, other peace mediation competence units are (according to the departmental principle) often not automatically involved, which makes cooperation difficult. And just as Germany is not a unitary but rather a multifaceted foreign-policy actor, some areas of action and actors in the field take the German mediation concept, including its inherent values and principles as a frame of reference for their actions, while others do not, either unconsciously or deliberately, due to a lack of information, expertise or possibly conviction. Depending on the respective reason, the consequence is therefore either to ensure a better flow of information about the existence of the mediation concept and expertise in place; to build specific skills in order to conduct the structural coordination processes still necessary for a comprehensive establishment of peace mediation or to translate the conceptual basis into administrative procedures and practical action; or to complete the necessary persuasive work.

In addition, among proponents of a political versus methodological understanding of peace mediation, there is a *mutual lack of knowledge about the other perspective*, which still exists despite the intensive, but still strongly person-dependent, exchange. The capacity for differentiation that peace mediators have developed for the methodological leverages of mediation has not grown in this form among politicians and diplomats (just as mediation experts usually have no comparable knowledge on the leveraging mechanisms of other foreign-policy instruments available to Germany). But if political actors know little about the existence and potential of mediation and still less about the concrete potential benefits of the processes involved, no need can be seen for them and no support will be requested.

Thirdly, for political actors mediation methodology is a foreign currency without any inherent value as long as its *specific benefit for political processes is not tangible enough*. Power-oriented actors view methodologically oriented, principle-based peace mediation – generally and especially for the lower tracks – as being quite timely and honorable. But in the end, they consider it ineffective as a concrete tool for governmental action. Proof is needed to counter this impression and to determine the extent to which it is true, respectively; flowery words such as mediation's canon of value creation, cooperation and consensus do not suffice, they rather trigger stronger calls for evident political impact. In our view, what is missing is not only solid effectiveness studies but also concrete, reliable own experiences with the effectiveness of mediation methodology, mediative process design and the specific value of multi-track approaches on the part of German political mediators: how, for example, a precise identification of the interests involved in a conflict can create new options for peace; how the use of specific communication techniques can actually improve understanding between conflict parties; or how the content of peace agreements can gain legitimacy and feasibility (with substantial added value also for the governmental level) through a synergetic linking of different societal levels. If one has not had this kind of effectiveness experience oneself (or at least received nuanced reports on key moments of specific processes from a trustworthy source), no arguments, however valid their formulation, will be really convincing. It is exactly such experiences that a written mediation concept alone cannot convey. So in the end, it is a chicken-egg problem: Without implementation, there is no experience of effectiveness; without an experience of effectiveness, there is no implementation. The people in demand in such situations, who are willing to experiment in low-risk contexts (as "early adopters"), are only slowly appearing on the scene.

Fourthly, two *different system-induced status aspects play a role*: Many political and diplomatic actors who shape events on Track 1 are fundamentally skeptical of integrated approaches that involve other social levels, actors and procedures in political negotiations. As much as it makes sense to limit participation under the often intense time pressure and on some issues, it seems to be neither compelling nor purposeful in other contexts. Moreover, the reluctance to take an inclusive approach goes beyond the methodology of peace mediation, affecting the entire so-called multi-track approach to crisis response. The big complex of questions – why (for reasons of justice, feasibility or sustainability) specific actors and specific measures should be involved (or not) in reacting to crises, to what degree they should be involved and in what status – remains largely unanswered, despite the "inclusive turn" of the last decade.

In addition, as in every political arena, rewards go to those who make a name for themselves and their department through successful processes. Cooperations reduce the success statistics one needs for one's own visibility. But since cooperation between the participating actors is an absolute requirement for successful mediation processes, one would have to establish *an integrated system of incentives* for the planning and implementation of peace processes that would proactively promote comprehensive teamwork, cross-departmental action and cooperative process design. These incentives would need to be both individual and collective.

Overall, it appears that the discrepancy is not the result of conscious decisions but rather of an interplay of factors inherent in the system that has not yet been fully understood, let alone controlled by any single actor. It is about more than mere non-communication and less than real competition; instead, it is about fundamental systemic and methodological gaps. Bridging these gaps could start with recognizing power not as a divisive motif (e.g., from the perspective of mediation ethics or realpolitik) or a contested one (from the perspective of internal organization) but rather as one that is shared between politics and methodology (with regard to conflicts): Both aim to have a concrete effect on ways of solving political conflicts, only at different points and in different forms. The key question indicated by the current discrepancy between the concept of mediation and political reality is whether, where and how these different forms of influence (can) interact in a meaningful way.

2. Possible Development Axes of Peace Mediation

We believe that at least three development axes are possible in response to this status-quo finding: targeted proof of the practical effectiveness of existing mediation methods and structures; a stronger normative regulation and enforcement of what is conceptually advisable; and a scientifically based review and conceptual advancement of the model of peace mediation, in order to adapt it even better to the needs of (German) foreign policy.

a. Evaluation and Experience of the Effectiveness of Mediation Methodology

One development axis could address the crux of the problem identified above: the lack of practical evidence and experienced effectiveness of differentiated peace mediation methods, which would make their concrete benefits more tangible for more political actors. Here, both the evaluation of previous processes and an active role in ongoing processes are possible (see Ian Wadley's approach to impact evaluation [2017]). Each option has its own challenges.

Evidence-based studies of empirical effectiveness[7] in this area always have to overcome a number of methodological difficulties.[8] One must

---

7 See, for example, Dominic Rohner, "Success Factors for Peace Treaties: A Review of Theory and Evidence", *Cahiers de Recherches Economiques du Département d'Économie* 8 (2018).

8 David Lanz, Martin Wählisch, Lars Kirchhoff, and Matthias Siegfried, "Evaluating Peace Mediation", *IIfP – Mediation Cluster* (2008).

bridge the so-called attribution gap that results from the ambiguity, indirectness or context dependence of cause-effect chains with regard to interventions in complex conflict systems:[9] How can one unambiguously and reproducibly determine which interventions – whether political or methodological[10] – have which effects under which circumstances and for which reasons? And, given the professionalization offensive in peace mediation, how can one determine the impacts of established structures, competency building, norm systems, applied skills, developed formats and implemented interventions on peace processes and their results?[11] These questions require methodologically innovative research approaches. In any case, if peace mediation is to occupy an established position in the field of political peace negotiations (in Germany and elsewhere), one cannot avoid a systematic evaluation of previous activities. Only by examining Germany's actions in different cases as a whole, by comparing and reflecting on them critically, can one distill the essential points that will be decisive for Germany's developing role.

A further massive obstacle to the systematic evaluation of previous mediation engagements is the access to inherently sensitive data from ongoing processes. Even though some individual studies have already been conducted in cooperation between politics and science,[12] a real, comprehensive mediation-effectiveness study would necessitate the release of data by

---

9 Daniela Körppen, Norbert Ropers, and Hans-Joachim Gießmann, eds., *The Non-Linearity of Peace Processes: Theory and Practice of Systemic Conflict Transformation* (Opladen: Budrich, 2011).

10 Isak Svensson, "Mediation with Muscles or Minds? Exploring Power Mediators and Pure Mediators in Civil Wars", *International Negotiation* 12, no. 2 (2007): 229–48; Jacob Bercovitch and Scott Sigmund Gartner, "Is There Method in the Madness of Mediation? Some Lessons for Mediators from Quantitative Studies of Mediation", *International Interactions* 32, no. 4 (2006): 329–54; Kyle Beardsley, David M. Quinn, Bidisha Biswas, and Jonathan Wilkenfeld, "Mediation Style and Crisis Outcomes", *Journal of Conflict Resolution* 50, no. 1 (2006): 58–86.

11 Anne Holper and Lars Kirchhoff, "Rethinking the Professionalisation of Peace Mediation", *Rethinking Peace Mediation. Challenges of Contemporary Peacemaking Practice*, edited by Christine Turner and Martin Wählisch (Bristol: The Bristol University Press, 2021): 355–72.

12 See Marko Lehti and Maiju Lepomäki, "The Era of Private Peacemakers. A New Dialogic Approach to Mediation. A Case Study of Three Finnish Private Organizations", *Working Paper Tampere University*, May 10, 2017; Laurie Nathan, Adam Day, João Honwana, and Rebecca Brubaker, "Capturing UN Preventive Diplomacy Success: How and Why Does It Work?", *Policy Paper and Case Studies Series* (New York: United Nations University, 2018); Rohner, "Success Factors for Peace Treaties: A Review of Theory and Evidence".

the ministries and individuals involved – data that has so far been considered too sensitive to be evaluated. And even if there are efficient means to protect confidentiality (anonymization, security checks, confidentiality agreements), this point is likely to remain a serious challenge.

For this reason, targeted methodological support and participation in the design of ongoing processes should be at least as effective in making the impact tangible. In contrast to the evaluation of past procedures, political actors themselves can directly test and experience how, for example, processes that are at an impasse can be set in motion again through mediation interventions. Since what matters at this point is whether a specific contribution is of practical help in a specific situation (and not whether clear, generalizable and reproducible cause-and-effect relationships can be proven), it would in fact be easier to make the impact tangible in this way. The challenges here lie in overcoming the institutional centrifugal forces mentioned above between actors influenced by power politics or mediation methodology, as well as intra-institutional rationales and dynamics.

In concrete terms, this means that models that involve seconding mediation experts who play a role in political processes must show tangible and visible added value. What matters here is to examine approaches based on (power) politics and on mediation methodology in an explorative and pragmatic way, until the resulting benefits enable the political side to grasp and estimate the role and contribution of the mediation method. In some cases, this may lead to the insight that the two approaches are mutually exclusive and require an either-or decision – for example, the use of sanctions, military intervention or support for one of the parties for political reasons. Such clarity in pragmatic, political and methodological as well as normative terms should enable an even better cooperation on the remaining points. The common reference point should be the goal and the cause (How can the process succeed best?), not the actors (Who or whose approach is better?). This engenders a complementary, rather than competitive, approach to (power) politics and method. This doubtlessly requires a leap of faith from the political side.

The direct experience of efficacy – political mediators learning and practicing mediation method themselves, as is common, e.g., in Switzerland[13] – may well require more preconditions. However, it is certainly effective,

---

13 OSCE.org, "Vermittlung eines Waffenstillstands. Interview mit Julian Thomas Hottinger, leitender Mediator, und Georg Stein, Mediationsberater im Eidgenössischen Departement für auswärtige Angelegenheiten der Schweiz", July 23, 2019, www.osce.org/de/magazine/433616 (accessed June 28, 2020).

because political and methodological thinking merge within a single individual.

b. Promoting Norms and Regulations for the Practice of Mediation

It is unclear whether it suffices to merely offer such a focus on *practice*, or whether one needs to experiment and then make decisions about whether and how certain approaches should be supported, incentivized or accelerated by *regulations*. Such a normative approach represents the second possible axis of development.

In general – not least in a country like Germany, which has, in principle, an affinity for norms – the regulation of a professional field of action is an option when the purpose is to influence, shape or change a behavior in order to establish a framework for action. A partial regulation or standardization of the field of peace mediation (which goes far beyond the *UN Guidance for Effective Mediation*) has already occurred.[14] Concerning (international) legal norms, it was ultimately inevitable that the elementary norms and values of the international community (and the large number of debates triggered by them) would find their way into the field of peace mediation, which was isolated and opaque for a long time and now claims professional status.

A second phase of (self-) regulation is, however, certainly imaginable, in which intra- and inter-ministerial collaboration, best practices to be observed and the spectrum of possible roles are codified more comprehensively and precisely. The latter in particular, a conceptual and functional differentiation of mediation approaches and actors, could take the field a big step forward. Above all, it would make sense to lay down uniform

---

14 See Fact Sheet on the subject of norms in this volume as well as Christine Bell, *On the Law of Peace: Peace Agreements and the Lex Pacificatoria* (Oxford: Oxford University Press, 2008); Timothy Donais and Erin McCandless, "International Peace Building and the Emerging Inclusivity Norm", *Third World Quarterly* 38, no. 2 (2017): 291–310; Sara Hellmüller, Julia Palmiano Federer, and Matthias Zeller, *The Role of Norms in International Peace Mediation* (Bern: swisspeace, 2015); Sara Hellmüller, Julia Palmiano Federer, and Jamie Pring, *Are Mediators Norm Entrepreneurs? Exploring the Role of Mediators in Norm Diffusion* (Bern: swisspeace, 2017); Philipp Kastner, *Legal Normativity in the Resolution of Internal Armed Conflict* (New York: Cambridge University Press, 2015); Alexander Ramsbotham, Achim Wennmann, and Conciliation Resources, eds., "Legitimacy and Peace Processes: From Coercion to Consent", *ACCORD* 25 (London: Conciliation Resources, 2014).

terms that make the complementary value of various approaches clear and make their implicit or explicit competition obsolete. Differences in normative convictions and methodological competencies (e.g., facilitative mediation vs. high-power diplomacy or third-party vs. fourth-party roles) could thus be understood as comparative strengths and work together if roles are assigned clearly. This could improve cooperation in conflicts, in the interest of the mediators as well as of the conflict parties and affected groups.

Clarity of roles using the example of the figure of the fourth party in peace mediation

"The fourth party is a party with a similar interest in conflict resolution as the third party, but with a different function [...]. Fourth parties can provide political, financial or logistic support to the third party. They are often states with an agenda of peace promotion or civil society organizations. The former usually operate at the official level ('Track 1'), e.g., organizing so called 'Group of Friends' or 'Contact Groups'."[15]

Regarding the question of whether stronger regulation (be it controlled by the parties themselves or by a superordinate player) is needed in peace mediation, we are, however, rather skeptical. An accentuation of the field of peace mediation through regulation would lead instead to increased discrepancy between "paper" and practice, not least because each individual case provides such great scope for discretion that the justification of exceptions would become the established practice. An overregulation of a field whose characteristic is a lack of conviction and experience of effectiveness on the part of important players, rather than a lack of normative orientation, appears inept. That is why we favor very restrained regulation, which, with a view to practical experience, should take at most one step forward when needed, but never two steps.

In concrete terms, this means operationalizing the current conceptual frameworks in a way that closely mirrors practice (from deployment plans to qualification concepts to rules for managing projects) and integrating them into existing systems (for example, in procedures for coordination and administration as well as incentive systems). This could possibly entail establishing a uniform, complementary terminology of approaches and roles in mediation, but otherwise relying on positive experiences of effectiveness rather than on norms.

---

15 Björn Gehrmann, "Third-Party Diplomacy", *HiCN Working Papers* 8 (2019): 6.

c. Reviewing and Adapting the Embedding and Functional Concepts

A third possible development axis is a critical review and adaptation of the existing conceptual approaches to anchor peace mediation in the German political system. A prerequisite for this would be an examination of the basic assumptions and strategies these concepts contain and a comparison with relevant political realities and developments. Alongside the above-mentioned development axis concerning efficacy, such a conceptual review would comprehensively measure how peace mediation fits into Germany's (or the Federal Government's) politically strategic, historical, organizational and operative profile, which is, of course, subject to constant change. It would also evaluate the added value, costs, preconditions and consequences that successful structural embedding entails, as well as which embedding strategies could accordingly be rejected or adopted.

Above and beyond that, examining how the mediation methodology functions when faced with the major challenges of today's political conflicts and advancing it accordingly could imply a real conceptual leap forward. In his contribution to this volume, David Lanz describes the dynamics that make it necessary to adapt the goals of mediation: "It is no longer a question of comprehensive conflict resolution but rather of partial measures within larger and longer-term processes, which are intended to contain and prevent violence and to stabilize the situation. Such an adaptation of objectives necessitates questioning established approaches to peace mediation. And it requires the ability to deal with difficult political and ethical dilemmas. For example, the question arises as to how mediators can engage with extremist groups while avoiding legitimizing their violent tactics." Against the backdrop of the realities of current crises, a (renewed) survey would be worthwhile in other significant places as well – for instance, concerning the balancing of the complex interaction of peace, justice, security and stability, or the enforcing of human rights and other norms.

In order to achieve such an adaptation of the goals and thereby ultimately the functions of peace mediation, the factors inherent to the methods and systems that determine and limit the efficacy of peace mediation in various contexts would have to be surveyed systematically and without prejudice. On this basis, the area/s in which mediation is (not) applied in today's political conflicts could be delineated more clearly, and the respective strategies for action could be derived.

The starting position for this is better today than it was just ten years ago, nationally as well as internationally. For many decades, political mediation in conflicts was considered to be a highly individualized matter and thus incapable of being analyzed on basis of reliable data; slowly, it has become the subject of academic study.[16] However, the still-erratic and fragmentary nature of the research field as well as the still persisting lack of a sufficiently representative and informative body of data[17] suggest that the potential for using scientific insights as the starting point for strategies to overcome the obstacles, conflicting goals and dilemmas that are characteristic of today's peace mediation interventions[18] remains untapped. Degree programs specializing in the topic have recently been intensifying research on current challenges in the field of peace mediation, but such studies –

---

16 Jacob Bercovitch, ed., "International Conflict Mediation: New Approaches and Findings", *Security and Conflict Management* 3 (London: Routledge, 2009); Julian Bergmann, *The European Union as International Mediator: Brokering Stability and Peace in the Neighbourhood* (London: Palgrave Macmillan, 2020); Chester A. Crocker, Fen Osler Hampson, and Pamela R. Aall, eds., *Leashing the Dogs of War: Conflict Management in a Divided World* (Washington, D.C.: United States Institute of Peace Press, 2007); J. Michael Greig and Paul F. Diehl, *International Mediation* (Cambridge, UK/Malden, MA: Polity Press, 2012); Lars Kirchhoff, *Constructive Interventions: Paradigms, Process and Practice of International Mediation* (Alphen aan den Rijn: Kluwer Law International, 2008); Susan Allen Nan, Zachariah Cherian Mampilly, and Andrea Bartoli, eds., *Peacemaking: From Practice to Theory* (Santa Barbara, CA: Praeger, 2012); Oliver Ramsbotham, Tom Woodhouse, and Hugh Miall, *Contemporary Conflict Resolution* (Cambridge, UK/Malden, MA: Polity Press, 2016).

17 Branka Panic, *Data for Peacebuilding and Prevention. Ecosystem Mapping: The State of Play and the Path to Creating a Community of Practice*, Center on International Cooperation (CIC), New York University, October 2020; Peter Wallensteen and Isak Svensson, "Talking Peace: International Mediation in Armed Conflicts", *Journal of Peace Research* 51, no. 2 (2014): 315–27.

18 See for example, Tobias Böhmelt, "Failing to Succeed? The Cumulative Impact of International Mediation Revisited", *Conflict Management and Peace Science* 30, no. 3 (2013): 199–219; Marieke Kleiboer, "Understanding Success and Failure of International Mediation", *The Journal of Conflict Resolution* 40, no. 2 (1996): 360–89; Anne Isabel Kraus (now Holper), Owen Frazer, Lars Kirchhoff, Tatiana Kyselova, Simon Mason, and Julia Palmiano Federer, "Dilemmas and Trade-Offs in Peacemaking: A Framework for Navigating Difficult Decisions", *Politics and Governance* 7, no. 4 (2019): 331–42; Autesserre, *Peaceland: Conflict Resolution and the Everyday Politics of International Intervention*; Catherine Barnes, "Dilemmas of Ownership, Inclusivity, Legitimacy and Power. Towards Transformative National Dialogue Processes", April 4, 2017, https://berghof-foundation.org/library/dilemmas-of-own ership-inclusivity-legitimacy-and-power-towards-transformative-national-dialogue-processes (accessed June 30, 2020); Kyle Beardsley, *The Mediation Dilemma* (Ithaca; NY: Cornell University Press, 2011); J. Michael Greig and Paul F. Diehl, "The Peacekeeping-Peacemaking Dilemma", *International Studies Quarterly* 49, no. 4 (2005): 621–45.

since they are generally prepared in the form of master's theses – can only examine particular fields in a synoptic or selective way.

> **Learning and researching peace mediation at the interface of politics and science**
>
> The Master of Advanced Studies in Mediation in Peace Processes program[19] is taught in close partnership with the ETH Zurich, Switzerland's Federal Department of Foreign Affairs, the foreign ministries of Germany, Finland and Sweden as well as the UN and is based on both theory and practice. Students learn, politically test and scientifically research mediation in violent political conflicts. Currently, research is being conducted on the following topics, among others: political models of power sharing and their application to specific conflicts; quantitative implementation of provisions in peace agreements; the role of religion in conflicts and peace mediation processes; learning experiences from multi-track approaches regarding the inclusivity of peace processes; the typology of ceasefire agreements and the forms in which they are negotiated; differences between regional organizations in peace mediation activities.

If the conditions under which peace mediation can function effectively are to be understood in a really new and reliable way, this topic must be better embedded in the field of peace and conflict studies.

The fact that in Germany these two fields have been only loosely connected to date might have to do with the theory-based tradition of political science in Germany, which – after the unprecedented abuses of power in 20th century – tends to be critical of power as such. Hence, it may have handed down to peace and conflict studies a certain skepticism towards a more practice- and policy-oriented scholarly analysis. Vice versa, the social policy-minded scholar-practitioner culture that is prevalent in peace mediation research in English-speaking countries occasionally tends to lead to a lack of interest in theoretical research. Today, both sides may be unaware of how broadly their own core issues are reflected in the work of the other side and fail to understand how profitable a stronger networking could be for clarifying these issues. After all, the differing approaches to theory and political practice could generate substantial insights and impulses for change on both sides.

Such peace mediation research could be situated within a new, more practice- and transfer-oriented, field of *applied* peace and conflict research.

---

19 https://mas-mediation.ethz.ch (accessed June 28, 2020).

Its task would be to systematically and critically evaluate peace mediation (and other forms of intervention) as outlined in the research agenda above and to develop innovative approaches to improving the practice of intervention. Considerable research gaps could be filled more quickly through systematic interlinkage with other key focal areas of peace and conflict studies (international relations, security research, etc.), and critical reviews and new approaches could be given a broader foundation.

d. Conclusion Concerning the Development Axes of Peace Mediation

When the three development axes and their respective potentials are considered together, significant further standardization or regulation of German mediation practice appears to make little sense. Rather, it seems to be time, on the one hand, to make the effectiveness of the mediation methodology tangible, and on the other hand to scientifically examine the structural embedding of peace mediation and its basic functioning in existing political systems, and to adapt it in practice, if necessary. Clearly, the political players must provide further answers and positionings in order to facilitate movement in the right direction at the right places. This positioning could be eased significantly through clearly outlined answers to the core questions, suggested below, on the differentiation of Germany's roles.

3. Core Questions About the Differentiation of Germany's Roles

Even though the discrepancy between concept and reality has already been mentioned, the bluntness of the following statement as a conclusive finding of this publication may be surprising – given a comprehensive mediation concept, numerous Fact Sheets and the attested, far-reaching and well-founded professionalization of peace mediation in Germany, which has long enjoyed international recognition: **Germany has yet to develop a tangible profile as an actor in peace mediation practice.**

In essence, while a method-based, balanced, norm-oriented understanding of mediation stands at the conceptual center of German foreign-policy planning, our conclusion is that it is not yet fully translated into political action. When, in the face of time-sensitive or geopolitically relevant conflicts, the "rubber hits the road", German foreign policy continues to rely on previous political experience and tried-and-tested forms of political influence instead of complementing those approaches with mediation competence and leverage. Sometimes, in fact, it relies on swift action instead of careful conflict analysis and process planning. Much of this is due to the above-described realities in the political arena, reasonable restrictions on the procedure, overriding geopolitical strategies and the complex international net of relations and is therefore simply inherent in the system.

However – as explained – this diagnosis does not indicate flaws in the concept but can be attributed to very tangible causes. Hence, we actually do not see it as a problem but rather as an opportunity: On the basis of what has already been achieved, a rapid, solid and prudent consolidation of roles can now take place, and is already becoming very apparent. In our view, a truly customized role differentiation would have to provide answers to three major and closely interlinked sets of questions, many of which are still being worked on in a fundamental way:

a) How does (an actor like) Germany react to crises and conflicts in light of fundamentally new realities in the international system? When is it right to take sides in a conflict, and when is it right to take a mediating third-party role?

b) What does a mediation profile of a middle power with a sensitive history and correspondingly charged domestic and foreign-policy terrain look like, if the strengths, weaknesses and conflicting objectives resulting from this are translated into the logic of mediation methods and politics?

c) And, intentionally switching back and forth between the micro and the macro level, which mediation and mediation support approach reflects most coherently the very fundamental values, strategies and resources of German foreign policy?

a. Positioning in the New (Post-) Multilateral Order

We detect one reason for the difficulties in developing a defined profile in the current international environment: States around the world are seeking appropriate ways to deal with the new political realities and the dynamics of a massively shifting multilateral order. Defining one's own position as a state in such an international arena, which is configuring itself anew in a dynamic process, and then – as one step among many – translating this position into a consistent profile in peaceful crisis intervention is a demanding task. It has much to do with the substantial redefinition and political fulfilling of responsibility in the new, multipolar international arena after the US ceased to be the dominant power player. And even though the question is primarily about foreign policy, the answer must take sensitive domestic-policy dynamics into account.

One consequence of the dissolution of multilateral commitments seems to be that the reluctance to fight out geopolitical conflicts on the backs of regional or national conflicts has continued to diminish (see the contributions by David Lanz, by Almut Wieland-Karimi and by Marike Blunck and Carsten Wieland in this volume).[20] The key question with which mediators are confronted here is: How can one break the vicious circles that develop through the overlapping, expansion, intensification and coupling of conflict systems resulting in proxy wars like those in Syria, Yemen or Ukraine? Only a third party with political weight *and* methodological skills can build the diplomatic framework, the road map, the guarantees and the bridges of trust that point the way out of the dilemma that characterizes many mediation attempts in today's proxy wars: Any direct or indirect use of power to bring actors to the table or to make them fulfill agreements at the same time endangers the impartial and voluntary nature of the process, qualities that are indispensable to the acceptance of mediation actors and hence to their capacity to act.

For peace mediation, one answer to those dynamics could mean explicitly and transparently recognizing the legitimacy and necessity of power politics as a premise for engaging in certain conflict contexts. To this end, clearer criteria are necessary to identify contexts in which the renunciation of facilitative peace mediation is the order of the day. The role of Germany as a force for the implementation of multilateral values must not be watered down by its role as a facilitating mediator – and vice versa.

Thus, what is needed is a differentiated, adaptive concept that defines the possibilities and limitations for action within German peace mediation, and in particular the criteria for determining the appropriate role for a given situation. Clarity is indispensable here, for Germany has "only one brand as an actor in peace mediation"[21], which must be shaped and credibly filled with life. Although this clear image can certainly encompass a spectrum of roles (which, however, must be defined), the selection of those roles should be made transparent and then fulfilled stringently and maintained persistently, in order to avoid the impression of arbitrariness and

---

20 See Francesco Mancini and Jose Vericat, *Lost in Transition: UN Mediation in Libya, Syria, and Yemen* (New York: International Peace Institute, 2016): 2; and the article by Blunck and Wieland in this volume.

21 Citing Björn Gehrmann, Team Lead Mediation & UN Peacebuilding Stabilization Desk, Federal Foreign Office, whereby the concept of the brand is understood here as a uniform representation of a differentiated set of properties.

the resulting loss of credibility. Precisely because of the volatility of the context, peace mediation requires stability in its conceptual core.

At the same time, in the current international order, new needs are arising for mediation engagement in regions, contexts and places that were previously non-existent or otherwise served by other actors – for example, multilateral negotiation processes in the areas of climate change mitigation, disarmament and distributive justice. Such an expansion of Germany's role from the curative type of mediation accompanying certain stages in a process to a comprehensive process responsibility in the field of "formative mediation" could prove to be an interesting additional effect of shaping Germany's peace mediation profile.

b. *Political-Methodological Mediation Profile of a Middle Power With a Highly Sensitive History*

The question of what the mediation profile of a middle power such as Germany – with its geostrategic interests, its minutely defined historical fields of responsibility and its substantial political and methodological resources – could look like in concrete terms is just as interesting in terms of mediation methodology as it is politically relevant: Why should – and how can – a middle power that is expected to play a strong international role in mediation and that actively seeks to take on that role combine its political weight with its expertise in mediation methodology? The *Peace Mediation Framework* already includes many answers:

> As a third-party mediator, Germany is closely committed to these principles, while at the same time taking into account its own policy interests. We do not engage as a mediator in, or supporter of, mediation processes out of purely altruistic motives; rather we act on the basis of our own interests and values, which we convey in an open and transparent manner to the conflict parties and the international community.[22]

> We are committed to the principle of multipartiality. We assess carefully whether our own interests in the course and outcome of a process or our obligations resulting from political alliances and multilateral treaties run counter to the interests of the conflict parties. If this is the case, we will choose a different role in the peace process concerned, such as supporting only

---

22 Federal Foreign Office, *Peace Mediation Framework* (Berlin: Federal Foreign Office, 2019): 1.

one conflict party or focusing on security-related efforts or military engagement.[23]

Other questions, including politically and methodologically relevant aspects arising from this, remain unanswered in the *Peace Mediation Framework*. This is not a failing of the mediation concept; these issues can only be clarified when political actors are confronted with them when applying the method. They can then develop answers during the political process. The fact that these questions have not yet been answered, however, results in a lack of methodological clarity. Its clarification will also strengthen Germany's political and strategic mediation profile. Open questions include the following aspects:

> In a conflict context, how does the commitment in principle to an inclusive, multi-track approach translate into concrete dealings with relevant civil-society actors who are *not* financed as project implementers and who are thus uninvolved?

> How cooperative or delimiting is the attitude towards other states and international, regional and non-governmental organizations that are actively conducting own mediation activities in the same conflict contexts?

> Does the German Nazi and colonial past create biases or responsibilities in contemporary conflicts that are incompatible with Germany's role as mediator? Does this simply exclude certain regions or conflict types from the portfolio, or, on the contrary, does this result in a particular focus?

> How far does the readiness for exchange and cooperation go with actors who do not share Germany's fundamental values? This question is reflected in decisions about which conflict parties are approached for direct exchange, and in decisions about which third-party alliances allow cooperative mediation engagements.

In short: Exactly which mediation approach or spectrum of approaches appeals to Germany?

---

23 Ibid.

c. Questions About the Motivation, Value Orientation, Responsibility and Strategy

The above-mentioned questions lead directly to the fundamental questions of goals, values, responsibilities and strategies that Simon J. A. Mason outlines in his contribution at the beginning of this volume. For Germany, these questions can currently be condensed as follows:

Motivation: What do German mediation activities aim for in terms of visibility and relevance; what are their goals with regard to political processes and conflict contexts?

At a time of a still propounded "America First" policy, to what extent does Germany seek to establish itself as an actor that stands for the *non*-use of its own power and generates its relevance through currencies *other* than its (context-specific) own weight, for example, by taking the side of the "common good" in the new multilateral order? In light of sensitive topics in domestic and international foreign policy (refugee crisis/Turkey, energy supply/Russia, rise of new-right voters, to name just three examples) as well as the resulting domestic-policy leverage on foreign-policy engagement, to what extent must mediation activities be subordinated at least in part to these priorities? Does Germany consider itself obligated to insist on the international system of norms that emerged after World War II, or does it tolerate, as in the case of Russia, massive transgressions for strategic reasons? These genuinely political questions demonstrate that a differentiated prioritization of domestic and foreign-policy interests always involves balancing the values and principles of German foreign policy, sending respective signals internally and externally and charting the course.

Role: Where must political power be used, and where, in turn, must it intentionally be limited; where can more leverage be achieved using mediation methods, and where is that not possible?

One thing is clear: In contrast to Switzerland, which occasionally punches above its weight with its facilitative approach on power-political Track 1, Germany may be punching below its weight when it opts to use mediation methodology rather than power-political leverage. Depending on the context of the conflict, such deliberate restraint tends to enable long-term, regionally and nationally anchored solutions, but at the cost of visibility and of the direct opportunity to influence short-term outcomes. In the case of strong escalation, and if many actors are involved militarily, a power-political and directive approach can be more effective in the short term.[24] It remains to be seen how Germany will seek to use its rich political and mediative potential to further stabilize international and regional systems in the future. One question that suggests itself is: Could Germany play a distinct role in mediating geopolitical proxy conflicts, as the contributions by Almut Wieland-Karimi, David Lanz, and Marike Blunck and Carsten Wieland propose?

Resources: How is German engagement in mediation guided, and which resources from which areas should be used to this end?

Which actors within the Federal Government should steer foreign-policy mediation efforts, based on which responsibilities and according to which criteria? How can coordination and cooperation with other relevant units be facilitated through simple routine procedures (in the sense of a standard operating procedure)? How exactly should the existing or potential internal and external support structures for mediation be used in such a standard operating procedure? How should the various forms of influential power and leverage that are available to Germany (expertise, funding, political weight, alliances, military peacekeeping operations) be employed to achieve the aforementioned goals?

Strategy: Where does German foreign policy have to upgrade its cooperation strategies accordingly, and where must necessary non-involvement be communicated?

Does Germany share the conviction that inclusive, positive peace can come about only if all levels of society are involved? Should a decidedly cross-track approach provide impulses for change, or should Tracks 2 and 3 be included only when needed and appropriate (see the article by Julia von Dobeneck in this volume)? How systematically does Germany seek to co-

---

24 Svensson, *Mediation with Muscles or Minds?*; Bercovitch and Gartner, *Is There Method in the Madness of Mediation?*; Beardsley, Quinn, Biswas, and Wilkenfeld, *Mediation Style and Crisis Outcomes.*

operate with other state and multilateral actors in mediation, or does it prefer to do so on a case-by-case basis (see the article by David Lanz in this volume)?

4. *Laboratory for a Middle Power With Multilateral Responsibilities*

The pending clarification and definition of the German peace mediation profile is unlikely to succeed if the key motivation and the questions about roles, strategies and values arising from it are not brought up clearly and continuously – ideally during the ongoing processes. The answers to these questions naturally depend on the case and the situation. However, every consciously weighed decision can help crystallize a basic stance, which then must be translated into the practice of mediation.

Since the motives will remain diverse and contradictory even in individual cases, one should not seek to make absolute either-or decisions. A meaningful goal for the remaining steps in the profile's refinement would therefore be to define a spectrum of activity regarding conflict types, priorities pertaining to the role as mediation actor as well as spelled-out combinations, delimitations and complementarities involving the interaction with other mediation actors. Similarly, the opportunities for combining political and methodological leverage must also be clarified. As long as the interaction of these two logics and their respective protagonists in German foreign policy has not been clarified and improved, considerable opportunities for added value in peace mediation will be wasted. Here the task is, for example, to find out how, in processes in which the effectiveness of previous power-political mediation seems to have been exhausted for explainable reasons (as in Ukraine), genuinely new leverage effects can be generated through differentiated process design based on mediation methodology.

In the current geopolitical situation, Germany is, given all the aspects mentioned, a kind of laboratory for what it means to create clarity regarding goals, roles and procedures in the tension between politics and methodology. How those representing Germany in future crisis interventions will respond to these core questions is observed with great interest internationally and could send an important political signal. What is at stake is nothing less than the politically consequential answer to the question: Which values (and, accordingly, which interests) are being validated by Germany choosing to exert its existing power in specific conflicts – or choosing not to do so?

The energy (but also the opportunity) to give answers must now be taken up, in a similarly concerted fashion as when the topic was initiated some years ago. And at the same time, as discussed above, the further conceptualization of peace mediation must not escape its own practical testing; a parallel step consists of incremental – occasionally even experimental – testing, through real, course-setting processes that are generated by good methodology.

It is no surprise that our final thought – and the attempt to present our tentative answer to the core question – moves towards orienting Germany's future mediation profile as explicitly as possible to the professional interplay of political and method-oriented actors, approaches and entry points. Germany could describe its approach to mediation in international discourse and the global political arena as principled, but pragmatic; method-based, but complemented with power-politics in a balanced way.

Depending on the context and interests, this profile would explicitly label Germany's peace mediation activities as sometimes primarily based on power politics, sometimes primarily based on mediation methods, or balanced between the two. The relevant "guard rails" of guiding principles and methods would consist of the Federal Government's clearly defined value structure for a mediating third-party role in conflicts, as well as the current German *Peace Mediation Framework*. In each individual case, the context of the conflict, the dynamics of the political process and Germany's own interests would have to be taken into account within the corridor arising from this commitment, in an intentionally pragmatic and flexible way. This would create a clear picture regarding the limits and the leeway for dealing with still-inherent dilemmas. Teams well versed in politics *and* mediation methodology would have to prepare the respective process design cooperatively and represent it transparently both internally and externally.

The decisive next step seems to be to spell out an adaptive model of German peace mediation in operational terms, and thus to establish a clearly defined German profile in the international mediation arena, which is constantly gaining relevance. This profile should intelligently blend the valuable power sources that Germany foreign policy obviously has with the methodological and normative leverages of contemporary peace mediation.

References

Autesserre, Séverine. *Peaceland: Conflict Resolution and the Everyday Politics of International Intervention.* New York: Cambridge University Press, 2014.

Barnes, Catherine. "Dilemmas of Ownership, Inclusivity, Legitimacy and Power. Towards Transformative National Dialogue Processes", *National Dialogue Handbook. Background Paper No. 1*, April 4, 2017. https://berghof-foundation.org/libra ry/dilemmas-of-ownership-inclusivity-legitimacy-and-power-towards-transformat ive-national-dialogue-processes (accessed June 30, 2020).

Beardsley, Kyle. *The Mediation Dilemma.* Ithaca, NY: Cornell University Press, 2011.

Beardsley, Kyle, David M. Quinn, Bidisha Biswas, and Jonathan Wilkenfeld. "Mediation Style and Crisis Outcomes", *Journal of Conflict Resolution* 50, no. 1 (2006): 58–86.

Bell, Christine. *On the Law of Peace: Peace Agreements and the Lex Pacificatoria.* Oxford: Oxford University Press, 2008.

Bercovitch, Jacob, ed., "International Conflict Mediation: New Approaches and Findings", *Security and Conflict Management* 3. London: Routledge, 2009.

Bercovitch, Jacob, and Scott Sigmund Gartner. "Is There Method in the Madness of Mediation? Some Lessons for Mediators from Quantitative Studies of Mediation", *International Interactions* 32, no. 4 (2006): 329–54.

Bergmann, Julian. *The European Union as International Mediator: Brokering Stability and Peace in the Neighbourhood.* London: Palgrave Macmillan, 2020.

Böhmelt, Tobias. "Failing to Succeed? The Cumulative Impact of International Mediation Revisited", *Conflict Management and Peace Science* 30, no. 3 (2013): 199–219.

Butler, Michael J. "Adaptive Peacemaking in Protracted Conflicts: Mediation in the Second Sudanese Civil War", *Global Policy* 10, no. 2 (2019): 93–100.

Coning, Cedric de, and Stephen Gray. "Adaptive Mediation", *ACCORD*, September 18, 2018. www.accord.org.za/conflict-trends/adaptive-mediation/ (accessed June 29, 2020).

Crocker, Chester A., Fen Osler Hampson, and Pamela R. Aall, eds. *Leashing the Dogs of War: Conflict Management in a Divided World.* Washington, D.C.: United States Institute of Peace Press, 2007.

Donais, Timothy, and Erin McCandless. "International Peace Building and the Emerging Inclusivity Norm", *Third World Quarterly* 38, no. 2 (2017): 291–310.

Federal Foreign Office. *Peace Mediation Framework.* Berlin: Federal Foreign Office, 2019.

Gehrmann, Björn. "Third-Party Diplomacy", *HiCN Working Papers* 8 (2019).

Göldner-Ebenthal, Karin, and Veronique Dudouet. *Dialogue with Salafi Jihadi Armed Groups: Challenges and Opportunities for Conflict De-escalation. Research Report.* Oxford/New York: Berghof Foundation, 2019.

Greig, J. Michael, and Paul F. Diehl. "The Peacekeeping-Peacemaking Dilemma", *International Studies Quarterly* 49, no. 4 (2005): 621–45.

Greig, J. Michael, and Paul F. Diehl. *International Mediation*. Cambridge, UK/Malden, MA: Polity Press, 2012.

Hellmüller, Sara, Julia Palmiano Federer, and Jamie Pring. *Are Mediators Norm Entrepreneurs? Exploring the Role of Mediators in Norm Diffusion*. Bern: swisspeace, 2017.

Hellmüller, Sara, Julia Palmiano Federer, and Matthias Zeller. *The Role of Norms in International Peace Mediation*. Bern: swisspeace, 2015.

Hirono, Miwa. "China's Conflict Mediation and the Durability of the Principle of Non-Interference: The Case of Post-2014 Afghanistan", *The China Quarterly* 239 (2019): 614–34.

Holper, Anne, and Lars Kirchhoff. "Rethinking the Professionalisation of Peace Mediation", *Rethinking Peace Mediation. Challenges of Contemporary Peacemaking Practice*, edited by Christine Turner and Martin Wählisch (Bristol: The Bristol University Press, 2021): 355–72.

Imbusch, Peter. "Machtfigurationen und Herrschaftsprozesse bei Norbert Elias", *Macht und Herrschaft: Sozialwissenschaftliche Theorien und Konzeptionen*, edited by Peter Imbusch (Wiesbaden: Springer Fachmedien Wiesbaden, 2013): 169–93.

Kastner, Philipp. *Legal Normativity in the Resolution of Internal Armed Conflict*. New York: Cambridge University Press, 2015.

Kirchhoff, Lars. *Constructive Interventions: Paradigms, Process and Practice of International Mediation*. Alphen aan den Rijn: Kluwer Law International, 2008.

Kleiboer, Marieke. "Understanding Success and Failure of International Mediation", *The Journal of Conflict Resolution* 40, no. 2 (1996): 360–89.

Körppen, Daniela, Norbert Ropers, and Hans-Joachim Gießmann, eds. *The Non-Linearity of Peace Processes: Theory and Practice of Systemic Conflict Transformation*. Opladen: Budrich, 2011.

Kraus (now Holper), Anne Isabel, Owen Frazer, Lars Kirchhoff, Tatiana Kyselova, Simon J. A. Mason, and Julia Palmiano Federer. "Dilemmas and Trade-Offs in Peacemaking: A Framework for Navigating Difficult Decisions", *Politics and Governance* 7, no. 4 (2019): 331–42.

Lanz, David, and Rachel Gasser. "A Crowded Field: Competition and Coordination in International Peace Mediation", *Mediation Arguments*, no. 2 (2013).

Lanz, David, Martin Wählisch, Lars Kirchhoff, and Matthias Siegfried. "Evaluating Peace Mediation", *IIfP – Mediation Cluster* (2008).

Lehti, Marko, and Maiju Lepomäki. "The Era of Private Peacemakers. A New Dialogic Approach to Mediation. A Case Study of Three Finnish Private Organization", *Working Paper Tampere University*, 2017.

Mancini, Francesco, and Jose Vericat. *Lost in Transition: UN Mediation in Libya, Syria, and Yemen*. New York: International Peace Institute, 2016.

Nan, Susan Allen, Zachariah Cherian Mampilly, and Andrea Bartoli, eds. *Peacemaking: From Practice to Theory*. Santa Barbara, CA: Praeger, 2012.

Nathan, Laurie, Adam Day, João Honwana, and Rebecca Brubaker. "Capturing UN Preventive Diplomacy Success: How and Why Does It Work?", *Policy Paper and Case Studies United Nations University*, 2018.

OSCE.org. "Vermittlung eines Waffenstillstands. Interview mit Julian Thomas Hottinger, leitender Mediator, und Georg Stein, Mediationsberater im Eidgenössischen Departement für auswärtige Angelegenheiten der Schweiz", July 23, 2019. www.osce.org/de/magazine/433616 (accessed June 28, 2020).

Panic, Branka. *Data for Peacebuilding and Prevention. Ecosystem Mapping: The State of Play and the Path to Creating a Community of Practice*. Center on International Cooperation (CIC), New York University, October 2020.

Ramsbotham, Alexander, Achim Wennmann, and Conciliation Resources, eds. "Legitimacy and Peace Processes: From Coercion to Consent", *ACCORD* 25. London: Conciliation Resources, 2014.

Ramsbotham, Oliver, Tom Woodhouse, and Hugh Miall. *Contemporary Conflict Resolution*. Fourth edition. Cambridge, UK/Malden, MA: Polity Press, 2016.

Reisman, Michael. "Myth System and Operational Code", *Yale Journal of International Law* 3, no. 2 (1977): 23.

Rohner, Dominic. "Success Factors for Peace Treaties: A Review of Theory and Evidence", *Cahiers de Recherches Économiques du Département d'Économie* 8 (2018).

Svensson, Isak. "Mediation with Muscles or Minds? Exploring Power Mediators and Pure Mediators in Civil Wars", *International Negotiation* 12, no. 2 (2007): 229–48.

Wadley, Ian. "Valuing Peace: Delivering and Demonstrating Mediation Results", *Mediation Practice Series* (2017).

Wallensteen, Peter, and Isak Svensson. „Talking Peace: International Mediation in Armed Conflicts", *Journal of Peace Research* 51, no. 2 (2014): 315–27.

Annex:
Peace Mediation Framework

Federal Foreign Office

PEACE MEDIATION
GERMANY

Peace Mediation Framework

I. Our approach to peace mediation

Peace mediation refers to the efforts by a third party accepted by all sides to facilitate the resolution of conflict through formal and informal negotiations and dialogue held on a voluntary basis. The procedures and instruments of peace mediation can be used to prevent, manage and resolve intra- and interstate conflicts at various levels of society ("tracks").

The mediation process is based on principles such as self-determination, respect, transparency and openness towards the outcome of the process. In addition, our approach to peace mediation follows the UN Guidance for Effective Mediation drawn up in 2012.

As a third-party mediator, Germany is closely committed to these principles, while at the same time taking into account its own policy interests. We do not engage as a mediator in, or supporter of, mediation processes out of purely altruistic motives; rather we act on the basis of our own interests and values, which we convey in an open and transparent manner to the conflict parties and the international community.

We are committed to the principle of multipartiality. We assess carefully whether our own interests in the course and outcome of a process or our obligations resulting from political alliances and multilateral treaties run counter to the interests of the conflict parties. If this is the case, we will choose a different role in the peace process concerned, such as supporting only one conflict party or focusing on security-related efforts or military engagement.

Assuming the lead role in a mediation process implies renouncing any parallel use of military or political pressure to increase the parties' willingness to negotiate or to enforce a one-sided outcome. In particular, when obligations resulting from political alliances and multilateral treaties exist, we assess carefully whether a German lead role is in the interest of all parties concerned.

However, being aware and making good use of the fact that Germany's political weight can have a positive impact on the conflict parties' commitment to a peace process constitutes an integral part of our approach. In doing so, we draw on past experiences where Germany has achieved a positive impact at local, regional and national level.

II. Embedding peace mediation into our stabilisation strategies

Whether by supporting third parties (project funding) or engaging directly, we use instruments such as mediation and dialogue to prevent or manage conflicts. These are essential components of coherent crisis management. Simultaneously, mediation processes can serve as a starting point for additional stabilisation and support efforts, for example, in cases of pending comprehensive transformation processes, such as demilitarisation, promoting the rule of law, and security-sector or constitutional reform. In such situations, mediating in conflicts means creating entry points for further engagement that allow us to deploy the whole range of instruments available to our Directorate-General for Humanitarian Assistance, Crisis Prevention, Stabilisation and Post-Conflict Reconstruction in a concerted manner. Subsequently, we underpin our efforts through follow-up support. Combined with financial resources at our disposal for crisis prevention and stabilisation efforts, we thus establish a sound basis for our mediation efforts.

III. Why we are expanding our efforts

Worldwide, there has been a marked increase in the need for professional negotiation and mediation. Today, many conflicts occur in increasingly complex and asymmetrical contexts that require a focused foreign policy with tailored and integrated instruments in the area of crisis prevention and response. Among these instruments, values-based, principled and methodologically sound peace mediation can facilitate precisely the kind of crisis intervention needed to pursue both peace-policy considerations and political interests when engaging in conflict resolution.

There are significant expectations in conflict regions and within Germany that we should play a strong and more active role as a mediator or a supporter of mediation and negotiation processes. In accordance with the guidelines, Preventing Crises, Resolving Conflicts, Building Peace (2017), Germany prefers civil conflict resolution measures whenever possible. The procedures and methods of peace mediation, along with the access generated by the process, can re-establish contact and trust between conflict parties and keep channels of communication open.

Peace mediation can help to bridge the societal and ideological divisions between conflict parties, particularly because its possible uses cover the entire spectrum from conflict prevention and supporting ceasefire negotiations to implementing agreements and the political reform processes arising from them. Germany regards peace mediation as a preferred foreign policy instrument for advancing the peaceful resolution of conflicts in regions of political importance to it, facilitating long-term access and positioning itself as a reliable partner – also and especially in light of current tensions within the multilateral system and a challenged international order.

The willingness, in principle, to also employ security-sector instruments when responding to crises makes a comprehensive approach possible. Our practice of dealing with our past – including the reconciliation with France and Poland – and our first-hand experience with the process of re-unification, as well as with federalism, are of interest in many crisis contexts. What also makes us an effective mediation actor is that we have the necessary instruments and financial resources to provide long-term and therefore reliable support as part of an overall strategy. This unfolds special relevance for a number of long-term processes that can typically result from mediation – namely, the demobilisation and reintegration of fighters, the drafting of a constitution, security-sector reform and/or stabilisation projects resulting from peace agreements.

Germany's position and responsibility within the international community, along with its desire to be an active agent for peace, set the parameters for its strong commitment to peace mediation.

The spectrum of possible German engagement – ranging from funding projects and conducting multilateral cooperation to taking the lead in mediation processes – enables and requires a context-specific and tailor-made approach to present day conflict settings.

IV. Forms of German engagement

We take a multi-dimensional approach:

German direct engagement in close coordination with our partners

When we engage directly as a mediator, we support various formats, send special envoys or conduct shuttle mediation, all with the aim of helping two or more parties to reach an agreement on a certain issue. In these efforts, we work closely with our partners, both governments and civil-society organisations. The prerequisite for any engagement is that we must be welcome as an agent for peace, bring added value through our political weight and do not duplicate any efforts by our partners. We ensure that our activities receive the broadest possible support from the parties involved, as well as from relevant stakeholders and multilateral actors (e.g., the UN, OSCE, EU and AU).

Supporting and coordinating mediation processes by other actors

Supporting third parties in mediation processes is a crucial part of Germany's engagement in the field of peace mediation. The third parties we support may already have direct access to key actors that allows them to react in a swift and informal manner to complex conflict dynamics. Furthermore, our approach to funding is often aimed at the level of civil society where direct and regular dialogue between conflict parties is just as necessary as it is at the high political level. When working with project partners, we emphasise close and strategic cooperation, especially in politically sensitive processes. We are engaged not only in hot spots such as Afghanistan, Syria and Iraq, but also in contexts where the focus is on conflict prevention or long-term transformation processes.

Supporting multilateral engagement and strategic cooperation at state level

We provide both funding and expertise to the mediation support units of the UN, the OSCE and the EU, and the processes they steer, and strive to deepen bilateral cooperation in the area of mediation. We believe that the UN, and in particular its Mediation Support Unit (MSU), should remain a strong mediation actor. We will advocate inter alia for this and for an expansion of mediation activities during our stint in the UN Security Council and afterwards. We recognise the important role the OSCE and the EU play in expanding mediation activities at regional level and support both the EEAS mediation team and the OSCE Conflict Prevention Centre's Mediation Support Team. With some bilateral partners, like Switzerland, we are implementing, inter alia, joint training initiatives.

Conceptual development/professionalisation

Germany's peace-mediation methodology is based on comprehensive and theoretically substantiated expertise and is also practised and shared through capacity-building efforts by a particularly diverse range of civil-society actors in this field. This expertise is closely integrated into the conceptual development of peace mediation. For example, we have been working closely with the Initiative Mediation Support Germany (IMSD) since 2014 on developing background material and building capacities. Since 2018, we have been collaborating with the European University Viadrina, with the express aim of creating an interface for knowledge transfer between academia and practice in the field of peace mediation.

V. Definitions of peace mediation and dialogue support, frame of reference

In contrast to **mediation**, which usually concludes with an agreement, **dialogue** processes focus on establishing contact and/or promoting understanding between conflict parties, without having to reach concrete agreements. Dialogues between members of the government and the opposition, between opposing civil-society actors, or aimed at including all levels of society (national dialogues) can help to prepare the ground and support peace processes, as well as to structure larger social change processes.

Mediation and dialogue processes can be assisted by **mediation support** teams. A mediation support team is available to mediators or dialogue facilitators and tends to comprise experts on conflict analysis, process design, constitutional reform, transitional justice, demilitarisation, reconstruction, logistics, etc. This support helps to ensure an effective process by analysing and addressing the issues inherent to the conflict and its lasting resolution in a professional way.

Mediation procedures and instruments can be part of **traditional diplomacy** and used by diplomatic staff. That said, mediation is not the same as diplomacy. For one thing, diplomats do not automatically possess mediation skills; rather, these must be acquired. Furthermore, diplomacy's remit extends much further than that of mediation. It includes, for example, bilateral negotiations, unilateral statements, the imposition of sanctions and the targeted use of political power to assert one's interests.

Our approach to peace mediation adheres to the United Nation's guiding principles for mediation (Guidance for Effective Mediation, 2012). In addition, we also bring some aspects of German foreign policy to bear. Our approach can be broken down as follows with regard to both the projects we fund and our own efforts:

Preparedness

Besides ensuring that our mediation teams possess the necessary skills and methods, before processes can begin, we make certain that the conflict analysis is comprehensive and takes diverse viewpoints into account and that the process design is based on realistic assessments.

Consent

Another important prerequisite for launching a peace mediation process is the willingness of all parties involved in a conflict to engage voluntarily in the process and with the mediator, as this is vital for lasting conflict resolution.

Impartiality

The mediating party must represent the interests of both or all conflict parties in the process equally. However, multipartiality must not be equated with neutrality.

Inclusivity

The inclusive design of a process can be the decisive factor for ensuring long-term success in the resolution of a conflict. Peace agreements often fail because key actors were not included. We decide whether or not to include a party based on the following questions: Can a party help to bring about a solution to the conflict? Is a party directly or indirectly affected by it? Can a party help to shape possible solutions, and will it be affected by their implementation? Whenever multi-track approaches or national dialogues can increase the likelihood of reaching a lasting and comprehensive solution, we believe these options should be pursued.

National Ownership

The content and outcome of a mediation process should be defined by those who are immediately affected – not by us or by third parties we support, as this would lower the prospects of ending the conflict. Wherever possible, we aim to take into account and support local approaches to conflict resolution.

Normative Frameworks

Mediation and dialogue processes are necessarily subject to certain norms. Compliance with or abuse of norms relevant to peace mediation may have consequences for actors, those affected and the viability of agreements. That is why, both in our own efforts and our support for third parties, we take particular care to ensure adherence to the norms of German foreign policy and accepted standards of international law.

Coherence & Coordination

The large number of actors in a highly competitive field must not be allowed to cause ineffectiveness, duplication or lack of coordination in the processes. We therefore advocate coordinating approaches efficiently and exchanging relevant information widely between third parties. We do this with the means at our disposal – as a member of the UN, the OSCE and the EU, as well as through our strategic partnerships.

Quality Peace Agreement

We believe that the issues addressed in a mediation process and included in the resulting peace agreement must also be the ones that lead to lasting resolution of the conflict. We therefore consider it essential that mediation and dialogue processes are enriched by the necessary expertise (mediation support).

Imprint

Editor

Federal Foreign Office

Werderscher Markt 1

10117 Berlin

www.diplo.de

June 2019

Author Biographies

Marike Blunck

Marike Blunck works in local conflict counseling at the Verein zur Förderung der Bildung – VFB Salzwedel e.V. Until early 2020, she was senior researcher at the Center for Peace Mediation at the European University Viadrina, where she was particularly active in Viadrina's Mediation Hub with the German Federal Foreign Office (FFO). Previously, she worked for the Berghof Foundation on national dialogues, where she co-authored the *National Dialogue Handbook*. She worked at the Conflict Prevention Program of the United Nations Development Programme (UNDP) in Nepal, where she was particularly involved in Track 2 dialogue processes, and supervised Civil Peace Service projects in Nepal and Myanmar. Marike Blunck is alumna of the Mercator Fellowship on International Affairs and the German Academic Scholarship Foundation. A trained mediator, she studied peace and conflict studies (MSc) at the School of Oriental and African Studies (SOAS) in London and international relations at Sussex University in Brighton.

Julia von Dobeneck

Julia von Dobeneck is a mediator and expert for systemic organizational development and holds a diploma in media sciences with specialization in law (TU Berlin). Since 2021, she leads the project „Strengthening Mediation Capacities" at the Center for International Peace Operations (ZIF). From 2015 to 2021, she was senior project manager and researcher at the Center for Peace Mediation at the European University Viadrina, where she led the operational side of Viadrina's Mediation Hub, focusing on the conceptional and methodological development of German peace mediation and accompanying selected mediation processes of the FFO. Previously, she conducted research on civil-society dialogue processes in Ukraine and worked as a dialogue facilitator and mediator in Kosovo. She teaches and advises in the fields of peace mediation and organizational development and was involved in the Initiative Mediation Support Deutschland (IMSD) until 2017, which she helped establish in 2012.

Sebastian Dworack

Sebastian Dworack heads the International Capacity Development Team at the Center for International Peace Operations (ZIF) in Berlin, which, inter alia, manages ZIF's peace mediation and mediation support portfolio. One focus of these activities comprises knowledge transfer on mediation practice in multilateral organizations and peace operations. As a member of the ZIF Expert Pool and a trained mediator, Mr. Dworack worked as a political advisor to EU and OSCE peace operations in several countries of the former Yugoslavia between 2002 and 2010. Afterwards, he was managing director of the Willy Brandt School of Public Policy at the University of Erfurt and coordinated projects to build mediation capacities in the Southern Caucasus and Eastern Europe in cooperation with the Potsdam University of Applied Sciences. He studied political science at the Ludwig Maximilian University Munich, the University of Edinburgh and the University of Bonn.

Dr. David Lanz

David Lanz holds a doctorate in political science and is co-head of the Mediation Program of the Swiss Peace Foundation swisspeace and a lecturer at the University of Basel. He has written about various aspects of peace mediation and is author of the book *The Responsibility to Protect in Darfur: From Forgotten Conflict to Global Cause and Back*, published by Routledge in 2019. Before his current role, David Lanz was seconded by the Swiss Expert Pool for Civilian Peacebuilding to the OSCE Secretariat in Vienna and helped to establish the OSCE Mediation Support Team.

Christoph Lüttmann

Christoph Lüttmann is a mediator and managing director at CSSP – the Berlin Center for Integrative Mediation. He specializes in peace mediation between political representatives on the communal and state level in conflict and transformation regions. Previously, he worked at the UN Secretariat, the Collaborative Research Center (SFB) 700 "Governance in Areas of Limited Statehood" and the Center for International Peace Operations. He has facilitated mediation processes in the Western Balkans, South Asia and Eastern Europe, focusing on preventive and post-conflict mediation between political representatives, support for "insider" mediators as well as the development of infrastructures for peace processes and alternative dispute resolution systems to strengthen the rule of law. He has trained personnel from various diplomatic services and international organizations.

Dr. Simon J. A. Mason

Simon J. A. Mason is senior researcher and head of the Mediation Support Team at the Center for Security Studies (CSS) at ETH Zurich. Since 2005, he has been working in the Mediation Support Project and, since 2011, in the Culture and Religion in Mediation (CARIM) project. He holds a doctorate in environmental sciences from the ETH Zurich and is a trained mediator. He has been involved as a trainer and facilitator in dialogue, mediation and negotiation workshops with actors from various conflict contexts, including Egypt, Ethiopia, Indonesia, Israel, Kenya, Libya, North Korea, Palestine, Sudan and Zimbabwe. He is senior advisor for the Master of Advanced Studies ETH Mediation in Peace Processes program and member of the mediation roster of the UN and OSCE. He has published on various aspects of peace mediation; with Dekha Ibrahim Abdi he co-authored the book *Mediation and Governance in Fragile Contexts: Small Steps to Peace*, published by Lynne Rienner Publishers in 2019.

Brigitta von Messling

Brigitta von Messling has been deputy head of teams training at the Center for International Peace Operations (ZIF) since 2015 and is the co-founder of the Initiative Mediation Support Deutschland (IMSD). Between 2017 and 2019, she headed the field office for the UN Verification Mission in Colombia (UNVMC) in Arauca and accompanied the implementation of the Colombian peace agreement. Previously, she worked for the UN in Liberia. In 2015, she contributed to the integration of mediation into German foreign policy as a mediation officer at the FFO. Between 2006 and 2010, she led mediation projects at the communal level for CSSP – the Berlin Center for Integrative Mediation in the Western Balkans. She studied conflict resolution (MA, MPhil) at the Peace Studies Department of the University of Bradford, UK and is a Rotary World Peace Fellow and member of the ZIF Expert Pool.

Dirk Splinter

Dirk Splinter is a mediator and licensed mediation trainer with 20 years of experience in the field. He has been a member of the management board of inmedio – institut für mediation. beratung. entwicklung in Berlin since 2001, and co-founded inmedio peace consult GmbH. He teaches at the University of Applied Sciences and Arts Northwestern Switzerland and the University of St. Gallen, among other institutions. In addition to mediation in organizations in German-speaking countries, his main areas of focus are mediation and dialogue in the context of development cooperation and peacebuilding in, for example, the MENA region (Middle East and North Africa), Ethiopia, Nepal and Sri Lanka. In recent years, he has been especially focused on Russian-Ukrainian dialogue and the Nagorno-Karabakh conflict. Dirk Splinter authored numerous publications and represents inmedio at the Initiative Mediation Support Deutschland (IMSD).

Luxshi Vimalarajah

Luxshi Vimalarajah is a scholar-practitioner in mediation. She is currently a senior advisor on mediation and devekioment at the Berghof Foundation. Previously she headed the Mediation & Dialogue Support Program at the Berghof Foundation. In the last 20 years, she was involved as a mediation and dialogue practitioner in a number of peace negotiations such as Sri Lanka, Nepal, Myanmar, Colombia, North Macedonia and Yemen. She also leads the conceptual work on National Dialogues and Insider Mediation (particularly work with Faith-based Insider Mediators). At Berghof, she was leading the project on Peace Processes and Constitutions which was jointly implemented by the UN-DPPA/MSU. She also serves as a negotiation and mediation trainer and coach and works with a number of bilateral and multilateral organizations and their mediation departments such as the OSCE, EEAS, and the World Bank. She represents the Berghof Foundation in the Initiative Mediation Support Deutschland (IMSD) and Mediation Support Network (MSN). Luxshi Vimalarajah holds a master's degree in political science from the Freie Universität Berlin.

Dr. Carsten Wieland

Carsten Wieland is a diplomat and scholar, UN consultant, Middle East and conflict expert with practical mediation experience. Between 2014 and 2019, he worked as a senior expert for three UN Special Envoys for Syria.

He is senior Middle East advisor of the Green Party Parliamentary Group in the German Bundestag, a fellow of the Geneva Centre for Security Policy (GCSP), a lecturer at New York University Berlin and a visiting professor at the Universidad del Rosario in Bogotá. He has published on Syria, nationalism, ethnic conflicts, Islamism and secularism. From 2006 to 2008, he was country director of the Konrad Adenauer Foundation in Colombia. As a correspondent for the German Press Agency (dpa), he reported from the USA, the Middle East and Latin America, where he later was head of corporate communications. Wieland studied history, political science and philosophy at Humboldt University in Berlin, Duke University in North Carolina and Jawaharlal Nehru University in New Delhi. Recent monographies include *Syria – A Decade of Lost Chances: Repression and Revolution from Damascus Spring to Arab Spring* (2012) and *Syria and the Neutrality Trap: Dilemmas of Delivering Humanitarian Aid to Violent Regimes* (2021).

Dr. Almut Wieland-Karimi

Almut Wieland-Karimi has been executive director of the Center for International Peace Operations (ZIF) since 2009. Previously, she worked for the Friedrich Ebert Foundation (FES) in various countries for many years, most recently as country director for the USA and Canada in Washington, D.C. From 2002 to 2005, she established the FES country office in Kabul, Afghanistan. She is a member of the International Advisory Board of the United Nations Institute for Training and Research (UNITAR), the Advisory Board of the Federal Academy for Security Policy, the German Armed Forces Command and Staff College and the Mercator Foundation. After pursuing Oriental Studies at the University of Bonn, she wrote her doctoral thesis at Humboldt University in Berlin on the role of religious leaders in modern Afghan politics.

Felix Würkert

Felix Würkert studied law at the Bucerius Law School in Hamburg and the Université Paris 1 Panthéon-Sorbonne. Since 2014, he has been a research assistant at the Chair of Public Law, in particular international and European law, at the Helmut Schmidt University of the German Federal Armed Forces in Hamburg. He recently completed his doctorate on peace mediation at the European University Viadrina. He has been a visiting fellow of the Global South Unit for Mediation at the BRICS Policy Center of the

Pontificia Universidade Católica, Rio de Janeiro. From February 2019 until April 2021 he did his legal traineeship, with internships including the UN desk of the German Foreign Ministry, the German Federal Constitutional Court and the Promotion of the Rule of Law and Justice in Africa Project of the Deutsche Gesellschaft für Internationale Zusammenarbeit (GIZ).

Editor Biographies

Dr. Anne Holper

Anne Holper is co-director of the Center for Peace Mediation at European University Viadrina and heads the *Tough Choices* cluster of Viadrina, ETH Zürich, swisspeace and the Kyiv-Mohyla Academy. As conflict researcher, mediator and trainer, she focuses on enhancing mediation, dialogue and decision-making methodology for the challenging realities of political processes. She consults the FFO on conceptual and methodological issues within Viadrina's Mediation Hub. From 2014 to 2015, she supported local dialogue actors in Ukraine. In her work as supervisor and coach, she accompanies various peacebuilding actors. As a fellow of the Center for Applied Policy Research (CAP) she has done part of her PhD research at Renin University of China. She collaborates with institutions as the Training for International Diplomats program of the FFO and the Mercator Foundation and has published on subjects as dilemmas, inclusion, norms, procedural justice, identity, interculturality and action research in peacemaking.

Prof. Dr. Lars Kirchhoff

Lars Kirchhoff is scientific director of the Institute for Conflict Management and co-director of the Center for Peace Mediation at European University Viadrina, where he has been active since 1999. As an expert on international law and a practicing mediator, he has specialized in the methodological and normative dimensions of peace processes and works on these issues with the FFO, the OSCE and various foundations. He has worked on the conflicts in Afghanistan and Ukraine, among others, as well as on various secession and territorial conflicts. His publications cover such topics as state sovereignty, political mediation, conflict resolution in Europe, transitional justice as well as dilemmas in peace mediation. He is a member of the mediation roster of the UN and OSCE, a member of the advisory board of the journal *Konfliktdynamik* and chairman of the jury for the German science, research and Socrates prize in the field of mediation.